A John Catt Publication

★ ★ ★

MUCH PROM1SE

Successful Schools in England

★ ★ ★

Barnaby Lenon

First Published 2017

by John Catt Educational Ltd,
12 Deben Mill Business Centre,
Old Maltings Approach,
Melton, Woodbridge IP12 1BL

Tel: +44 (0) 1394 389850

Fax: +44 (0) 1394 386893

Email: enquiries@johncatt.com

Website: www.johncatt.com

ISBN: 978 1 911382 23 2

Set and designed by

Theoria Design

Praise for Much Promise:
Successful schools in England

"Higher standards, school autonomy, exams that stretch, getting the basics right – all the education reforms we have undertaken in recent years have been based not on ideology but simply on what works. That is what Barnaby Lenon explores in this fascinating assessment of all that is good (and bad) in education today. A must-read for teachers, parents, policy-makers and anyone interested in making sure that all children are able to reach their potential."

David Cameron, UK Prime Minister, 2010–2016

"A tour-de-force! A thorough summary of evidence, research and analysis combined with eminently accessible practical examples to reflect on. Really got me thinking, with loads for serving school leaders to reflect on. Just need one or two politicians to take note. Highly recommend."

Andy Buck, Leadership Matters

"This is a book that promises much, and delivers in every sense; for anyone involved in schools, regardless of whether they are free, academy, comprehensive, or independent, this is essential reading."

David James, Deputy Head, Bryanston School, and editor of *World Class: tackling the ten biggest challenges facing schools today*

"A wonderful practical guide on what makes a successful school. The analysis is sharp and detailed, covering all angles. It makes you think twice about assumptions you might have. If you don't have time to visit lots of schools or do the research yourself, then this is the book for you. It is excellent to have all of this in one book!"

Katharine Birbalsingh, Headmistress, Michaela Community School, London

"This is essential reading for anyone who cares about education. Barnaby Lenon's wealth of experience comes through on every page, as does his knowledge of current research. This is a forensic examination of what schools need to do in order to deliver at the highest levels, as well as what to avoid. It ruthlessly hunts down myths about education and slays them, offering instead practical advice gleaned from some of the UK's top schools. A copy of this should be in every staff room."

Robin Macpherson, Head of Professional Learning, Wellington College

"When I go to a lecture by a leading politician or pundit, I expect one or more of three things – good stories of direct experiences, sound analysis, provocative reflections. I seldom find all three together, and frequently walk away having experienced none. Not so Barnaby Lenon's book. All three jostle for position on every page. I can see educational researchers getting very grumpy about it – where are the references? Where is the research synthesis to support the sweeping conclusions? That is to miss the point of the text. I love the single line judgements, all deriving from the author's rock solid pedigree in running schools and working at the top level of policy. Those judgements derive from his accumulated professional experience, and are rightly provocative and stimulating. He deals with concerns of parents and children, society and the State – and understands absolutely the complexity of national arrangements in which system-level drivers combine with the acts of individuals to make a difference to quality. Parents, politicians, teaching professionals should read this book, not to gain a definitive view of all aspects of education, but to be pushed into thinking about why the system looks and behaves the way it does, and to be galvanised into action to separate curriculum snake-oil from hard-won professional knowledge."

Tim Oates, Group Director ARD, Cambridge Assessment

Contents

To Penny, India and Flora

Introduction

The English education system shows much promise. For the top 50% of academic pupils high quality school exams are followed by successful entry to good universities. The progress made by girls and ethnic minorities in the past 30 years has been tremendous, as has the increase in the proportion of students from poorer homes making it to university.

But the system is less good for the least academic 50%, much less good for boys and many of those from poorer homes. As the country leaves the EU and seeks to become competitive globally, we will need an education system which gets the bottom 50% to a significantly higher level in terms of English, maths, work ethic and vocational skills. We have to be more ambitious.

We know we can succeed because hundreds of good schools are already proving it can be done. But we are a long way from the standards of technical and vocational education which would strengthen the English economy and provide a more satisfying life for many of our pupils. Which is why it is fair to characterise the system as showing promise.

I have written thousands of end-term-reports describing my pupils as showing promise: a word which conveys a helpful level of optimism without firmly predicting a successful outcome.

For 35 years I taught largely in independent schools. In recent years I have been involved with both independent and state schools. The two sectors are in competition but have much to learn from each other. Independent schools have the advantage of more income per pupil, state schools have the advantage that they can attract applicants without the impediment of fees.

In recent years heads and trustees of some state schools have been to visit independent schools and learn from them. When I became the chairman of governors of a state school I decided to do the same thing in reverse. First I went to see charter schools in the USA and then, with the much valued help of Lizzie Noel and Rebecca Coulson, I went to interesting schools in England, especially those that get outstanding results with disadvantaged pupils. In this book I describe what they do.

I had great guidance from Professor Pam Sammons and Professor Steve Strand at the Department of Education in Oxford, and help with data and background research from Donna Stevens, Jonathan Parkes and Shun-Kai Chan at the Independent Schools Council.

Who controls the state educational system in England?

1. *The Department for Education together with the Treasury* determines the funding per pupil for schools and the measures which will be used to decide whether there should be central government intervention in a school. These latter measures are called the *floor standards*. For example, in 2016 the floor standard for primary schools in England was: '65% of pupils must meet the expected standard in reading, writing and maths and the school must achieve a value-added score above a certain threshold in each of these subjects.' The floor standard for secondary schools was a Progress 8 score of -0.5 (page 282). There is also a group of secondary schools classified as 'coasting' with Progress 8 measures below -0.25.

    In addition to the floor standards are *performance tables* which give a wide array of data relating to every school, state and independent. The performance tables are there to benefit parents thinking about schools but they are badly explained. Schools are ranked on several measures against other similar schools.

    Since 2010 the Government has accelerated the programme of *academisation* started by the previous Labour government, taking schools out of local authority control and handing them independent governors. Many of these academies are now in groups of schools called Multi-Academy Trusts (MATs).

    The Department for Education also takes decisions about the way schools can be set up, and in recent years has favoured the establishment of *free schools* – schools set up by local parents or teachers, by other good schools and Academy chains, by businessmen, by local authorities or by universities. Those hoping to set up free schools have to prove they have the capacity and expertise before they are allowed to proceed. Once they open, free schools are academies and no different from any other academies.

    The new National Curriculum and even the detail of the subject specifications (the syllabuses) have been decided by ministers advised by subject specialists.

2. *Local authorities.* Most primary schools and many secondary schools are still managed by local authorities but the number is steadily declining as schools are taken over by Academy trusts. This, together with budget cuts, means that the services which local authorities used

to give schools are diminishing too. Local authority schools are called *maintained schools* and the National Curriculum is binding on them in a way it is not binding on academies.

3. *Academy trusts* – the trustees who have been given the go-ahead by the Department for Education to run schools, either singly or in chains. They have more freedoms than maintained schools.

   The first wave of academies was 2002–2010. These were schools which had been doing badly and were called *sponsor academies*.

   The second wave, after 2010, were schools rated good or outstanding by Ofsted; they are called *converter academies*.

4. *The Church.* About one third of the 20,000 state funded schools in England are faith schools, of which 68% are Church of England schools and 30% Roman Catholic. Many of these were founded and paid for by the Church but were subsequently funded by local authorities, leaving us with a situation where the church and local authorities were in dual control. In recent years the Church of England has sponsored many schools taking Academy status and this has increased their power and responsibility.

5. *Regional Schools Commissioners* work for the Department for Education and advise on the state of education in their region – what to do about failing schools, how to increase capacity where pupil numbers are rising, helping schools convert to Academy status, encouraging schools to join or form MATs.

6. *Ofsted* inspects schools and grades them. If a school receives a bad grade it will be reinspected within a relatively short period. If a school is found to be very bad or fails to improve, the Department for Education may take steps to turn the school into an Academy or replace the governors.

   Ofsted has a degree of independence from government.

7. *Teaching training* comes in various forms. Universities run courses for both undergraduates and postgraduates. Many of the best schools run Teaching School Alliances or SCITTs (school-centred initial teacher training) where they offer teaching training across a group of local schools.

8. *Ofqual* regulates the exam system and has a good degree of independence from government. *Exam Boards* and their co-ordinating body, JCQ (Joint Council for Qualifications) set public exams including GCSE and A-levels.

All qualifications are placed into one of nine levels so users understand their relative degree of difficulty, Entry level then 1 to 8. GCSEs grades 4–9 are level 2, A-levels are level 3, an honours degree is level 6, a doctorate level 8.

9. *The Institute for Apprenticeships and Technical Education* manages what it says in its name. Employers have an important role in helping the Institute set up and run vocational courses and apprenticeships.

10. *The Education and Training Foundation* helps colleges and teachers deliver vocational courses and functional skills qualifications.

11. *The Standards and Testing Agency* sets primary school tests.

12. *Universities* influence the education system by determining the qualifications they require for admission.

My written evidence submitted to All-Party Education Select Committee, December 2015

What is the purpose of education for children of all ages in England?

1. The main purpose should be to transmit important human knowledge in a way which will ensure the student is able to recall a good proportion of it in the years after school.

2. Important knowledge is that which provides essential life skills, which allows pupils to understand the world, which provides a basis for developing related interests after school, and which leads directly or indirectly to employment.

3. Essential life skills can in large measure be taught by parents. Where parents fail, it is up to schools to plug the gap – the ability to read and write well, the ability to speak well, basic numeracy, basic IT skills, the ability to concentrate, to memorise, to work hard, to be an effective part of a team, to be resilient in the face of difficulties, to be organised, to form good relationships, to live a healthy life. For those with good parents, the essential skills a school will teach include English, mathematics and a small amount of ICT. For those with less good parents, schools have much more to do, including teaching pupils how to behave, how to organise themselves, how to eat well and be healthy.

4. Enabling pupils to understand the world is the particular function of history, geography, science and religious studies. These subjects allow us to make sense of the world and our place in it. They give life perspective.

5. Providing the basis for developing interests after school is a function of all school subjects. All subjects have the capacity to do this, including sport, art, design technology, drama, music, languages and literature – areas of human endeavour that are part of what makes life worth living. Latin and Greek are two completely 'useless' subjects which bring great enjoyment to some of our most able pupils. Many pupils I taught joined the armed forces – an interest they developed at school through the cadet force. The areas of the Harrow curriculum which inspired Churchill were art, history and the Harrow rifle corps – the basis of lifelong interests salvaged from a curriculum which otherwise passed him by.

6. Several school subjects can lead, after further training, to employment – including computer coding, design technology, A-level sciences and FE college vocational courses. Specialisation in vocational subjects should begin at age 16, not before.

7. The purpose of school education is that which can be achieved in 10,000 hours. Not all purposes of education can be achieved in that time. If you spend time specifically teaching character or citizenship or British values or PSHE then something else has to be cut. Parents and politicians are always quick to suggest that schools solve the problems of society by 'teaching it' but never say what should be cut to make room. The multiple purposes of education exceed the time available.

8. People responding to this consultation will rightly say things like 'the purpose of education is to create nice people or good citizens'. These are reasonable aspirations but are largely the responsibility of parents. If you take your eye off the main game – improving children's knowledge – then you tend to lose the match. All schools aim to create nice people and good citizens but that comes as a by-product of the main function of the school.

9. There will be some who say 'the purpose is to produce a fairer society'. No, that should not be the purpose, it should be an important side effect of educating all children well. If you make fairness a principal purpose you lose sight of the main game.

How well does the current education system perform?

10. International comparisons tell us three things: as a country we place less emphasis on mathematics but more emphasis on other subjects than East Asia; we do well at the top of the ability range compared to other high-performing jurisdictions; and we do particularly badly at the bottom of the ability range. The fact that our pubic exam results correlate closely with social class means that pupils from disadvantaged backgrounds do badly compared with their peers in England and compared with pupils from disadvantaged backgrounds in East Asia.

11. The priority for this country should be to improve the public exam results of the bottom 30% of pupils, including white working-class boys.

12. Getting a grade C/4 in a GCSE is easy. All my life I have taught less able boys who, by a combination of firm discipline and attractive teaching, can be got to a much higher level than a GCSE C/4 grade. The secret of the success of many good schools is that they start from the assumption that all pupils can and must achieve a high grade. The large number of pupils in England who fail to gain good GCSEs is, in part, a result of low aspirations. The fact that they can do better is demonstrated for us by those schools who achieve excellent results with disadvantaged pupils.

13. The English system allows pupils to specialise in a limited number of subjects at the age of 16. This is a good thing. As long as they have an adequate level of literacy and numeracy, the ability to specialise allows pupils to focus on subjects they like and can be good at. This brings motivation and being motivated matters greatly. Forcing pupils to study a range of subjects after the age of 16, such a maths, science and a modern language, would be demotivating for many and prevent them from studying subjects in which they could do well.

14. We do not place enough emphasis on the ability to speak well. Pupils from disadvantaged homes may achieve exam results but this will not translate into good jobs if they cannot speak well.

15. In many schools inadequate emphasis is placed on sport, societies and activities which develop qualities of leadership and team work. Too little time is devoted to them. Too much weight is placed on exam results because of the DfE accountability measures and too little weight is given to the non-examined qualities by Ofsted.

Chapter 1

Successful Schools

A summary of research

*There is always a well-known solution to every human problem —
neat, plausible, and wrong.*

H. L. Mencken, 1920

Of course it is not easy to define what we mean by a successful school. Good exam results are a convenient measure but are greatly influenced by the background of the children. Schools in middle-class areas get better results than schools in disadvantaged areas but may still be failing to stretch their pupils.

Very good exam value-added (a measure of progress over time relative to all other pupils who were at the same performance level at the start of the time period) seems a better measure because a school normally only gets good value-added if the teaching is good. Having said that, it is easier to get good value-added with more motivated and able pupils.

Having a good record in terms of student destinations is important. Student destinations (*ie* which universities or vocational courses they go on to) are a measure of the quality of both exam results and careers/UCAS advice.

Ofsted inspection report grades are another measure. Ofsted grades should be a reliable indicator for parents and often are. But the Education Policy Institute published a report in 2016 which looked at school inspections between 2005 and 2015; they found, as previous researchers have done, that Ofsted inspection grades correlate too well with raw exam results. Schools with few disadvantaged pupils get good results and good Ofsted grades, schools with disadvantaged pupils get worse raw exam results and worse inspection grades. Too little attention is being paid to value-added (progress): middle-class schools with weak value-added are getting better Ofsted grades than schools in disadvantaged areas with good value-added (Hutchinson, 2016).

Soft skills also matter greatly. As the cachet of going to university has waned somewhat, parents have become more aware of the significance of soft skills. Sutton Trust research into Assisted Place holders at independent schools (1980–

97) found that these pupils displayed much more self-discipline, self-reliance, ambition, curiosity, better communication skills, cultural sophistication and self-confidence than their state school peers with similar levels of attainment. This, they concluded, was why the Assisted Place holders went on to better careers and higher earnings (Sutton Trust, 2012). So schools should also be judged on the extent to which they promote the development of soft skills, partly through activities like sport.

Some schools have good average results but there is a big *range* hiding behind that average. The most successful schools achieve good results for all types of pupils – all year groups, all ethnicities, boys and girls, able and less able, those from disadvantaged as well as more prosperous backgrounds.

How well do we do compared to other countries?

Since the mid-1990s there have been three main tests which allow us to make comparisons between countries. TIMMS is the Trends in International Mathematics and Science Study; PIRLS, the Progress in International Reading Literacy Study; and PISA, the Programme for International Student Assessment. The three sets of tests are different and produce different rankings of the countries concerned, a fact which tells us about the dangers of relying on any one test.

England performed badly in TIMMS maths in 1995, coming below the international mean in both years 5 and 9, prompting the introduction of the National Numeracy Strategy for primary schools a few years later. Since then performance in maths has improved significantly in both year groups, but particularly in Year 5 where it is now significantly above the international mean.

The 2015 TIMMS looked at maths and science knowledge for 9/10-year-olds and 13/14-year-olds in 57 countries (Greany *et al*, 2016). East Asian countries came top by some way and the gap between these countries and England is widening. Yet pupils in England performed, on average, significantly above the international mean in maths and science in both years 5 and 9: 10th in Year 5 maths out of 49 countries; 9th in Year 9 maths out of 39 countries; 14th in Year 5 science out of 47 countries; and 8th in Year 9 science out of 39 countries.

Three issues stood out for England from the 2015 TIMMS results: that pupils in England make relatively little progress in maths between years 5 and 9 compared to some countries; that far higher proportions achieve high scores in both subjects in the highest performing countries; and that England has wider gaps between more and less advantaged pupils than most other high performing countries.

PISA, the best known of the three international tests, is funded by the OECD (Organisation for Economic Co-operation and Development). The programme started in 2000 with tests happening every three years. PISA is the most rigorous project ever undertaken to assess what makes schooling effective.

PISA tests are computer-based, administered to a sample of 15-year-olds in each country and cover reading, science and mathematics; 15-year-olds are chosen because at this age most children in most OECD countries are reaching the end of compulsory education. The tests are not directly linked to the school curriculum.

Additional questions are asked to discover something about the schools the pupils go to, their socio-economic background and their attitude to school.

PISA in England is administered by NFER, the National Foundation for Educational Research. Schools which are not chosen in the sample can pay to do the PISA test as 'extra' schools. All schools are given feedback about their results. In 2015, 5194 pupils in England took the tests.

Since 2006 PISA standards in England have been stable over time in absolute terms but falling relative to other countries. There has been a sustained decline in average science scores in Wales and average maths scores in Scotland during the last decade. While other countries – particularly Asian nations – moved ahead, the UK has, in the words of the OECD's Director of Education, 'stagnated'. The 2015 results placed the UK 13th out of 72 countries in science, 17th in reading and 26th in maths. British 15-year-olds' maths skills are more than two academic years behind 15-year-olds in Singapore and China.

The OECD equate 30 PISA test points to a year of additional schooling. So if we take PISA 2015 maths for example, England scored 493, Singapore 564 – 2.4 years difference.

In maths our lowest achieving pupils are much worse than the lowest achieving pupils in many other countries. In 2015, 22% of UK pupils did not reach level 2 in maths which means that they 'cannot solve problems routinely faced by adults in their daily lives'.

PISA results have had a very important influence on school systems throughout the world. In 2010 the UK Government kicked off reforms in England with a White Paper in the foreword of which the Prime Minister said: '*What really matters is how we're doing compared with our international competitors*'.

This same thought influenced the 2011 National Curriculum Review where Tim Oates stated: '*The content of our National Curriculum should compare favourably with the curricula in the highest performing jurisdictions...*'

The most valuable thing about PISA is identifying countries which have greatly improved their scores so we can see what they did to produce this improvement. After bad results in 2000 – *der PISA Schock* – Germany adopted well-defined centralised curricula with specific content for each age group and this had the effect of raising their scores for both achievement and equity (the difference in scores between different sub-groups of children).

The big worry about PISA is that it is simply too influential, partly because the press love league tables of the sort PISA generates. PISA does not measure creativity, or a dozen other qualities that make happy and successful people. But many jurisdictions have PISA targets as part of their national plan and some, such as Dubai, use PISA scores as a way of promoting their country to potential investors and employees.

It is naïve to assume that Asian countries do well simply because of something that happens in their classrooms. It could well be their wider culture which is responsible for the academic success of their pupils. So requiring British schools to adopt the classroom methods of Asia is what social scientists call a 'category error'.

In some countries the PISA tests have higher status than others and these countries have adapted their curriculum to try and boost their PISA scores. Their success in the PISA scores does not mean they have 'the best' schools.

Many of the jurisdictions which do best are small and socially homogeneous: Shanghai, Hong Kong, Singapore, Finland, Taiwan. It is wrong to compare these with large and much more ethnically diverse countries.

PISA publishes huge numbers of reports based on correlations between PISA scores and other variables. For example, PISA claimed that high-scoring jurisdictions gave schools greater autonomy (and this influenced the current UK Government). But we all know that correlations do not prove cause and effect – Janet Ouston (1999) showed that the number of pot plants in a school correlated well with exam results. Some of PISA's conclusions may be misleading.

And you have to read the fine print to know that PISA rankings have a big margin of error. A country might in truth be 'between 19th and 27th' but will always be reported in the newspapers as being 23rd.

Why do schools in China, Taiwan and Japan do better than schools in the USA?

To study this further see Stevenson and Stigler (1992) and Crehan (2016) for comparisons with England.

Cultural factors

1. The Chinese and Japanese attach more importance to academic success. Schools can count on all parents to give academic support to their children.

2. The Americans believe in the importance of intelligence; this has the consequence that if a child is doing badly, low ability is blamed and this reduces motivation. The Chinese and Japanese believe in the importance of effort. If a child is doing badly it means the teachers and pupils have to try harder. This increases motivation.

3. In America schools are expected to do everything – health education, social education *etc.* In East Asia parents are expected to do these things, allowing schools to concentrate on teaching traditional subjects.

4. In America teachers lack status. In China and Japan they are regarded as important professionals.

5. In America parents feel disengaged from school life; in China and Japan they are closely involved with their child's schoolwork.

6. Americans are unrealistically optimistic about the academic level reached by their children.

School factors

1. In America teacher training is quite superficial and there is no common body of knowledge (unlike other professions). In China and Japan much teacher training happens in schools and continues for years under the supervision of experienced teachers.

2. In America class sizes are small; this means that, for the system to work financially, teachers have to teach long hours. In China and Japan class sizes are bigger, freeing teachers to have more time planning high quality lessons and learning from other teachers. The average contact hours for an American teacher is 26.8 hours a week, 17.7 in Japan.

3. In America the emphasis is on the individual child; much energy goes into supporting disadvantaged or troubled children. In China and Japan the

emphasis is on the group and there is much more whole-class teaching. In America teachers studied by Stevenson and Stigler were found to be teaching the whole class 46% of the time (the rest of the time they were with individuals or small groups); in Taiwan the figure was 90%. Whole-class teaching produces better progress for all children.

In America teachers believe that the best teachers are those who show sensitivity to the needs of children; in Japan and China they think the best teachers are those who explain things clearly.

4. In America academic education starts at a young age when many children lack the cognitive ability to succeed. In China and Japan early years education focuses on developing vocabulary, socialisation and learning classroom routines – things which make academic learning much more successful when it does begin.

5. In America schools try to cover a big syllabus quickly. In East Asia they take it slowly and ensure every child has mastered the work before moving on.

6. In America, because they believe in the importance of genetic intelligence, children are put into ability sets. In Japan and China, because they assume all children can succeed, they are not. This becomes a self-fulfilling prophecy.

7. In America there is no common curriculum across the states, so resources have not been developed and fine-tuned in the way they have in Japan, where all children study the same syllabi. Textbooks are far better in China and Japan.

8. In America the school day is seven hours compared to more than nine hours in Japan and China. The school year in America is 180 days compared to 240 days in Japan.

9. In America children do much less homework.

10. In America children have inadequate breaks between lessons; as a result they cannot concentrate.

11. In China and Japan children are taught disciplined routines – such as how to be ready at the start of a lesson. In America this doesn't happen and as a result much time is wasted.

12. In Asia there is more emphasis on dividing the children into groups within the class and each group is responsible for policing its own behaviour and working together to do well academically.

McKinsey surveys the world

Sir Michael Barber served as Chief Adviser to the Secretary of State for Education in the UK during the first term of British Prime Minister Tony Blair. Subsequently, and under Barber's direction, the consultancy firm McKinsey conducted some good international comparison research: *How the world's best-performing school systems come out on top* (2007), and *How the world's most improved school systems keep getting better* (2010).

First and most interestingly the reports identified those things which do NOT seem to improve the education of pupils much:

1. Reducing class sizes does not have much impact

It has long been shown that there is no good correlation between class sizes and results (page 67). In the USA the student-teacher ratio fell from 58 pupils per teacher to 42 between 1970 and 2005 with no improvement in reading scores.

One reason for this is that reducing class sizes requires schools to employ more teachers. There are only a limited number of good teachers so the more teachers we are forced to recruit the greater the number of weaker teachers who will obtain jobs in schools.

Most teachers prefer small classes to larger classes for obvious reasons and will always vote for class-size reduction. But in fact it is much better for your child to be in a large class with an excellent teacher than a small class with a weaker teacher.

2. Streaming or setting by ability damages less able children

While able children may well benefit from setting, children placed in bottom sets often do worse than they do in mixed ability groups.

3. The starting age of education does not have much impact

In Finland education starts at age seven and pupils attend school for only four hours a day for their first two years. Yet by the age of 15 they are at the top of the European PISA scores.

Of course this finding may be less true for children from poorer backgrounds who receive less education at home. In England at least there is plenty of evidence that early years intervention can make a huge difference to such pupils.

4. The degree of central government control does not have much impact

In Singapore, a country with outstanding educational performance, schools are centrally controlled. In Finland, another high-achieving country, schools are independent of the state.

What does improve the education of pupils is teacher quality. The 2007 McKinsey report says, '*The available evidence suggests that the main driver of the variation in student learning at school is the quality of the teachers.*'

This will seem obvious but it is obviousness of a kind which is well worth repeating. In order to deal with England's greatest educational problem (the underachievement of the bottom 30% of boys) we do not need to reorganise schools or overhaul the curriculum. We need to create or recruit really good teachers who will teach that bottom 30%. And it is especially important at primary level because once a pupil falls behind they stay behind. In England few pupils who fail to achieve the expected minimum level in tests at the age of 11 go on to achieve good GCSE results.

The McKinsey reports suggest that there are two ways of ensuring that teachers are high quality:

1. Only recruit good teachers

The most effective countries make it hard to gain entry to a teacher training course. In Finland only the top 10% of graduates are allowed to become teachers and only one in ten of the applicants for teacher training is accepted. Because of this the status of teaching as a career has risen – and so the country moved into a virtuous circle.

All the best-performing educational systems, including England's, pay their young teachers well. People do not go into teaching for money, but in terms of the status of the profession, having starting salaries which are close to the national norm for graduate jobs is important.

Teacher recruitment is fallible: some of those taken onto teacher training courses will be found to be weak. So most of the best-performing educational systems make it possible for schools to sack weak teachers without too much difficulty. The system in England was strengthened by the decision that teachers could not achieve their licence to teach (Qualified Teacher Status) until they had passed a year's probation.

2. Develop the staff you have recruited so they all remain good teachers

But the McKinsey research across many countries showed that it is difficult to improve teachers or get them to do things differently. Most teachers, once they have established a way of doing things, are reluctant to change.

Those countries which had successfully managed to improve the teaching ability of existing teachers did so in a number of ways:

- Expert teachers are sent into classrooms to observe and give one-to-one feedback on what they had seen. That worked.

- Teachers generally work alone. But in the best schools teachers collaborate with others in the creation of lesson plans, resources and by observing each other. Teachers coach one another. Reflecting on best practice becomes a normal part of school life. In Finland teachers are given one afternoon a week for meetings with their colleagues. That works.

- The English national literacy strategy started in primary schools in 1998 and focused on each child having one hour of English a day. A network of experts were trained to go out to schools and train individual teachers in the use of the synthetic phonics method of learning to read. Within three years there were significant improvements in reading ability. So that worked.

- All the research shows that it is very hard for a school to be successful without a good headteacher, and that good headteachers can transform weak schools. The best performing schools in the world allow headteachers to have the time to coach their teachers. They do less admin, more teacher training. That works.

McKinsey found that all good school systems have certain things in common:

1. They have high expectations of all pupils. They set clear and high expectations for what students should achieve. They believe all pupils CAN do well … bright pupils will move faster, but less bright pupils are prevented from succeeding only by lack of effort and poor teaching, not by their ability.

   In Finland, if you fall behind you are taken out of lessons and given one-to-one or small group tuition until you catch up. An incredible 30% of all students receive this support in any one year. The extra tuition is done by specialist teachers who receive an additional year of training and higher salaries than other teachers. Because such a high proportion of pupils receive the extra help it is destigmatized – sometimes the best students are also sent for extra lessons, so it is not only about academic failure.

2. They place a great emphasis on literacy and numeracy at primary school.

3. They ensure that educational targets are measurable and monitored so that schools can be held accountable for their results.

But is Finland really so great?

The story of Finland is a good example of the complexities of understanding the causes of school success. When the PISA 2000 results were released in December

2001 Finland emerged as the top performer in the world. People flocked to the country to work out what it was that they did so well. They looked at the schools as they were and came up with a number of conclusions which they carried back to their own countries: Finnish schools have high degrees of autonomy; there is no national inspection or testing; there are no private schools *etc.*

Tim Oates (2015) and Gabriel Heller Sahlgren (2015) looked closely at the 'Finnish miracle' and concluded that in fact the achievements of Finland in PISA 2000 were the result of reforms made in the 1960s, 1970s and 1980s. In the immediate post-war period Finland was poor, it had experienced civil war and the nation lacked a cultural identity; the government sought to use education to tackle all three problems. Finland's schools improved very rapidly, as fast as countries like South Korea and Singapore in the 1980s. Reforms pushed Finnish school standards to a high level but by 2000 many of these reforms had been abandoned – and Finland has been falling in the PISA rankings since 2000.

In other words, a system may be doing well as a result of things which happened in the past. Drawing conclusions by looking at how things are done now can be a mistake. It takes years to improve a system and years for a system to lose the benefits of such improvement.

For example, Finland's schools today are quite autonomous. But up to the 1990s the system was centralised and controlled by the state. The national curriculum was very prescriptive and detailed. All textbooks had to be approved. Teachers had to undergo lengthy training and were required to keep a log of what they taught hour by hour to prove they had taught the mandatory content. Pupils were expected to be obedient and work hard. Decentralisation began in 1985; test scores show that Finland's academic rise took place during the period when the system was most centralised.

The Indian High School, Dubai: a school with 13,000 pupils

I visited this school because its immense size and because it is one of the highest achieving schools in Dubai and the world according to PISA data. Pupils range in age from 3 to 18.

The school started in 1961 when Dubai was little more than a village on a creek at the edge of the desert. It was funded by a few local businessmen to provide education for the Indian expat community and based on the Indian national curriculum and exam system. There have only been two Principals since that date; the more recent is Dr Ashok Kumar who has been in post for 22 years.

Most schools in Dubai are private and many are for-profit. Regardless of their type, all schools are inspected annually by the Dubai Government's excellent school inspection service, the KHDA (Knowledge and Human Development Authority) which currently uses a six-point scale. The Indian High School has received the highest rank (outstanding) for several years.

The school charges parents £800 a year — a small sum compared to the £20,000 charged by some other top schools in Dubai. Most of the parents are well paid so this figure is well below what the market could bear. They are a not-for-profit school. They keep the fees low in four ways:

1. They have class sizes of 30 (25 in kindergarten). This is perfectly manageable as pupil behaviour is good. The pupils come from supportive middle-class Indian families.

2. With 13,000 pupils they have great economies of scale.

3. They recruit teachers from India. They are paid above the Indian rates but not much above because Dubai residents pay no tax. All are found accommodation before they arrive.

   Much of their recruitment of teachers is done by existing staff recommending former colleagues. Dr Kumar and his colleagues then interview them by Skype and the best are visited in their school in India and observed teaching.

   Unlike many international schools, their staff retention rate is excellent. Dr Kumar attributes this largely to the school's caring approach to teachers; for example, if a member of staff is ill, the school will sometimes pick up the medical bill.

   Most teachers take on private out-of-school tuition and this can more than double their salary.

4. Textbooks and other resources are charged as extras.

They manage 13,000 pupils in the following ways:

1. The school is divided into four sections by age and each section has a section-head who is the equivalent of a headteacher.

2. Girls are there 7.20am to 1.20pm. Younger boys are there 9am-3pm, older boys 1.20pm-6.40pm.

3. They have 160 school buses.

4. They have a team of staff whose only job is to independently audit the efficiency of the support services such as catering, IT, medical services, cleaning, transport and all suppliers.

Pupils take the Indian CBSE (Central Board of Secondary Education) exams when they are 16 followed by five examined subjects when they are 18. After 16 pupils specialise in one of arts/humanities, commerce or sciences, taking the All India Senior School Certificate Examinations.

After school pupils go on to universities in Dubai, the UK, USA, Canada and Australia.

If a pupil misses a lesson they are expected to come in on Saturday 8.30–11.30am to catch up. They are not charged for this but the teachers *are* paid extra for Saturday lessons.

Every classroom has a digital projector. Pupils are allowed their own devices but tablets are connected to the school server and firewalls prevent them accessing unsuitable sites. The school prefers pupils to learn from textbooks, knowing that they are a more efficient way of communicating information than a screen.

All new teachers do 15 days of training before they start and all existing teachers must do 18 hours of CPD a term.

Peter Matthews (2009), *Twelve outstanding secondary schools*, Ofsted

This research set out to provide evidence-based answers to the question: 'why do some schools succeed brilliantly against all the odds while others in more favourable circumstances struggle?' Matthews chose 12 highly-successful schools, all rated 'outstanding' by Ofsted, all with above average rates of pupils on free school meals.

He identified the fact that schools go through stages of improvement and the successful characteristics of these schools could be classified by three such stages:

Features of schools which achieve, sustain and share excellence, drawn from the 12 outstanding schools

Achieving excellence	Sustaining excellence	Sharing excellence
Having vision, values and hight expectations	Continuity of leadership	System leadership
Attracting, recruiting, retaining and deleloping staff	Maintaining a strong team culture	Partnering another school facing difficulties and improving it
Establishing disciplined learning behaviour	Continually developing teaching and learning	Acting as community leader to broker relationships across other schools
Assuring the quality of teaching and learning	Developing leaders	
	Enriching the curriculum	
Leading, and building leadership capacity	Improving literacy	Developing and leading a successful school improvement partnership
	Building relationships with students, parents and the community	
Providing a relevant and attractive curriculum		Working as a change agent or expert leader: National Leaders of Education
Assessment, progress- tracking and target-setting	No student left behind	
Inclusion: students treated as individuals		

Source: Matthews, 2009

Of course what we want to do is spread examples of good practice to other schools but this is not as easy as it seems for several reasons:

- it depends on the willingness of heads to accept that another school is better than their school in some ways and to have the humility and determination to copy those things which work.

- reading about the methods used by other schools is not enough. Much depends on the detail. So, for example, saying that good schools have 'high expectations' tells you little because most heads probably think they have high expectations. Only by seeing what the schools with the highest expectations *actually do* does this phrase have real meaning. Heads who are serious about this simply have to visit other schools.

- in the end if you don't have teachers with the ability and passion to teach well, you will not achieve the standards of the best schools.

The London effect

In the late 1990s London schools were the worst in the country. Today they outperform schools in the rest of England, achieving the highest proportion of students obtaining good GCSEs, the highest percentage of schools rated 'outstanding' by Ofsted and the highest GCSE attainment for pupils from poorer backgrounds.

Research by Greaves *et al* (2014) showed that the higher GCSE results of disadvantaged pupils in inner London compared to the rest of the country after 2004 can be largely explained by their higher Key Stage 2 results at the end of primary school education. The explanation for the good GCSE schools in London after 2004 should therefore be related to changes in London's primary schools in the late 1990s and early 2000s. Initiatives such as the London Challenge were unlikely to be the major explanation as they happened too late.

The improvement in London's Key Stage 2 scores at age 11 occurred almost at the same time as the National Literacy and Numeracy Strategies were rolled out, and London local authorities made up many of the pilot areas for these programmes. According to Greaves this was the reason the GCSE results improved.

CfBT (2014) also looked at the reasons London schools improved so rapidly between 2000 and 2014 but came to different conclusions. They found that four school improvement interventions provided the impetus for improvement – London Challenge (2003–2011), Teach First (after 2003), the Academies programme (after 2002) and improved support from local authorities. They also found that the improvement was NOT due to advantages that London had over other regions such as the social class make-up, ethnicity of pupils or a buoyant jobs market.

Burgess (2014) concluded that much of the improvement was due to the ethnic make-up of the children. In 2004 45% of Year 11 pupils in London were white British, the worst performing group. By 2012 only 36% of Year 11 pupils in London were white British (compared to 84% in the rest of England). Other ethnic groups, with better motivation, had pulled London up. However, this argument misses the point that in London the GCSE performance of white British children, not just ethnic minorities, shot up after 2002.

In contrast Blanden *et al* (2015) found that while differences in the ethnic mix of pupils can explain a sixth of the higher level of performance, more was explained by rising prior attainment (pupils entering secondary school with better age 11 test scores) and because London schools were doing better and better at achieving good results with FSM pupils.

In the London Challenge, managed by the Department for Education, the exam results of socially similar schools in London were compared and this made it possible to challenge underperformance on the compelling grounds that if other schools were doing much better with a similar intake of students, significant improvement was possible. The use of data, therefore, generated both optimism and urgency about the need for change.

An important element was buy-in by schools, driven by a moral imperative to improve the results for disadvantaged pupils. Improvement work was to be done *with* them, not *to* them.

The focus *was on training existing teachers to be more effective.* This was done by external experts and by the best teachers in the area. The main COST was providing cover for the teachers to have time off to be trained or to train.

The training happened in Teaching Schools. The host school teachers gave the training to 15 or so teachers from the schools being supported. A teacher in each supported school was appointed the in-house mentor to help the trainee develop back in their own school.

Each school is different and had an adviser to offer bespoke solutions for that school. The advisers were often former HMIs, senior educational consultants, former heads or directors of children's services. They were experts who knew how to fix a problem. They worked in partnership with the head. They built a capacity for further internal improvement after they stopped.

So the key elements of the London Challenge were:

- a focus on data and data literacy
- the culture of accountability
- the creation of a more professional working culture
- a collective sense of possibility
- highly effective practitioner-led professional development

Another important element was the creation of a generous inner London pay scale, which helped retain good teachers in the capital.

An Ofsted report summarised the effect of the London Challenge:

'*Working with teachers from other schools with similar challenges, outside the confines of their home school, enabled frank discussions of strengths and weaknesses in their own teaching, free from concerns about performance management or the disapproval of peers. In particular, a high proportion of time was dedicated to reflecting on and reviewing their own teaching, and their understanding of pedagogy. This taught teachers to become reflective practitioners and they began to share that skill with their colleagues at their home school, under the guidance of the school mentor.*' (Ofsted, 2010)

The Academies programme also helped to raise standards in London because it removed some of the worst-performing schools from local authority control and, in the most successful cases, transferred them to very effective groups of independent trustees.

Teach First also helped because it recruited some of the brightest graduates coming out of university and put them in the worst London schools – they now make up about 6% of all London teachers and a much higher proportion in inner London.

Some local authorities, such as Tower Hamlets, also did a great job by improving the support they gave to schools and replacing many underperforming headteachers.

The CfBT study also attributed part of the success of London to exceptional leaders – London Challenge led by Tim Brighouse, Teach First led from the beginning by Brett Wigdortz. Successful Academy chains, such as Ark Schools and the Harris Federation, have been led brilliantly, as have some individual local authorities.

So, the success of London was probably a complex combination of different factors.

An experiment in Canada that went wrong

Starting in 1999, schools in Quebec implemented a new curriculum and new ways of teaching. The reformers wanted students to *'find answers to questions arising out of everyday experience, to develop a personal and social value system, and to adopt responsible and increasingly autonomous behaviors'.*

And *'Instead of passively listening to teachers, students will take in active, hands-on learning. They will spend more time working on projects, doing research and solving problems based on their areas of interest and their concerns. They will more often take part in workshops or team learning to develop a broad range of competencies.'*

A decade later Haeck *et al* (2014) found that the reforms, far from improving learning, had hugely decreased test results, as well as increasing anxiety and hyperactivity among pupils:

'Our data set allows us to differentiate impacts according to the number of years of treatment and the timing of treatment. We find that the reform had negative effects on students' scores at all points on the skills distribution and that the effects were larger the longer the exposure to the reform.

Lower performing students were impacted more severely, and the effects grew larger as students progressed from primary to secondary school. These large negative effects are worrying, and suggest that the reform may have harmed those most in need.'

Haeck's research is one of many studies which suggests that people who believe in discovery learning, collaborative learning and child-centred learning are wrong.

Standards fall in France

Hirsch (2016) studied the decline in educational standards in primary schools in France after 1989. For many years French primary schools had been amongst the most successful in the world, teaching a detailed and centrally prescribed curriculum which ensured all French pupils learnt the same subject knowledge to a good standard. But in 1989 France passed a new law – the *loi Jospin*, named after the French education minister – which required primary schools to stop teaching the national curriculum and begin teaching a locally determined curriculum instead. Furthermore, individual schools were encouraged to develop their own version of their local curriculum, called their *projets*.

The *loi Jospin* reforms also encouraged schools to pay more attention to children as individuals and to shift the emphasis from subject knowledge to general skills such as critical thinking.

The French Ministry of Education now has 20 years of data about the performance standards of ten-year-olds since the *loi Jospin* and these show a steep decline on all measures. It affects all social-economic groups but is worst amongst the poorest students – gaps in performance between the rich and poor have widened.

Hirsch is clear that the causes of this decline are the same as the causes of the decline in standards of American schools after 1960. Between 1960 and 1980 scores in American schools fell by more than 25% of a standard deviation at all grade levels (a large amount) and have since remained low and stable. International studies such as that by Elliott Medrich (1992) have shown that school systems which keep young children in lock-step in terms of curricula, like Japan where all children follow the same syllabi at the same time, produce happier schools and much more successful pupils.

According to Hirsch, the three ideas which lay behind the decision to move to a catastrophic child-centred and skills-based approach to education were:

1. The ideas of Jean Piaget (1896–1980) that early education should be appropriate to a child's age, that some school topics are 'developmentally inappropriate' for children of a particular age. Hirsch argues that this is false science and that what may appear to be a child's immaturity is often just a lack of knowledge about the world, worst amongst children from low income families. Holding back more demanding topics from children on the pseudo-scientific assumption that they are not 'ready' for them is damaging the education of poorer children. Jerome Brunner (1960) and Robert Siegler *et al* (2003) have shown how developmental psychology does NOT support the notion of treating children differently according to their developmental level.

2. Individualism: the idea that all children are different, with different interests and learning styles, so they should be taught as such, with individualised instruction replacing whole-class teaching. Such teaching is called 'differentiation' and has been one of the characteristics of teaching expected by Ofsted inspectors in England. Hirsch shows that the problem with individualised instruction, nice as it sounds, it that it is a less effective method of teaching than whole-class instruction. If you are dealing with one individual child then at that moment you are not teaching the rest of the class. Daniel Willingham (2005) and Lynn Waterhouse (2006) have shown that there is no evidence for the idea of individual learning styles. Whole-class instruction in which pupils are focus on the same work is a far more effective method of instruction than individualised instruction.

3. The belief that the aim of education is the teaching of general skills such as critical thinking, problem solving, teamwork and creativity rather than subject knowledge. Hirsch rejects this idea as especially harmful. Research by Feltovich *et al* (2006) showed that there are few general skills which can be applied to several subjects. Most skills are *domain-specific*, that is they apply to a particular part of the syllabus within individual subjects. Thinking skills cannot be separated from subject content.

In his famous radiation experiment, Duncker (1935) showed that when people were shown how to solve a problem in one domain they were unable to solve the same type of problem in another domain. The experiment involved asking the question:

'Suppose you are a doctor faced with a patient who has a malignant tumour in his stomach. It is impossible to operate on the patient; but unless the tumour is destroyed the patient will die. There is a kind of ray that can be used to destroy the tumour. If the rays are directed at the tumour at a sufficiently high intensity the tumour will be destroyed. Unfortunately, at this intensity the healthy tissue that the rays pass through on the way to the tumour will also be destroyed. At lower intensities the rays are harmless to the healthy tissue but they will not affect the tumour either. What type of procedure might be used to destroy the tumour with the rays, and at the same time avoid destroying the healthy tissue?'

Duncker showed that however much the respondents knew about analogous situations, such as military tactics in a war, they were unable to answer this question unless they had a good knowledge of how radiation works. The skills are domain-specific.

Many well-known schools have statements on their websites which say things like 'we want all our pupils to have excellent critical thinking and problem-solving skills'. They say less about what the pupils will actually be learning in science, history or French.

When schools like Michaela (page 242) and West London Free School (page 233) talk about their 'knowledge curriculum' they are really saying something very straightforward – every child needs to know a basic body of knowledge if they are to function effectively as adults, knowledge that middle-class families take for granted. For less advantaged pupils the school must teach them. This is not 'merely learning facts' because teaching knowledge can be fun and, because it must be committed to the long-term memory to have much value, it is tough and rigorous. Children who KNOW a lot of history, geography, French, maths, music and science are better able to develop useful skills, such as analytical thinking, and are obviously more educated people. Educational success is defined by what pupils learn.

Hirsch (2016) explains that the main focus of *primary*-level education should be the acquisition of vocabulary taught in the context of traditional school subjects. Children from middle-class homes pick up a wide vocabulary and knowledge of the world from their parents. Children from poor homes are at such a disadvantage in this respect that they will never catch up unless the school helps them. It is relatively ineffective teaching vocabulary by rote – it needs to be taught in the context of specific subjects where children can come to understand the meaning of the words by hearing and using them in context.

A school that transformed itself without changing the staff

In most schools there are one or two 'star' academic departments where the results far outshine those of other subjects. This was the case with the history department at Robert Clack School, a split site, mixed, 11–18 comprehensive in Dagenham on the edge of London. The catchment area for the school has the largest percentage of council housing and one-parent families in England and Wales. In 1993, the school was in the bottom percentile of schools in the south-east of England in terms of the A–C pass rate at GCSE, with only 8% of pupils gaining five or more grade Cs or above.

Chris Woodhead, the Chief Inspector for Schools, described the school before its transformation as *'Quite simply one of the worst in the country. Bullying was rife, drugs were peddled, discipline was non-existent'* (Woodhead, 2000).

But the history department stood in contrast to this. Results at both GCSE and A-level were good and the subject was popular. Interviewing students, Haydn (2001) found out why:

'You could tell that they all worked together. There was no messing about; you never felt that it was a waste of time.'

'You knew that there was a good chance that you would do well, and get a good exam result.'

'There was never any of the "pass the time stuff" that you got in other lessons.'

'You didn't mess with them, everyone knew that if you did, it would be sorted.'

The department was very well led by Paul Grant and in 1997 he was appointed to be headteacher. The challenge was to transfer the lessons of one department to the whole school. By 1999 the school's exam results were already much improved, the school was more popular and an inspection report was glowing. Grant was tough with disruptive pupils and their parents with the consequence that behaviour improved and teachers felt they could teach, some for the first time. Exclusions ran at 100–200 a month in the early stages of Grant's headship and the support of the local authority for this was essential. A new code of conduct was introduced for pupils. Staff were looked after and supported.

Now it was possible to teach without disruption, teachers really enjoyed their work. *'The recent history of Robert Clack School suggests that the welfare and job satisfaction of teachers, and the extent to which they feel supported, are factors which influence educational outcomes, and which need to be taken into consideration in moving schools forward.' (Haydn, 2001).*

The school developed a culture where staff supported each other rather than blamed each other. There was a culture of collaboration. In such an atmosphere teachers who might have been labelled 'weak' became effective.

So the key point is that this was a school that revolutionised its performance without changing the staff...

'*The recent history of Robert Clack High School suggests that schools need to look within themselves as part of the quest for improvement, rather than relying predominantly on the analysis of comparative data on school performance, wholesale staff changes, the importing of a 'heroic' leader, and other external interventions.' (Haydn, 2001)*

Turning round a failing school

Hill, A., Mellon, L., Laker, B., Goddard, J. (2016), How to Turn Around a Failing School, *Harvard Business Review*

Hill *et al* are from the Centre for High Performance at Oxford and Kingston universities. They studied changes made by 160 UK academies after they were put into remedial measures by Ofsted.

Here are their conclusions based on the effective (and ineffective) practices they uncovered:

'**Don't improve teaching first.** *This was a very common mistake. Many schools tried to improve teaching while still struggling with badly behaving students, operating across a number of sites or having a poor head in charge. You can't expect teachers to sort out all the problems themselves* – you need to create the right environment first.

Do improve governance, leadership, and structures first. Otherwise, you're putting great teachers in a position where they fail – they'll waste time doing or managing the wrong things.

Don't reduce class sizes. While reducing class size works, it is not the best use of resources. It is expensive and you can create the same impact by improving student motivation and *behaviour, which takes fewer resources. They found class sizes of 30 performed as well as class sizes of 15 when standards of student behaviour had been addressed.*

Do improve student behaviour and motivation. *The best way to create the right environment for good teachers is to improve student behaviour and motivation. They found that the fastest way to do this is to exclude poorly behaved students, even build a new, smaller school for these students. However, while this "quick win" produced immediate results, it was not the best long-term solution. The better, more sustainable practice was to move poorly behaved students into another pathway within the existing school, so that they can be managed differently and reintegrated into the main pathway once their behaviour has improved.*

Do create an "all through" school. *Keep students from the age of five until they leave at ages 16 or 18. In this way, school leaders can create the right culture early on and ensure that poor behaviours never develop. It also makes teaching at secondary school level much easier, as you don't have to integrate older students with different views about standards.*

Don't use a super head. *Many academies parachuted in a "super head" from a successful school to turn themselves around. Although this had a positive short-term impact, it didn't create the right foundations for sustainable long-term improvement. These "super heads" tended to be involved only for one to two years and focused their changes on the school year (ages 15–16) and subjects (mathematics and English) used to assess performance, so they could make quick improvements, take the credit, and move on.*

In every case, exam results dipped after the "super head" left and only started improving three years later.

Do improve all year groups. *Although schools can improve short-term performance by focusing on classes with imminent exams, they will not create sustainable improvement unless they invest in all age groups and subjects.*

Don't expect inner city schools to be more difficult. *Another common view is that it is more difficult to turn around an inner city school. However, we found it is easier, as they have greater access to good leaders, teachers, and students.*

Do invest more in rural and coastal schools. *It is more difficult to attract good leaders, teachers and students in rural and coastal areas. Improvement was much slower in these regions.*

Don't expect spending more money to solve your school's problems any faster. *More resources can help to overcome specific challenges, such as attracting good leaders and teachers, but at least in these 160 British academies, what mattered most to the overall speed of improvement was making the right changes in the right order.*

...But, at the same time, don't expect to improve without spending more, at least in the short term. *To improve student learning, schools must have the basic resources they need to improve student behaviour, pay higher salaries to attract good teachers, and employ staff to manage parents so teachers can spend more time teaching and leaders can spend more time leading. Expect financial performance to dip in the short-term. Pursuing financial performance over operational performance will not serve students well in the long term.' (Hill et al, 2016)*

Does school type matter? Academies and maintained schools

The last Labour government saw the beginning of the process of transferring responsibility for running state schools from local authorities to independent groups of trustees (the latter schools to be called Academies) under the Learning and Skills Act 2000. The process was greatly accelerated by the Coalition government after 2010.

The evidence about the success of Academies is as yet mixed – some are brilliant, others less so – but most Academies and Academy chains are quite new and it is unfair to judge any of them too quickly. As Chapters 8–17 tell us, there are outstanding local authority schools and outstanding Academies. The Academy Trusts with a strong central vision and control, like Ark and the Harris Federation, get the best results. In 2015 at Key Stage 4 more than half of MATs had value-added scores that were significantly below average, but many contained historically underperforming schools (DfE, 2016).

Silva, Eyles, Heller-Sahlgren, Machin and Sandi at the London School of Economics researched the GCSE performance of Academies (Eyles *et al*, 2015). Once a school becomes an Academy, the nature of its pupil intake can change – so any improvement can be due to *either* improved teaching and systems *or* more able pupils joining the school. For this reason they only looked at the performance of pupils who were already at the school before it became an Academy.

The first Academies, pre-2010, were failing schools and were called 'sponsored academies'. Their GCSE results have, not surprisingly, improved – by the equivalent of one grade in five subjects. The post-2010 Academies are called 'converter Academies'. For those that were already Ofsted-graded outstanding schools, results have improved by the equivalent of one grade in two GCSE subjects. For those that were Ofsted-graded good, satisfactory or inadequate on conversion there has been no improvement in results.

In 2016 the Education Policy Institute (EPI) and the London School of Economics published research using eight-year performance data, comparing the results of 205 sponsored Academies approved after May 2010 and 49 schools which were not Academies at the time. They found that results at Academies improved in the year immediately before and the year after conversion, but this boost appeared to 'taper away to zero' within about three years.

They could not be sure why there was a pre-conversion bump in results, but said it could be explained by an intensive focus on GCSE results in the year before conversion to avoid being taken over by an Academy sponsor.

The academisation programme has been of great benefit to many schools. A good proportion of the worst schools have improved. Many of the best schools have continued to flourish as they gained greater independence. However, becoming an Academy is not necessary nor sufficient for a school to improve. Some non-Academies are doing very well, some Academies are doing badly. Academisation is a useful tool but it is not a panacea.

Becoming at Academy was supposed to be a way of increasing a school's autonomy. In fact for some individual schools there is less autonomy than they had under local authority control: they are now under the thumb of a Multi-Academy Trust.

What about free schools? Although some free schools have been a failure, on balance free schools are more likely to be rated as 'Outstanding' by Ofsted than other state schools – 28% compared to 21% in 2016. They are outperforming all other types of state school at Key Stage 1 and the 16–19 free schools are the best-performing state schools in terms of A-level results.

However, at GCSE in 2016 the 32 free schools had an average Progress 8 score of -0.02. In mitigation, these schools were in the first wave of free schools and this was their first year of GCSE entry. Schools should not be judged on their performance in year one.

In 2017 the Government announced its intention of opening specialist sixth-form maths free schools across the country. There are two such schools at the moment – King's London and Exeter. The number of students is small – fewer than 100 pupils took A-levels in both schools combined in 2016 – and the very narrow choice of A-levels on offer makes it unlikely that such schools will make a great impact.

Studio Schools are a particular class of free schools; there are about 40 of them. They are small schools for pupils aged 14–19 who wish to follow vocational courses. They have strong links to local employers and focus on preparation for jobs; the employers help with mentoring, work placements and course design. They have a curriculum with a large element of project-based learning. A wide range of industries and professionals are involved in the schools – from space to computer games, construction to engineering, sport to healthcare and accountancy. Their biggest problem is the start age of 14 – it is very hard to recruit pupils at this age, unless their existing school is keen to see them leave.

Seventeen per cent of free schools in 2016 were for pupils with special needs and the great majority have been set up in the more deprived parts of England.

Several of the schools described in Chapters 8–17 are free schools.

Multi-Academy Trusts

Multi-Academy Trusts are groups of academies – that is, schools which are independent of local authority control. We know from abundant research (such as that of the Education Policy Institute in 2016) that being an Academy or MAT does not in itself raise standards. However, being part of an effective MAT can have a very beneficial effect on schools. Research by Matthews *et al* (2014) looked at this.

'One multi-academy federation, for example, uses its own school improvement model for transforming under-performing primary schools. The model focuses entirely on teaching and learning.'

This is what they did:

'First the headteacher and any deputy or assistant headteachers were given four weeks to show what change they can make to the school. The MAT director was clear about the changes he expects to see in classes and in children's books, for example. If they cannot manage this they are moved on.

Prospective heads are often concerned about two issues: will the MAT want to run the school instead of them and what support will they have? They are reassured on both counts. The model is focused on outcomes. Principals have the resources and the power to run their own schools.

Once appointed, the head will receive a set-up grant for the school together with an allocation of support for information technology, finance and human resources; an allocation of advisory teacher days; and access to support for middle leadership. They will also get a business manager for two days a week, since "the budgets of inadequate schools are usually in a mess".

The focus on teaching is relentless. Teachers with several years' experience that are still teaching unsatisfactory lessons have to improve rapidly. The federation has its own bespoke 'requiring improvement' to 'good' programme which gives them weekly support in the classroom over six weeks with advisory teachers. Teachers with several years' experience that are still teaching unsatisfactory lessons have to improve rapidly or face pre-capability steps.

There is also an 'ambassador programme' for very good and consistently good teachers who can become leaders of learning. This programme amounts to six hour-and-a-half twilight sessions working in peer pairs with videoed teaching, supported by sessions and resources on leadership and what makes a great leader of learning. These programmes are very popular and often draw out capable but hitherto 'reserved' staff from these poor schools that have frequently been dominated by inadequate teachers.

Monitoring of and by the schools is rigorous. Schools are expected to assess pupils every six weeks and report to parents every six weeks. The advisory team meets weekly, but undertakes a six-weekly scrutiny of each school's pupil-level data. They write a commentary for the principal on the basis of these data, which are then discussed with the principal. In this way, no child in any of the schools can slip through the net and make insufficient progress undetected. Performance management is focused on the progress of key named children.' (Matthews et al, 2014)

The advantages of good MATs are:

- they can impose a faster and stricter regime of school improvement than school governing bodies or local authorities ever have.

- they will provide external support, not just for the obvious things like finance but also expert teachers in every subject.

- they can provide good training and career development within the MAT, including growing future heads. This helps them to retain the best staff within the MAT. Many will have Teaching Schools and Schools Direct partnerships which also helps with the supply of teachers.

Grammar schools, Direct Grant schools and academic selection

The 1944 Education Act set up the tripartite system of grammar schools, secondary modern and technical schools. In 1965 all three types started to be closed in favour of comprehensive schools.

In the 1960s and 1970s the most successful schools in England were the Direct

Grant schools, often ancient grammar schools like Bradford Grammar, Leeds Grammar and Manchester Grammar. These were independent schools who admitted pupils on the basis of a good score in the 11+ exam. Children from lower-income families had their fees paid by their local authority. The Direct Grant scheme opened up the best independent schools to ability rather than wealth.

The grant was abolished by the Labour government of 1974–79 and most of the Direct Grant schools became fully fee-paying, which increased the number of fee-paying parents and denied opportunity to many poorer children.

There is a myth that state grammar schools were the great social mobility ladder before 1975. In fact, grammar schools took very few pupils from the working classes and those few tended to do quite badly. Because secondary moderns were so bad, there is every reason to believe that their counterpart, the grammar schools, entrenched socio-economic class. Fewer than 0.3% of those who left grammar schools with two A-levels before 1975 were from the unskilled working class.

In 2016 the Government announced the reintroduction of grammar schools. In that year there were only 163 grammar schools in England out of some 3000 state secondaries, and a further 69 grammar schools in Northern Ireland. They have 167,000 pupils, 5% of all state-funded pupils, and are mostly in middle-class areas.

Chris Cook's research (2013 and 2016) shows that in local authority areas with grammar schools, the minority of students in the area go to the grammar schools and do better than they might have done in a comprehensive, but the majority left in the comprehensive schools do worse than they would have done had the grammar schools not existed.

The reason that comprehensive schools do less well in areas with grammar schools nearby is that all the brightest pupils have been stripped out. This makes it harder to push pupils towards the top marks and harder to attract good teachers. Those who have been rejected by the grammar schools (the great majority) are demotivated. Cook's research into Kent and Medway, an area with grammar schools, shows that poorer children lag further behind than they should do, richer children move further ahead – and the losses at the bottom are much larger than the gains at the top.

'The highest performing school systems in the world, according to the PISA tests, are comprehensive. So are England's highest-performing boroughs and counties – especially when you look at results for poorer children.' (Cook, 2016)

OECD research (PISA, 2014) found that there is a strong negative association between levels of pupil motivation and the degree to which countries sort students into different schools by ability. On the whole the highest achieving countries maintain comprehensive systems.

Burgess (2016) compared GCSE results in Buckinghamshire, which has grammar schools, with Hampshire which does not and found that middle attainers did less well in selective systems.

Porter and Simons' research for Policy Exchange (2014) showed that very few students from low-income backgrounds make it into grammar schools so it cannot be argued that grammar schools help social mobility. The reason for this is that so few pupils on free school meals (FSM) are in the top 20% academically by the age of 11. And middle-class parents employ tutors to prepare their children for the entrance exams. The Education Policy Institute (2016) found that 2.5% of pupils in selective schools are eligible for FSM, compared with 13.2% across all state-funded secondary schools. Thirteen per cent of grammar school pupils went to private schools before they moved to the grammar and 85% had private tutoring to prepare for the 11+ exam.

The PISA 2105 tests also found *'little support for the notion that pupils from disadvantaged backgrounds are more likely to succeed if they live in a country with an academically selective secondary education system...'* (Jerrim and Shure, 2016).

Arguments against grammar schools have also focused on the 11+ test, taken when pupils are aged ten or 11. It has been shown that such tests have a significant margin of error so many pupils were and are assigned to the wrong school. Furthermore, testing at 11 assumes that pupils do not change much after that age.

It might come down to the fact that some people believe in what is best for society as a whole (anti-grammars). Others believe in what is best for individuals regardless of society as a whole (pro-grammars); they aim for the best fit between individual people and their education, worrying less about the collective impact.

Coalition and Tory governments between 2010 and 2016 opposed grammar schools. They argued that it was better to focus on making comprehensive schools work well for the more able (as well as the less able). Schools such as King Solomon (page 220) have shown it can be done. Around half of pupils eligible for free school meals in inner London achieve five or more GCSEs at A*–C, double the proportion outside London. Grammar schools seem to offer an opportunity to improve and stretch the brightest pupils, but this comes at the cost of increasing inequality. Inner London, by contrast, has been able to improve results amongst the brightest pupils *and* reduce inequality. This suggests that London schools offer more lessons on ways to improve social mobility than do grammar schools.

Some schools are partly selective. Watford Girls Grammar is an example: 25% of the pupils are selected on the basis of an entrance exam and 10% on musical ability, the rest by distance from the school. In 2016 GCSEs 55% were graded A*/A and 90.6% A*–C with a Progress 8 score of + 0.47.

All analysis of the effectiveness of grammar schools is compromised by the fact that 74% of grammar schools are single sex. Where being single sex influences results, it is hard to disentangle this influence from that of selection by ability.

What about the political benefits of allowing more grammar schools? The mass of swing voters are the provincial lower middle class – C1/C2 voters. Because there are so many in this group all parties know that they are the priority. They account for half the population of England and half of most swing seats. In opinion polls the C1/C2 support grammar schools, even though their children are not going to get in. They associate grammar schools with tradition, school uniform, academic rigour and good discipline. So even if grammar schools are unlikely to improve social mobility or academic results generally, a party seeking votes may be tempted to introduce more of them.

It is also important to note that academic selection does not only happen with entry to grammar schools at age 11:

- there is selection within schools into streams and sets, and this often determines which subjects pupils will take and, for GCSEs, which tier of exam they will sit.

- there are many comprehensive schools who are allowed to select up to 10% of their pupils on the basis of their ability in a specialism, like science.

- schools select pupils in part by the proximity of their homes to the school. For schools with good results this drives up house prices. In this way social selection becomes established: only wealthier parents can afford to live near the best schools.

- schools with a religious character may apply religious criteria when selecting pupils and when they do the entry is always more middle class than it would be if these criteria were not used.

- almost all state sixth forms are academically selective. Most comprehensive schools in England only allow a limited proportion of their Year 11 pupils to continue on to A-levels. So those who argue for comprehensive education are really arguing on behalf of pupils aged 11–16.

So there is plenty of selection taking place without grammar schools.

Finally, let us remind ourselves that the most academically selective schools get the best exam results AND THIS IS NO GREAT SURPRISE. Those who admire schools at the top of the league tables are in part admiring their marketing, their reputations and their admissions policies. Their teachers may be excellent, *but not necessarily.*

Further Education Colleges

Seventy-one per cent of 16- to 18-year-olds continued in full-time education in 2015 (DfE, 2016). The main providers were FE colleges (484,000 students), school sixth forms (433,000 students) and sixth form colleges (157,000).

So FE colleges are a *very important* part of the education system in England. Every year about 100,000 16-year-olds enrol at an FE college to do technical or vocational courses. And yet they are rarely talked about in the media and receive scant attention from politicians. Their funding has been cut, their courses are of mixed quality. In 2016 Ofsted reported that in more than half of FE colleges inspected in the previous year, study programmes were 'less than good' (Ofsted annual report 2015/16). In many teaching was not demanding enough and attendance at lessons was low.

In his final speech as Chief Inspector of Schools Sir Michael Wilshaw made the point. Referring to the skills shortage in the UK and the poor quality of many FE colleges he said: *'For half a century, the FE sector has been the Cinderella arm of the education service...We can no longer afford to accept mediocrity on such a grand scale'* (Wilshaw, 2016).

He was being pessimistic: Ofsted's own data shows that there are many good FE colleges. But the FE sector generally needs better funding and more attention – it is so important to a big proportion of our post-16 students.

University Technical Colleges

There are about 50 UTCs in England, sponsored by universities and local employers. They are for pupils aged 14–18. A UTC curriculum includes one or two technical specialisms, which are linked to the skills gaps in its region. For example, Silverstone UTC, which opened in September 2013 on the Silverstone racetrack, specialises in high performance engineering and event management.

As well as their core academic subjects, students study GCSEs, A-levels and other relevant qualifications matched to these specialisms. UTCs have a special focus on science, technology, engineering and maths and their technical, academic and practical learning is designed to be applied in the workplace.

UTCs have struggled to attract pupils because at the age of 14 few pupils wish to change schools and few schools encourage their pupils to leave. But they are a good idea. In the future they may adapt to taking more pupils at age 16.

State boarding schools

There are 40 state boarding schools in England, mostly for pupils aged 11–18. They are rarely mentioned by the media or government. Most are designed for UK parents who need boarding for their children (for example, where both parents work long hours or change job location frequently – such as members of the armed forces). A few take overseas pupils as a source of income. These schools often get good academic results and their fees are generally a third of those of independent schools.

Boarding schools have two other advantages. They create a strong sense of community within which many pupils thrive, and they are able to offer a far wider and deeper range of cocurricular activities than day schools. Walker (2016) surveyed 8000 pupils and found that those at boarding schools had become more socially adept as a result of their boarding experience and had a stronger sense of belonging to the institution, especially their boarding house.

Independent schools

Independent schools educate 7% of all pupils but 14% of those taking A-levels. Their fees average about £13,000 a year for a day place.

Independent (private, fee-charging) schools have been around for much longer than state schools. Most have made a huge effort to fund pupils from poorer homes in recent years, so although their fees are high many parents do not pay them.

Reforms to the English education system have often mimicked best practice in private schools: the whole notion of independence (= Academies, free schools), a focus of traditional academic subjects, character development, soft skills, extracurricular activities. The iGCSE, much loved by private schools, was the model for the recent GCSE reforms.

Research into value-added at GCSE from the CEM centre at Durham (Ndaji *et al*, 2016) showed much higher levels of value-added in independent schools than in state schools and suggests that attending an independent school is associated with the equivalent of two additional years of schooling by the age of 16. If independent schools were measured on international PISA outcomes, they would outperform the best European nations and be on a par with Japan and South Korea.

The PISA 2015 tests found that in England the top performing schools were independents even after controlling for the effect of social class. *'Their performance in science puts them level with 15-year-olds in the top-performing countries, such as Singapore. Independent school pupils are also around a year of schooling ahead of the next highest achieving group in England, converter academies'* (Jerrim and Shure, 2016).

Based on A-level points per subject, the 2016 results showed than of the top 100 schools in England, 81 were independent schools (DfE performance tables 2017). The average A-level value-added for independent schools was +0.15 compared to -0.12 for state schools.

HEFCE research in 2015 found that of independent school pupils, 82% got firsts and 2:1s, compared to 73% for state school students (HEFCE, 2015). On all key measures *(achieving a degree; achieving a first or 2:1 degree; continuing to employment or further study; achieving 'graduate-level' employment)* independent school pupils at university do well.

A 2015 report from the Sutton Trust and upReach charities found that six months after finishing university, private school graduates in high-status jobs were earning £670 per year more than those from the state sector in the same high-status positions, even after taking into account any differences in age, gender, university attended and degree obtained. Three years later, this gap has grown such that a private school graduate is on average earning £2,198 per year more than the comparable state school graduate.

Half of this difference can be explained by factors such as prior academic attainment and the type of university attended, but the remaining half cannot – and is likely to be down to non-academic factors such as articulacy, assertiveness and other important soft skills.

A third of pupils at independent schools are on a reduced fee. Several schools have spent the last ten years building up bursary funds. For example, in 2016 Manchester Grammar School had 220 bursary holders and the AVERAGE bursary was 93% of the fee.

And as 40% of UK independent school pupils have parents who did not themselves go to an independent school this is not about the perpetuation of a small elite.

Twenty-nine per cent of pupils at independent day schools are from a minority ethnic background (ISC Census). In many independent schools in London and Birmingham the majority of pupils are non-white – and their schools are providing them with the ladder to prosperity their parents or grandparents envisaged and hoped for when they came to this country.

Oxbridge

Given the weight accorded by the media to the proportion of pupils from different types of schools going to Oxford and Cambridge, it is worth reminding ourselves of the stats.

Oxford and Cambridge undergraduate acceptances 2015/16		
	%	
School type	Cambridge	Oxford
Comprehensive	19.8	31.7
Grammar	17.1	2.7
Sixth form college	6.7	7.8
FE college	1.9	1.5
UK independent	27.5	37.7
Overseas	18	9.2
Other	9	8.9
Total (n = the actual number)	100 = n.3449	100 = n.3216

Sources: Oxford university admissions statistics, 2015; Cambridge university admissions statistics, 2016

The House of Commons Library has analysed the figures historically (Bolton, 2014) and found that the proportion of state pupils at Oxbridge was 26% of home pupils in 1959, 37% in 1964, 43% in the early 1970s, 52% by 1981, rising ever since. The idea that fewer state school pupils go to Oxbridge now than in the heyday of the grammar schools is a myth.

KIPP and Ark

KIPP stands for the Knowledge is Power Programme in the USA. There are over 180 KIPP schools, located in low-income parts of America. Fifty-seven per cent of their pupils are African-American and most of the rest are Latino. They expect all their students to aim to go to university and they have a high degree of success. In addition they aim to develop the character and personality of their students focusing on zest, grit, optimism, self-control, gratitude, social intelligence, and curiosity.

KIPP schools are examples of what in America are called charter schools – schools that receive government funding but operate independently of the established state school system. There are over 7000 charter schools in the USA. Evidence on charter schools thus far appears mixed. Most successful are the No Excuse charter schools which have high behavioural expectations, strict discipline and longer school days. Such schools have been found to improve test scores radically among disadvantaged children.

In 2016 Ark was running 34 schools in England of which Burlington Danes (page 225) was their first. The chain includes King Solomon Academy (page 220). They are the highest-achieving chain in England: Ark students are twice as likely to achieve five good GCSEs as the national average. Ark schools are influenced by the ethos of the charter schools in America.

School personality

I have been fortunate enough to work in schools which have a strong personality. Because so many schools are new – new start-ups like free schools, fresh starts like academies – they are still developing their personality.

School personality comes in many forms but it hits you as soon as you walk through the gates. Personality is a good thing because it generates loyalty to the school and a strong sense of community.

Where does school personality come from?

It may come in part from a calendar of high-profile events. In addition to Speech Day there is a regular pattern of events which students look forward to and which often involve parents – like debating competitions, poetry reading prizes, singing and instrumental competitions, plays, art and design technology exhibitions, church services, high-profile speakers, fund-raising runs. Once a pattern is established and sold effectively it soon becomes part of a 'tradition'.

Some heads recommend singing as a way of establishing a sense of school community. Of course you need a good music teacher who is able to grip large numbers of pupils. But you cannot beat compulsory singing competitions or compulsory participation in a great choral work like Verdi's *Requiem* for creating a strong positive spirit in a school – even if you do have to hire a few musicians.

All the best schools feel that they do things differently from other schools – 'the John Perryn way' (page 212), the 'King Solomon School way' (page 220), 'the Michaela way' ('*we reject the way most schools do things*'). There is nothing more important than for children to feel proud of their school and to feel it is the best.

The House system

In boarding schools the House is the place where you live. At Eton and Harrow, in the period I worked in those schools, the parents chose the House as well as the school. Indeed there were a good number of parents who felt that the choice of House was more important than the choice of school. If they didn't get their choice of House they might look at another school.

They were right to do so. In a traditional boarding school the House parent has a great influence on the performance of pupils in the House, in just the same way as parents have a big influence on the performance of their children. And of course the House parent/House Master/House Mistress determines the atmosphere of the House. A weak House parent permits indiscipline and that inevitably results in unhappiness. Good House parents become respected friends for life.

The impact of the House parents can be seen most obviously when one House parent retires and another begins. I have seen Houses transform their exam results, their sporting success, their level of music or drama, in a year. So one of the problems boarding schools have is recruiting enough good House parents.

In boarding schools Houses are places where you live. But many school competitions are organised on the basis of Houses. In the schools in which I have worked the level of inter-House rivalry was so great that the Head Master had to take special measures to cool things down. At Harrow I had to ban boys from training for a cadet force assault competition before 6am. The master in charge of rugby looked on slack-jawed as pupils who were of modest ability during inter-school rugby competitions became beasts of speed and handling ability in the inter-House rugby sevens competition. Teenage boys are not noted for their willingness to sing in front of other teenagers, but at Harrow the singing competitions are the most popular of all.

Stevenson and Stigler (1992) write well about the motivating force of being part of a group. In America schools and parents take pride in the notion of their children as individuals. In China and Japan there is a much greater emphasis on being a member of a group, including sub-groups within classes. Pupils are motivated by a strong wish to ensure their group does well. This is exactly the benefit of loyalty to a House.

In day schools Houses are mainly used to generate this sort of motivation. It is harder for them because their Houses are an artificial construct with little other purpose, but with good staff in charge it can be made to work.

A word about innovation

In 2005 I went to visit Capital City Academy in Brent with a view to setting up partnerships with Harrow. The school had opened in 2003 as one of the first and most expensive academies, designed by Norman Foster. In common with a number of academies opened in the Blair years it had needed to demonstrate that it was 'innovative' in order to get the go-ahead. But the school was a disaster in the first year and the head had to be replaced. The new head told me that his job was 'to turn it back into a normal school.'

Time and time again I have seen examples of Academies that are innovative – with very large classes, for example, or masses of computers used for teaching – and these innovations have left them weaker than they might be. Like the schools in Knowsley, the local authority with the worst educational record in England. In 2005 the authority decided to build seven new secondary schools based on their view that local pupils had a 'preferred learning style' which meant they did not like to sit at desks, preferring to move around when being taught. Classrooms were built without walls. Curtains on runners created different zones. The schools opened in 2009 and of course many of the intervening years have been spent trying to turn the schools ('centres for learning') back into normal schools with walls and corridors.

There is nothing wrong with being innovative if it works. But governments should never insist that funding follows schools just because they are innovative because *many innovations fail*. Ninety per cent of the time what is needed is for a school to do established things well – excellent discipline, dynamic teaching, regular testing, and a vibrant programme of cocurricular activities.

Government performance tables

Performance tables published by the Department for Education are in part information for prospective parents, in part a tool used by the Department to influence state school behaviour.

Department for Education performance tables of exam results can be misleading – some of the schools with the best exam results appear low in the league table.

Only the first sitting of a GCSE 'counts' for the current performance tables. This is because the Government was (rightly) annoyed with schools putting pupils in early for exams and then resitting if necessary. So the performance table results of many schools understate how well they have actually done – many pupils take a GCSE early (the one which counts in the table) but go on to gain a higher grade thereafter. Whitmore High School in Harrow is an example of an outstanding school whose performance is not accurately reflected in the DfE performance tables because GCSEs are taken early.

International GCSEs are not counted in the government league tables and so the most ambitious schools, who put pupils in for iGCSEs because they are more stretching than GCSEs, are penalised. Many good schools, such as

Harrow, Winchester and Eton, put pupils in for iGCSE maths and English and are recorded as having no passes in those subjects. The reason most iGCSEs are not counted is that the Government wishes to discourage state schools from offering them. They are worried that if state schools opt for the iGCSE this will undermine the take-up of the reformed GCSEs, the first exams for which are sat in 2017 and 2018.

On the whole a school's raw GCSE and A-level results reflect the nature of the pupils. More academically selective schools obviously do better which is why the performance tables have a score for value-added, or progress, which IS valuable and partly a reflection of the quality of teaching. But value-added is far from a perfect measure of a school's performance because pupil attainment is not only determined by prior attainment and school effectiveness (the two components of value-added). Other things influence that, including the pupils' home lives.

In England progress or value-added is measured at Key Stage 2 by looking at progress in maths, reading and writing between the ages of seven and 11. Later it is used by comparing a child's Key Stage 2 results in reading, writing and maths with their GCSE results using the Progress 8 measure (progress in your best eight GCSEs) which is valuable, although it gives a double weighting to English and maths because Ministers think these are twice as important as other subjects (which they may be, who knows?). Value-added at age 18 is measured by comparing GCSE results with A-level results.

The Progress 8 measure, like all single measures, has flaws. A very small number of weak pupils' results cancel out good scores by many more pupils. So pupils with special needs will have a disproportionate impact on the score and this is unfair, not least on schools who may be making tremendous progress with special needs pupils relative to their ability.

The Government also uses measures of the proportion of pupils doing well in what at GCSE they call EBacc subjects (maths, English, sciences, computer science, modern languages, history and geography) and at A-level they call 'facilitating subjects' – those which are favoured by the Russell Group of good universities. These are both an attempt by the Government to nudge schools towards mainstream subjects and it has worked – a brilliant example of the Government achieving change at no financial cost.

The use of performance measures and Ofsted grades to determine the future of individual schools has put pressure on weak schools to improve – a good thing. However there have been a few unwanted consequences caused by *perverse incentives:*

- The main measure before 2016 was the proportion of students who gained five GCSEs grade A*–C. This encouraged schools to focus on the C/D boundary pupils and neglect those who were either well below a C grade or well above.

- Because of the importance of GCSE performance measures many state schools have reduced the Key Stage 3 to two years (it is supposed to last three years, from the age of 11 to 14) and have pushed Key Stage 4 to three years. This means that pupils have, in some subjects, studied a narrower curriculum than they might otherwise have done. Pupils drop subjects like history and geography when they are 13 rather than 14.

- The Progress 8 measure encourages schools to exclude weak pupils. A small number of pupils with severe special needs depresses a school's Progress 8 more than a larger number of pupils making good progress raises Progress 8. This discourages schools from taking and supporting these children.

- The importance of Ofsted grades has meant that too much time is spent by governors and heads focusing on 'preparing for the next Ofsted' at the expense of more worthwhile things. For example, Ofsted attaches less weight to extracurricular activities and this is one reason why sport, music, drama, cadet forces and societies are weak in too many state schools. Or to put the point another way, school leaders have increasingly come to believe that if they are doing well in government measures they are doing all the right things.

The school you go to is less important than the individual teachers you have

Within-school variation in the progress of pupils is greater than between-school variation. PISA results suggest that England has one of the highest levels of variance within schools in the world: less than 30% of the performance variation lies between schools; the rest is within schools (OECD, 2016). For example, 77% of the variability in science scores for PISA 2015 in England occurred within schools, 23% between schools (Jerrim and Shure, 2016).

A Department for Education study showed that at Key Stage 2 in-school variance was five times greater than between-school variance, at Key Stage 3 it was 11 times greater and at Key Stage 4 it was 14 times greater (Department for Education, 2010).

Put another way, parents would be much better off if they could choose their children's teachers rather than choosing their school. This is especially true of pupils from low-income families:

'*The effects of high-quality teaching are especially significant for pupils from disadvantaged backgrounds: over a school year, these pupils gain 1.5 years' worth of learning with very effective teachers, compared with 0.5 years with poorly performing teachers. In other words, for poor pupils the difference between a good teacher and a bad teacher is a whole year's learning.*' (Sutton Trust, 2011)

This is why those schools and MATs that focus on consistently good practice within their schools are right. Teachers are told exactly what they are expected to do and they are closely monitored. As Jonathan Simons (2016) said, 'factory schooling' is a term deployed pejoratively but consistency within schools brings great benefits to the pupils.

There is too much emphasis on debate about school types in England (grammars, maintained, academies *etc*) when in fact what goes on in individual classrooms matters much more.

Chapters 8–18 are my reports on visits to a number of schools which have been identified as being especially successful, for different reasons. They are not 'the best schools in England'. They are just a selection of schools which have very good exam results or very good progress scores or seem to be making a success of an innovative approach to education. Each was chosen for a specific reason, to illustrate a particular point. I could have added a hundred more.

Chapter 2

Successful Teachers

When you talk about teaching it is difficult not to sound as if you are stating the obvious. Because...well, you are. And yet it is obviousness of a tricky kind.

Jonathan Smith, 2000, *The Learning Game*

When I started teaching (at Eton) we had little in the way of induction or training. The first lesson I taught was the first lesson I had ever taught. New teachers found a piece of paper from the Head Master in their pigeon holes; this is it:

HINTS ON TEACHING AND DISCIPLINE

1. Relations with Boys

Be friendly without being matey. Boys should not be called by their Christian names in class. When talking to boys about a colleague refer to him as "Mr X" or "your Tutor", and insist that they do likewise. Avoid being drawn into discussing your colleagues or other boys (*eg*, those in authority such as House Captains); boys are skilled at luring you into indiscretions and at playing one master off against another. When a boy says "Mr X says it's all right if you say so", it's wise to check with Mr X. Don't allow boys to come up and talk to you disrespectfully, and, if you observe discourtesy at any time, tell the boy concerned on the spot and tell his House Master. In fact if every master's complaint about the boys' conduct were replaced by on-the-spot reproof the community would greatly benefit.

It is not possible to like all boys equally. But you should do your best to treat all with absolute equality, certainly in all formal situations, and as far as possible in informal situations too.

As a master you share a responsibility for the maintenance of discipline. You have a copy of the Masters' Book and School Rules

---

which you should make yourself familiar with. If you see a boy breaking a minor rule, deal with it yourself and tell his House Master what you have done; if it is serious, send him to report himself to his House Master and tell the House Master that you have done so. If you come across a boy out of bounds, do not hesitate to ask to see his permission. Discipline is resented only when its application is bad.

In all matters concerning boys it is sensible to keep in touch with House Masters and Tutors, especially if you are having difficulty over their work or behaviour. For they can tell you about such relevant factors as a boy's home background, and his intellectual and other strengths and weaknesses.

2. Control in School

First learn the boys' names: you will find this easier if you sit them in alphabetical order starting from the front row. This has the further advantage of breaking up tiresome cliques or pairs of boys. When you come into the room, insist on the boys' being seated and silent. Be punctual in starting lessons and insist on boys' punctuality and tidiness; also that they bring the right books in. Don't hesitate to apply mild sanctions to get your way, and always give the offender a "ticket" to be signed by House Master or Tutor and ensure that you get it back.

Above all, be consistent in your attitude and demands. Boys respond to stability and consistency; they like to know where they stand, and they mistrust capriciousness and unreliability.

Punishment: be explicit in warning them and firm in carrying it out. Late work should be corrected but not marked. Inform House Masters and Tutors of all punishments by making the offender take a "ticket" or "tear-over" for their signature. For bad work the best punishment is "do again", and if the second attempt is poor, have double the amount done a third time. When you have work done again, set a time limit for it to be handed in by. For misbehaviour after a warning, give a stiff punishment; when in doubt consult the House Master. If you are dissatisfied with the behaviour of a class as a whole, see me if the boys are in D and above, and the Lower Master if they are in E or F.

Try to avoid requiring boys to leave the classroom. This should only be done in extreme circumstances and is more often than not a confession of failure on the master's part. If it is necessary, you should tell the House Master. You may like to arrange with the House Master and Tutor to "complain" of the boy to me or the Lower Master.

In general, err on the side of strictness to start with; you can always ease up later. Boys will always get away with what they can.

Cheating: particularly in the Lower School, minor cribbing is likely, and should be eradicated immediately.

3. Teaching Methods

Consult your Head of Department freely, and don't be afraid to ask advice on even small points of teaching technique. If you have not done a Certificate / Dip. Ed. year, invite your Head of Department or some other colleague to come and "sit in" on you, and ask if you can do the same on him.

Other help can be got by visiting other schools, from Ministry of Education pamphlets on the teaching of individual subjects, and journals of particular specialisations, *eg*, the publications of the Association for Scientific Education.

A period of 45 minutes is surprisingly short; you need to plan the use of your time in advance carefully. In particular, leave enough but not too much time for *testing* the knowledge your class have acquired.

At all levels boys are quick to judge a master by his care in *correcting* their written work and his *promptness in returning it*. In D, E, and F (Years 11, 10 and 9) it is more important to be prompt than detailed. When giving back work, make a few public comments on it; in D, E, and F collect the marks publicly also.

Regard it as your duty to insist on legibility and clear lay-out and to correct the English of your boys' work whether it is an English class or not, and insist on correct spelling and punctuation, *etc*. Except for tests, there is much advantage in getting boys to do written work in exercise books. Their progress can then be followed through the term or year.

Be careful not to go too fast for the average boy. When boys fail to understand, do not show irritation, *still less indulge in sarcasm*. Another mistake commonly made by the beginner is to lecture rather than teach.

Don't dodge or shelve a genuine enquiry. You may need or wish to defer an answer till another occasion, or you may need to confess ignorance. But a genuine attempt should be made to find the answer by an agreed time.

4. Reports

Order Cards (fortnightly report cards) for D, E, and F (Years 11, 10 and 9) and half-term reports should be short and clear.

End-of-term reports mean a great deal to most parents, and while they should be candid they should be worded so as not to cause unnecessary distress. There should be no signs of personal animosity. To write reports which are neither platitudinous nor offensive takes time. Try to avoid stereotyped formulae: no two reports should be the same. Distinguish between a boy's industry and ability. Parents ought to receive an assessment of their son's progress and achievement, and, if possible, some indication of what is preventing him from doing as well as he might. Assessments are more convincing if they are relative *eg,* to the level of the class, his performance last term, his prospects in an external exam, but be careful of the last until you have had some experience of such exams. Where you criticise unfavourably, try to find something, however small, to mention on the credit side; and reflect that too severe a criticism may reflect on your own capacity as a teacher. In no circumstances should a strongly adverse report be the first thing heard of a boy's poor work. It is safer, easier, and quicker to write a final report if you have made a few notes towards it in your mark-book during the term. You can also collect the boys' exercise books just before you write your reports.

The main headings to consider when writing a boy's report are his ability, originality and initiative, interest in the subject, industry, perseverance, organisation and presentation of his work, and his attitude (co-operative or not, *etc.*).

It is worth while keeping some notes of what you have written in order not to repeat or contradict yourself the following term.

Typed reports should be signed in ink. Biro should not be used.

5. Invigilation is a duty, not an opportunity for doing other work or reading.

This was all wise, and easier to appreciate now than it was then.

I went straight from university to teaching via a short spell buying and selling coconuts out of a railway arch in Waterloo. I had no intention of remaining a teacher but I realised very quickly that this was the perfect job for me. I was a keen geographer and just loved working with my subject, learning more every day. As the years rolled by I would spend about half the school holidays reading and preparing lessons ... bliss.

I loved the acting element. Every lesson could be a show. I loved the fact that I could make a difference. I knew how to do well in exams and I knew how to teach my pupils to do the same. I loved the competitive element – could my classes do better than other sets? I loved the rapport with pupils and colleagues.

Finally I loved the fact that I was part of a good system – a good school but more importantly a very good department. In the 1980s over 100 boys chose A-level geography in my school each year. We were a strong team who made the subject interesting and fun.

Good teachers

Research shows that the most important influence on pupil progress is the quality of the teacher, as opposed to things like the school type or the brilliance of the head. We know that with a weak teacher a pupil makes six months' progress in a year compared to the average. With a great teacher a pupil makes 18 months progress in a year – so the difference between the two is 300% (Slater, Davies and Burgess, 2009).

It is quite difficult to identify good teachers by just interviewing them. A teacher's own educational record does not correlate well with an ability to teach. This is why it is important to see applicants for teaching jobs teach classes before they are appointed. One of my heads of modern languages was fairly quiet and rarely engaged in conversation – it was hard to see him being a great teacher. Yet in fact he was one of the most inspiring teachers his fortunate pupils would ever come across – dynamic, animated, tough, and brilliant at his own subject. But based solely on an interview he would have been unappointable.

Schools often ask pupils to comment on the performance of prospective teachers' sample lessons – possibly a mistake because pupils tend to favour sample lessons for the wrong reasons.

Atteberry, Loeb & Wyckoff (2013) used New York City value-added data to measure the effectiveness of over 3000 teachers of maths and English over the first five years of their career. They found:

- Most teachers improve with experience.
- The teachers who were most effective to start with remained the most effective after five years.
- A teacher's performance in their first two years of teaching is a far better predictor of future performance than anything else.

This suggests that it is difficult to improve a teacher and that a beginner-teacher starts with or without the attributes necessary for success – such as subject knowledge, empathy and the ability to communicate well. Teachers can be improved, but the best way of ensuring you have good staff is to appoint the best ones in the first place.

When I started teaching I was on a two-year probationary period. The purpose of a probationary period is for an employer to determine if a (new) employee is suitable for a job and for an employee to determine if they want to stay in the job. There is no statutory limit on the length of a probationary period but, given the purpose of probationary periods, it is expected that employers will be reasonable when determining this.

Let me echo Jonathan Smith's words: much that one can say about teaching is obvious. But if it is so obvious why is everyone not as good as Jonathan was as an English teacher at Tonbridge? Because implementing the obvious is difficult. I did woodwork O-level and love DIY so I completely understand how to make a table, but I also know that making a table is very difficult, very skilful and takes years of practice to do well. I cannot make a table.

So what does the research tell us about teacher effectiveness?

All teacher effectiveness studies suffer from a flaw identified by Brophy (1979), among others. After reviewing the extant research on teaching he said, '*The influence of context is being recognized as more and more important. [Thus] there do not appear to be any universal teaching competencies ... that are appropriate in any and all circumstances.*' In other words, teacher A may be better than teacher B with low ability or disruptive pupils, teacher B may be better than teacher A with able and well-behaved pupils.

Nevertheless, there are some useful pointers in the research.

Coe, R., Aloisi, C., Higgins, S. and Elliot Major, L. (2014), *What makes great teaching? Review of the underpinning research*, Sutton Trust

This is a well-known meta-survey of over 200 previous pieces of research into teacher effectiveness. The authors found that the two factors with the *strongest* evidence of improving pupil attainment were:

- Teachers' content knowledge, including their ability to understand how students think about a subject and identify common misconceptions.
- The quality of instruction, which includes using strategies like effective questioning, the use of assessment, reviewing previous learning, using model answers, and giving adequate time to practise topics so that pupils firmly grasp concepts.

Four other factors associated with good teaching were:

- Classroom climate – the quality of the relationship between the teacher and pupils, a teacher with high expectations but one who recognises pupils' self-worth, a teacher who attributes success to effort rather than ability.
- Classroom management – a teacher who manages behaviour well, who makes efficient use of lesson time, whose rules are all aimed at maximising learning.
- Teacher beliefs – the best teachers know why they are doing things in the way they are. In maths teaching, for example, the best teachers know what good numeracy looks like and they know how children learn it.
- Professional behaviour – good teachers reflect on and develop professional practice, support colleagues and liaise with parents.

Specific practices which have good evidence of improving attainment include:

- Challenging students to identify the reason why an activity is taking place in the lesson.
- Asking a large number of questions and checking the responses of all students.
- Spacing out study or practice on a given topic, with gaps in between for forgetting.
- Making students take tests or generate answers, even before they have been taught the material.

Common practices which do *not* improve pupil results include:

- Using praise lavishly.
- Allowing pupils to discover key ideas by themselves.
- Grouping students by ability.
- Presenting information to students based on their 'preferred learning style'.
- Using re-reading and highlighting as ways to memorise material.

- Ensuring pupils are active rather than listening passively if you want them to remember something.
- Efforts to raise confidence or low aspirations.

How does one assess teaching quality? Coe *et al* suggest there are three 'moderate validity' methods:

1. Lesson observation. Lesson observation is used in most schools to help teachers improve. It is also used by inspectors to gauge the quality of teaching. If lesson observation is to be used the observers need to be trained.

Lesson observation has three weaknesses – it is quite subjective and is therefore not ideal if the results are high stakes, such as determining a teacher's pay. Secondly, having an adult in the room scrutinising you will inevitably affect the teacher's performance – you are unlikely to see a 'typical' lesson. Thirdly, successful teaching sometimes depends on the cumulative impact of work over several weeks; one lesson observation will not capture that.

2. Value-added models measure progress over time. You would never judge teachers on their raw exam results because some teachers teach subjects taken by very bright pupils (like Latin) and can expect top grades. Another teacher may teach a bottom ability maths set and can expect relatively poor grades.

Value-added measures the progress a child makes from one year to another *relative to the ability of other children* who were at a similar starting point at the beginning. So we can measure progress from Key Stage 1 (age 7) to Key Stage 2 (age 11) and so on.

Some teachers get better value-added than others but variation in value-added teacher by teacher is difficult for researchers because it requires them to obtain class lists – which is not publically available information.

The validity of value-added analysis is affected by various things:

- David Berliner (2014), a professor at Arizona State University, found that individual teacher's value-added scores were very variable according to the class they were teaching. This was because of the impact of *exogenous variables* such as the nature of the pupils and characteristics of the neighbourhoods in which students live. Girls, for example, work harder and make more progress than boys. So when a teacher has more girls in a class they achieve more value-added. A weak teacher with an able class may achieve more progress than a strong teacher with a low ability class.

  Hirsch (2016) makes the point that in English language teaching particularly, a high proportion of what children know comes from their parents. The value-added measures are to some extent measuring the effectiveness of the child's parents. Teachers of middle-class children will inevitably gain much higher value-added scores. Teachers are not the only agent affecting student achievement in their classrooms.

- The quality of the child's *previous* teacher. If the child had a brilliant previous teacher he will already be at a higher level at the start of the cycle than he 'should be' and this will depress the value-added score of the next teacher. Westminster School in London sometimes has poor A-level value-added. A-level value-added is based on progress since GCSE but in this case is hard to achieve because their excellent teachers ensure that their pupils achieve the top grades in most subjects at GCSE.

- The size of the group being looked at. Value-added measures are not statistically significant if the group size is small. In a small class just one or two children can have a big effect on the average value-added.

3. Student ratings. Pupil ratings of teachers are used in increasing numbers of schools and in all universities.

Coe *et al* also concluded that three other methods of assessing teachers had limited validity:

1. Headteacher judgement

2. Teacher's self-report

3. Analysis of lesson plans, teacher assignments and pupils' work

Sammons, P., Kington, A., Lindorff-Vijayendran, A. and Ortega, L. (2014), *Inspiring teachers: perspectives and practices*, CfBT

Thirty-six teachers nominated by their schools as being inspiring were observed to explore their practices. Seventeen of these were then interviewed and there was a survey of 203 pupils.

The main characteristics of inspiring teachers were found to be:

- enthusiasm for teaching
- positive relationships with children
- they are committed professionals who continue to learn and improve their own practice

The main characteristics of inspiring lessons were found to be:

- enthusiasm
- good behaviour management
- clear instructions

- good lesson pace
- gave formative feedback
- intellectual challenge – students are stretched
- high expectations
- trust between the teacher and pupils so that pupils are not embarrassed to speak up
- goal-focused activity – they never lose sight of the aim, which is making progress in the subject
- using a wide range of teaching strategies to create variety

Other characteristics of good lessons were:

- asking pupils questions by name and encouraging all pupils to contribute
- pupils knew what to do at the beginning and end of lessons without being reminded
- there was a strong sense of teacher authority
- teachers had strong subject knowledge
- lessons were made enjoyable

Sammons, P., The EPPSE project, a lecture in Oxford, 24 May 2016

The Effective Pre-School, Primary and Secondary Education (EPPSE 3–16) project is a research study that has followed the progress of 3000+ children since 1997 from the age of 3 to 16 years.

They found that good GCSE outcomes correlated with, in rank order:

1. Schools which placed a big emphasis on learning.
2. Schools with good behaviour.
3. The amount of homework time in Year 9. 25% of boys spent 1–2 hours a night compared to 32% of girls, one factor explaining the gender gap in results.
4. The qualities of the headteacher.
5. The school's physical environment.
6. A feeling that the school valued students.

They also found that pupils on free school meals had a less positive view of school than others: they were less happy and had less academic self-confidence. This tended to reinforce their disadvantage.

Matthews, P., Rea, S., Hill, R., and Gu, Q. (2014), *Freedom to lead: a study of outstanding primary school leadership in England*, National College for Teaching and Leadership

The authors did an analysis of 20 outstanding primary schools as well as 84 Ofsted inspection reports. The findings were:

1. The basic tenets of the best primary school heads are:

- All children can succeed – most can reach level 4 by age 11.
- Primary schools determine life chances. Children who do not reach level 4 in English and maths at 11 struggle with GCSEs.
- Background should not limit outcomes. Some schools with many disadvantaged pupils achieve excellent results.
- Successful schools do the right things consistently well.
- Almost all teachers can be good or better. CPD matters.
- Teaching needs clear learning objectives, effective instruction for all, feedback and assessment.
- School leadership is key to raising standards.
- The best heads model good teaching.
- The best support for teachers comes from other expert practitioners.
- The quality of the curriculum makes a big contribution to the children's interest, engagement and learning.

2. The best heads...

- have a single-minded focus on teaching and learning.
- are driven, determined and committed.
- have high expectations.
- have a no-excuses policy.
- are good at communicating.
- trust and empower staff.

3. What a leader needs to do depends on the stage the school is at. An inadequate school needs rapid control of behaviour, firm action. A 'requires improvement' school needs to build capacity, harness good practice, raise aspirations. A good school needs refinement – ensuring all teaching and learning is good, ensuring the needs of every pupil is met. An excellent school needs renewal – building on outstanding practice.

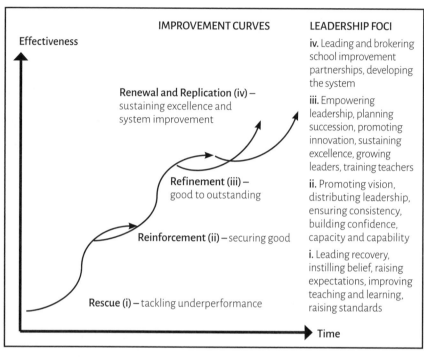

IMPROVEMENT CURVES

LEADERSHIP FOCI

Effectiveness

iv. Leading and brokering school improvement partnerships, developing the system

Renewal and Replication (iv) – sustaining excellence and system improvement

iii. Empowering leadership, planning succession, promoting innovation, sustaining excellence, growing leaders, training teachers

Refinement (iii) – good to outstanding

ii. Promoting vision, distributing leadership, ensuring consistency, building confidence, capacity and capability

Reinforcement (ii) – securing good

i. Leading recovery, instilling belief, raising expectations, improving teaching and learning, raising standards

Rescue (i) – tackling underperformance

Time

Source: Matthews, Rea, Hill, and Gu, 2014

Common features of outstanding teaching and learning were felt to be:

- Stimulating and enthusiastic teaching which interests, excites and motivates pupils and accelerates their learning.
- High expectations of what pupils can do.
- Consistency in the quality of teaching across the school.
- Development of good learning habits with many opportunities for pupils to find things out for themselves.
- Highly structured approaches to reading, writing and mathematics.
- Well-planned lessons that provide for the differing needs of pupils.
- Stimulating classroom environment.
- Frequent praise and a valued reward system.
- Well-trained and deployed teaching assistants.
- A close check on learning during lessons, with effective marking and assessment.

- Clear evidence of progress.

The Education Endowment Foundation Toolkit

educationendowmentfoundation.org.uk/toolkit/

The Education Endowment Foundation Toolkit is research into 'what works and what doesn't work' in raising standards of achievement of disadvantaged pupils aged 5–16. It is sponsored by the Sutton Trust and the Department for Education.

The Toolkit is written by Professor Steve Higgins, Dr Maria Katsipataki (School of Education, Durham University), Professor Rob Coe (CEM Centre, Durham University), Dr Lee Elliot Major (The Sutton Trust), Robbie Coleman and Peter Henderson (Education Endowment Foundation).

The research evidence for the effectiveness of each 'intervention' is expressed in terms of the COST per pupil each year of the intervention and the number of months of PROGRESS the intervention gives the average child in the study.

The results represent averages across many schools. What is true of many schools on average may not be true of any one school – so the toolkit should be treated as an aid to thinking about your school, not a directive.

Impact vs. cost

Source: CEM, Durham University

	Average progress made in a year because of the intervention
Things which don't work	
School uniform policy	0 months
Setting and streaming	-1 months
Longer lessons (double periods etc)	0 months
Repeating a year	-4 months
Efforts to raise aspirations	0 months
Performance pay for teachers	0 months
Improving physical environment of the school	0 months
Things which don't do much harm or much good	
Homework in primary school	1 months
Mentoring	1 months
Arts participation	2 months
Individualised instruction *Individualised instruction is giving different tasks to each child*	2 months
Using different learning styles	2 months
Sports participation	2 months
Extending school hours	2 months
Summer schools	2 months
Things which produce improvements but are expensive	
Smaller classes (very expensive)	3 months
Digital technology	4 months
Improving behaviour	4 months
Early years interventions (very expensive)	5 months
One-to-one tuition	5 months
Small group tuition (2–5 pupils)	4 months
Outdoor adventure learning	3 months
Parental involvement	3 months

Teaching assistants	1 months
Social and emotional learning	4 months
Things which produce significant improvements at limited cost	
Collaborative learning *Students working together in small groups*	5 months
Homework in secondary schools	5 months
Mastery learning *Subject matter is broken down into units and there is a test at the end of each unit. Students must do very well in the test before they move on to the next unit.*	5 months
Oral language interventions *Focusing on spoken English; especially good for younger children and those from disadvantaged backgrounds*	5 months
Use of phonics to teach reading	4 months
Reading comprehension *Especially good for older pupils not making progress*	5 months
Meta-cognition and self-regulation *Meta-cognition is giving children a range of strategies they can use to monitor and improve their own academic development. Self-regulation is developing the ability to motivate oneself to learn.*	8 months
Feedback *Feedback is information given to pupils about how they are doing against their learning goals.*	8 months
Peer-tutoring *Pupils work together in pairs or small groups to give each other explicit teaching support.*	5 months

The figures above change over time as new evidence comes in.

The toolkit is one of the most used pieces of research in British schools. However, as with all such lists of 'what works' the challenge is implementation. Teachers are slow to change their ways and anyway much depends on the detail of how any particular intervention is actually used.

In the Education Endowment Foundation *Parent Engagement Project*, 2016, 16,000 students in 36 English secondary schools took part in a randomised controlled trial delivered by the University of Bristol and Harvard University. Selected parents were sent an average of 30 texts over one school year (roughly one a week) with content ranging from dates of upcoming tests and warnings about missed homework, to information about what their child had learnt that day. In these ways parents became more engaged in their children's school work.

Pupils whose parents received the texts made an additional month's progress in maths compared with a similar group whose parents didn't get the texts. Absenteeism was reduced too.

Hattie, J. (2009), *Visible Learning*
Hattie, J. (2012), *Visible Learning for Teachers*

John Hattie is Director of the Melbourne Education Research Institute at the University of Melbourne, Australia. *Visible Learning* is a synthesis of more than 50,000 studies covering 240 million pupils. Hattie compares the impact of many influences on students' achievement and finds:

- *What doesn't work?* Reducing class size, individualized instruction, extracurricular programmes, ability grouping, student control over learning, summer schools, using different learning styles.
- *What's neither bad nor good?* Team teaching, open vs. traditional classes.
- *What helps a bit?* Enquiry-based teaching, computer-assisted instruction, homework
- *What helps a bit more?* Cooperative learning, direct instruction.
- *What helps a lot?* Clear feedback to students, good student-teacher relationships, high expectations for each student, the teaching of study skills, the teaching of learning strategies.

In *Visible Learning for Teachers,* Hattie's central point is that the most effective teachers are those who focus on the impact their teaching is having – they constantly assess their own work as well as that of their pupils. Most of the most effective teaching methods are not accidents: they are deliberate strategies adopted by teachers who are assessing the impact of their work.

The best teachers:

- do not necessarily have better subject knowledge than less good teachers but they do have a superior understanding of how to organize and use their subject knowledge. They are, for example, better able to combine new subject knowledge with pupils' prior learning. They are better able to relate their subject teaching to other subjects the students are studying. They know where pupils are most likely to stumble.

- create a classroom atmosphere in which it is acceptable to make mistakes. This is important because pupils learn from mistakes only if they are not nervous about them. They create a climate where pupils want to learn and do well.

- seek and use feedback about the effectiveness of their teaching so they know when interest is waning or when pupils do not fully grasp a concept.

- believe all their pupils can do well. They involve and respect their pupils.

- enable their pupils to not only do well in assessments but to develop deep understanding of the subject and a desire to succeed. They set challenging goals rather than 'do your best' goals.

The best teachers are passionate about teaching and learning. '*The key components of passion for the teacher and for the learner appear to be the sheer thrill of being a learner or teacher, the absorption that accompanies the process of teaching and learning, the sensations of being involved in the activity of teaching and learning...*'

Hattie's results suggest that school reform should concentrate on what is going on in the classroom and not on structural reforms.

Hattie is also completely right when he points out that reading his book will not make much difference to most teachers. He says: '*Talking is one thing; action is the other. To put the ideas in this book...into action requires having an intention to change, having knowledge of what successful change would look like, and having a safe opportunity to trial any new teaching methods. This often requires some specific coaching.*'

Class size effects

Class sizes in the UK are quite large – an average of 25 at primary schools compared to an OECD average of 21.

There are mixed opinions amongst researchers about the merits of smaller class sizes. PISA research suggested that small class sizes do not raise standards. They point out that some of the highest-achieving jurisdictions have large class sizes, such as China with average primary class sizes of 37. Andreas Schleicher has often said that the policy should be to 'put the best teachers in front of large classes'.

The McKinsey research (pages 19–21) echoes this. John Hattie reported that the average effect size for class size and student achievement, based on hundreds of studies, was positive but small.

The Education Endowment Foundation toolkit (page 63) summarises the research in the UK and concludes that smaller class sizes raise standards, especially at primary level, but not by much and at tremendous cost.

By contrast, the CSPAR study (Class Size and Pupil-Adult Ratios project, Blatchford, 2003) looked at Key Stage 1 and 2 pupils (about 31,000 in total) in the UK. They found that children in smaller classes got more individual attention, were more involved and less passive and there was less poor behaviour. Teachers found that with large classes they were frustrated because they could not meet pupils' needs, it was harder to spot problems with individual pupils, harder to give good feedback, harder to set individual tasks for pupils. Pupils with special educational needs had less overall teaching, less individual attention and did more work with teaching assistants. The CSPAR conclusion was that smaller classes lead to higher academic attainment.

The American STAR Project (Student-Teacher Achievement Ratio), (Finn and Achilles, 1990) looked at a cohort of 12,000 students in Tennessee between 1985 and 1989. They found that small classes did better academically and especially benefitted minority ethnic students, so reducing the achievement gap. In smaller classes young children from poor homes found it easier to learn how to learn. The students were more engaged, they received more individual attention, there were fewer disciplinary problems. Smaller classes generated a stronger sense of group membership, children were more able to support each other, teacher stress and teacher turnover was less. Teachers spent less time on behaviour management and less time on paperwork.

The California Class Size Reduction (CSR) Program to reduce class size began in 1996 when California's state legislature passed a reform aimed at cutting class size in the early school grades from what had been an average of 28 students to a maximum of 20. While the Tennessee STAR program was a carefully controlled experiment involving 12,000 students, the California program was implemented state-wide for 1.8 million students. Jepson and Rivkin (2002) found that, all else being equal, smaller classes raised student achievement. Reducing class size by 10 students raised the percentage of third-grade students who exceed national median test scores by about four percentage points in mathematics and three percentage points in reading. However, all else is not equal when you hire thousands of new teachers. Separating out the effects of new teachers from the effects of smaller classes, Jepsen and Rivkin found that having a new teacher reduced the percentage of students who exceed the national median by roughly three percentage points in both mathematics and reading. So in many schools, class size reduction meant zero gain, at least in the short run. The bottom line was that California implemented a $1.6-billion-a-year programme that yielded only modest gains.

Lorin W. Anderson, Professor Emeritus at the University of South Carolina, Columbia, reviewed existing research in a lecture in 2016. He found that class effect size varies depending on:

1. Differences in the sizes of the classes being compared (*eg* 25 vs. 5; 25 vs. 15; 40 vs. 20).

2. Differences in ages/grade levels of students. Younger = larger effect size.

3. Differences in the socio-economic status of students. Poorer = larger effect size.

4. Differences in the subject matter (*eg* reading vs. arithmetic). Effects more likely to remain over time for reading than for arithmetic.

There is another important point about class size which is well analysed by Stevenson and Stigler (1992). Countries have finite resources to spend on education so there is always a trade-off between class size and hours spent teaching. In countries with smaller classes (America, the UK) simple economics means that teachers have to spend more time in front of pupils and have less time for preparation and CPD. In countries with larger classes like China (38–50 in a class) the system can afford to allow teachers to teach less and have more time to prepare.

The reduced teaching load of teachers in East Asia is important. It means that they have the time to devise excellent lessons and to observe others teach. Of course they have to be able to cope with larger classes – but they do cope, partly by ensuring pupils are well behaved and follow clearly established routines. One reason the pupils behave is that the lessons are excellent so pupils are engaged.

Gates Foundation (2010), *Learning about Teaching: Initial findings from the Measures of Effective Teaching Project*

This study estimated the value-added results of 3000 teachers and also asked the students to complete surveys of their experiences in these classes. In the classes with the most effective teachers pupils said that:

1. Teachers kept control: 'students in this class treat the teacher with respect.'

2. Teachers care for pupils: 'my teacher really tries to understand how students feel about things.'

3. Teachers explain things clearly.

4. Teachers raise the bar: 'in this class we learn a lot every day.'

5. Teachers make lessons interesting.

6. Teachers allow students to speak up and share their ideas.

7. Teachers check to make sure the pupils all understand.

However, a continuation of this study (2012) found quite weak correlations between multiple measures of teacher behaviour and student test scores. For example, in mathematics, across several years, the correlation of teacher behaviour with pupil value-added scores ranged from 0.12 to 0.25. Across different classes taught in the same year by the same teacher the correlations ran from 0.16 to 0.26 – all very low.

The reason the correlation was weak was that factors *other than* the teacher have a big impact on pupils' value-added scores. High ability classes nearly always make more progress than low ability, for example. Identifying the characteristics of 'the best' teachers may be the holy grail, but it is extremely difficult to achieve.

The Heart of Great Teaching: the Pearson, Global Survey of Educator Effectiveness (2016)

Pearson surveyed 13,000 citizens in 23 countries, asking the question: "What do you think are the most important qualities of an effective teacher?"

The most common response, regardless of country, gender or other factors, was that relationships between teachers and students matter most.

Top 5 most valued qualities for teachers across all 23 countries:

- The ability to develop trusting, compassionate relationships with students
- Patient, caring, and kind personality
- Professionalism
- Subject matter knowledge
- Knowledge of the students

Top 10 most valued qualities for teachers in England were:

- Ability to develop trusting, productive relationships
- Patient, caring, kind personality
- Engaging students in learning
- Subject matter knowledge
- Knowledge of the students
- Professionalism
- Classroom management

- Ability to make ideas and content clear
- Dedication to teaching
- Teaching skills/pedagogical practices

This can be set alongside with Stevenson and Stigler's research (1992) which showed that teachers in America put 'sensitivity to the needs of individual children' as the most important quality of a good teacher while teachers in Beijing emphasised 'ability to explain things clearly'. American teachers emphasise individual differences and the importance of building self-esteem while Chinese teachers see themselves as skilled performers, delivering a lesson as effectively as possible.

Doug Lemov's micro-techniques

Successful teachers do not all use the same methods with children. However, most would agree with the pedagogical techniques described in Doug Lemov's books *Teach like a Champion* and *Practice Perfect*. Doug has observed hundreds of the most successful teachers in the most difficult schools in America, working out in detail what makes them so great. He has isolated the *micro-techniques* which make all the difference to student learning and behaviour, such as careful routines for the distribution and collection of classroom materials. He recommends specific drills as a way of practising these techniques.

Many of Lemov's techniques are used in the schools described on pages 212–276. All teachers should have a copy of Lemov's books and the accompanying DVDs.

Teacher training and CPD

In England there are numerous types of teacher training:

Number of teacher trainees recruited for academic year 2016/17 (source: DfE)

Post-graduate courses

University courses 11,992

SCITTs (School Centred Initial Teacher Training) 3057

School Direct (unsalaried) 7470 – These are based in schools and pair up with universities or SCITTs.

School Direct (salaried) 3159

Teach First 1375 – Designed to attract good graduates who will work in disadvantaged areas.

Undergraduate courses 5195

All types of teacher training lead to one thing – Qualified Teacher Status. In universities there is a qualification is called a PGCE (post-graduate certificate in education) but the PGCE gives you QTS, which is what matters.

In recent years the Government has moved much teacher training from universities to good schools. It is too early to say if this is a good thing or not. What is certain is that as a country we still lack the confidence of the East Asian countries, who have longer and more carefully planned teacher training programmes. We have still failed to make teacher training as attractive an option as it is in countries like Finland.

In England 10% of teachers retire or choose to leave the profession every year; that is 35,000 teachers. Most leave because of poor behaviour or because they wish to improve their work-life balance. So each year at least 35,000 teachers need to be recruited, the same size as the British Navy. Even this figure does not take account of the expectation that pupil numbers will rise by 13% between 2016 and 2025. There are serious teacher shortages in some parts of the country, especially in sciences, modern languages and design and technology. The majority of Teach First graduates drop out within three years.

There are 500,000 trained teachers in the UK who are not currently in teaching; many of these might return to the profession if they were offered part-time work. Many have a university loan the repayment of which will be triggered by a full-time job but not by a part-time job.

Several of the schools described in Chapters 8–18 take additional measures to find good teachers. Some are Teaching Schools so they are able to recruit from the annual pool of trainees. Some that are not Teaching Schools nevertheless recruit direct from universities and train the teachers themselves. Some appoint teaching assistants who are, over time, trained up to become full-time teachers.

The Carter Review of teacher training (2015) found that the average quality of teacher training was quite good, although the number of different routes was confusing. Their main concern was the absence of subject-knowledge development on some training courses – a grave omission and something which distinguishes England from countries thought to have strong teacher training like Finland and Singapore. Even teachers with a degree in a subject often lack the breadth of knowledge to cope with the National Curriculum. Primary teachers, especially, need breadth across a range of subjects.

Teacher-shortage subjects like maths and physics are often taught at secondary level by teachers with a degree in a different subject. Such teachers need a great deal of subject-knowledge training which they do not always get at present.

Nor, the review found, is there enough emphasis on behaviour management or on child and adolescent development or on assessment methods. Poor behaviour is a common reason why teachers leave the profession so behaviour-management is clearly an essential element of training, yet the Carter Review found one university where this matter received one hour of advice in the year-long teacher training course.

In *Beyond the Plateau* (2016), Matt Hood blamed poor quality professional development for the fact that many teachers are not progressing to become the excellent teachers he claims they could be. He argues that there are *three myths* that need busting.

1. Teachers are born, not made

Matt makes the point that successful teachers are of many types which it why it is odd to believe that it is the teacher's inborn personality that matters. What is more, his experience shows that good training can create very effective teachers.

2. If you know it, you can teach it

The second myth is that if you know something you can teach it. No, you have to know *how* to teach a subject. Subject knowledge is not enough.

3. Teaching isn't hard

No, teaching is a phenomenally hard task that takes years to master.

'Compared to middle leadership, classroom teaching lacks a clear progression route to mastery; its lower status and pay progression is poorer.' (Hood, 2016).

With these thoughts in mind he called for a new US-style institute for advanced teaching in the UK specifically for staff in challenging schools and run by successful schools in disadvantaged areas. This would be far more effective than the current scatter-gun approach of CPD.

Much of the best CPD is subject-based: courses led by subject associations and exam boards. Much of the best CPD is simply visits to other good schools; more can be learnt spending an hour in another school than attending any number of talks in a conference centre.

Teachers in Singapore are entitled to 100 hours of CPD a year and teach fewer hours a week than teachers in England. We are miles behind in this respect. In East Asia teachers teach fewer hours than do teachers in England and spend more time talking together about the details of how to teach topics successfully.

The question of teacher autonomy and teacher quality

When I started teaching, many independent schools quite deliberately avoided applicants for jobs who had had training. It was felt that good teachers could do the job based on their subject knowledge; pedagogy was something you could pick up as you went along.

Michaela Community School (page 242) believes that there is a specific way of teaching which is effective and that it is essential for all their teachers to teach in the same way. So they are trained to teach in this manner. The Michaela approach is arguably the safest – you know exactly how each teacher should be performing. It means that you don't have to rely on 'outstanding' teachers to do the job. Outstanding teachers are thin on the ground and it is more secure to take teachers with plenty of potential but limited experience and train them in 'the Michaela way'.

Does this rob the teacher of autonomy? Only to some degree. To be a good pianist you have to be taught to read music and play the piano. Pianists all over the world are being taught to read the notes and press the keys in a similar way. Ultimately this releases their creativity rather than stifling it. Michaela teachers have plenty of opportunity to express their individuality, to interact with individual pupils and to develop their own subject knowledge.

Teacher quality is not the only influence on pupils' achievements

Chingos and Whitehurst (2012) have shown that there are two variables which determine how well pupils learn: teacher quality and the curriculum/syllabus they teach. A good teacher asked to teach a weak syllabus may be less effective than a weaker teacher asked to teach an excellent syllabus.

In the USA some of the most successful projects designed to help young children from poor homes learn to read have been based not on teacher quality but on highly scripted, high quality syllabuses (Hirsch, 2016).

Middle management

The key to success in schools is often the efficacy of the middle managers, especially year heads and heads of individual subjects. So often the latter do not seem to be given a full range of responsibilities, yet they are better placed than senior managers to carry them out.

Here is a good job description taken from a London comprehensive school:

DUTIES AND RESPONSIBILITIES OF A HEAD OF SUBJECT

1. Curriculum and assessment

1.1 To establish schemes of work and to monitor their use by staff.

1.2 To establish arrangements for the assessment of students' work and progress, including the setting, marking and grading of internal exams and the setting and assessment of coursework. To ensure data is recorded regularly. To examine differences in results between sets and to look for explanations.

1.3 To maintain contact with subject developments outside the Academy and to bring them to the attention of colleagues.

1.4 To foster, by example, a spirit of academic enquiry within the department. To maintain links with a subject association and to join the local branch.

1.5 To select the examination syllabi offered in your subject.

1.6 Every year to supply staff with a current copy of the GCSE and A-level syllabus they are to teach towards.

1.7 When exam results are published, to arrange for remarks and for the return of scripts.

2. Staff

2.1 To be involved in the appointment of new staff to the Department, by drafting advertisements, job descriptions and departmental notes, drawing up a short list and taking part in interviews.

2.2 To provide and oversee an induction programme for new members of the Department.

2.3 To deploy staff to teach sets within the Department in a way that puts the interests of pupils first.

2.4 To arrange for the observation of teaching as a part of the processes of induction and appraisal and as a matter of good practice, and to provide constructive feedback to staff concerned.

2.5 To ensure that homeworks are set and of the correct length for each year group; homeworks to be marked promptly and according to Academy policy; stand-by homeworks to be available in the event of absence or omission.

2.6 To arrange for the appraisal of members of the Department to be carried out as directed by the Principal and to assist staff in following up appraisal recommendations.

2.7 To devise and review annual professional development objectives for the Department, and to make arrangements for appropriate Inset.

2.8 To ensure that at least one staff member is an external examiner each year.

3. Students

3.1 To use performance data to track the progress of all students.

3.2 To ensure that all members of the department teach appropriate subject skills and that pupils are expected to produce work with high standards of accuracy and presentation.

3.3 To ensure that pupils are taught in appropriate groups, whenever possible.

3.4 To ensure that staff are aware of pupils with learning, medical, social or other difficulties and that appropriate support is provided.

3.5 To monitor closely the progress of pupils who are borderline examination candidates and to provide opportunities for extra support.

3.6 To advise students with university applications to read your subject or one closely related.

3.7 To manage and monitor students doing an EPQ related to your subject.

4. Organisation of the Department

4.1 To hold, and to keep records of, regular meetings in a way that promotes the exchange of ideas, and informs and develops good practice. To send a copy of the minutes to the Principal.

4.2 To delegate tasks so as to create a sense of teamwork within the Department and so as to ensure that experience is acquired for the future development of the Department.

4.3 To organise cover when staff are absent and to ensure that work is set when a teacher is absent.

4.4 To liaise over the allocation of teaching space to staff.

4.5 To ensure that rooms are properly treated and secured, that the Academy safety policy is operated throughout the Department.

4.6 To keep accurate inventories of fixed assets in the Department.

4.7 To appoint and manage ancillary staff.

4.8 To manage the agreed departmental budget and to follow accounting procedures as required by the School.

4.9 To liaise with the library over the provision of suitable texts.

4.10 To run a subject-based society with visiting speakers & to oversee all subject-based extracurricular activities, clubs, visits and exchanges.

Textbooks

In England 10% of 10-year-olds are issued textbooks; in South Korea, 99%. In secondary science 8% of pupils in England are issued with textbooks compared to 88% in South Korea, 92% in Taiwan.

Why are English schools not using textbooks? Cost is a factor, but as important is the growing use of copied worksheets and handouts. Worksheets have certain advantages (bespoke to the class, pupils have to focus on that one piece of paper) but some disadvantages (easily lost, rarely organised in the file). Textbooks are dying out because more materials are now available online. And the emphasis in schools on differentiated learning has discouraged the notion of 'one resource for all'.

The demise of textbooks is a downward spiral – if schools don't buy textbooks, publishers cannot afford to produce them. In the past a small number of outstanding teachers earned a good living producing wonderful, captivating textbooks and these people are now being lost to the system.

So what's so good about textbooks? Textbooks are better than online resources or paper handouts in several ways:

1. They are easier to issue (two minutes at the start of the year) and much easier to refer back to ('let's return to page 45 which we did last October').

2. They are a big part of the solution for the child who joins a course late or who misses a large piece of work.

3. They are a resource which parents can use to help their children.

4. The best textbooks contain exercises, questions and worked examples – perfect for setting homework and for testing understanding.

5. For sixth formers especially, learning to make notes from texts is a vital skill they will need at university. With the advent of handouts, fewer and fewer students are learning to make notes.

6. Textbooks are far better for revision than handouts (many of which will have been lost).

7. Textbooks CAN be used for differentiated learning – all pupils use the same book but work through it at different rates.

8. The best textbooks, like those used for maths in Singapore and Shanghai, lead the pupil and teacher through the syllabus in ways which are extremely effective. They save the teacher hours of lesson preparation time as all the essential materials have been written for you by experienced teachers.

If you ask people aged 40+ if they can remember textbooks they used at school the answer is usually 'yes'. But more than just the title of the book, they can remember individual pages and diagrams in the text. Will today's children be able to say the same of handouts?

Textbooks of the past had a huge impact on education. They not only reflected exam board syllabuses, they influenced them. The best textbooks *were the curriculum. They determined the level to which the better students worked.* Especially at A-level the materials put out by exam boards do not pin down exactly what a child has to know – the level of detail and depth. It is textbooks that do that.

A good example would be Robert Peal's recent Key Stage 3 history textbooks: in-depth coverage written in a completely accessible way.

As Nick Gibb MP says in the foreword to Oates (2014):

'*Behind every short sentence setting out the content to be taught, there is inevitably scope for divergent interpretation.*

In the Key Stage 2 science curriculum, for example, requiring 9-year-old pupils to be taught that "unsupported objects fall towards the Earth because of the force of gravity" could be taught superficially or in a way that conveys a genuine understanding of the science involved.'

School libraries and school textbooks should be regarded as a vital resource in all schools. Good books go into depth, they elaborate on and clarify what has been taught in schools. They lodge in your mind.

Oates (2014) looked at over 200 teacher textbooks, teacher guides and student workbooks, from Hong Kong, Singapore, Finland, Massachusetts, England, and Alberta. Maths was a key focus, but subjects included geography, physics, chemistry, biology, history, literature and first language learning.

Oates shows that textbook use has declined in the UK compared to higher performing jurisdictions. A 2011 survey, for example, found that in England 10% of maths teachers use textbooks as 'the basis for instruction' compared to 95% in Finland. The equivalent figures for science were 4% and 94%.

In addition the quality of UK textbooks has declined. They have increasingly become revision guides. This has happened because this is what the market demanded: schools are under pressure to get their pupils good grades so all the focus tends to be on exam preparation. What is more, many of these books are 'endorsed' by individual exam boards; it is extremely hard for a school to ignore a text written by a chief examiner and endorsed in this way.

I have a collection of textbooks going back to the 1960s. Older textbooks are much longer and went into more depth than modern books. Older textbooks rarely mentioned exams while modern books seem to be largely about revision for specific exams.

Oates explains that part of the problem is that in England there is a great deal of hostility towards the notion of government-approved or government-recommended textbooks. In other high-performing countries it is commonplace for the government to ensure that textbooks are written well (by experienced teachers) and stretch pupils.

Project-based learning in secondary schools

Some secondary schools use project-based learning. This allows pupils to research and write-up their own projects which normally cross across more than one school subject. They have the potential to make pupils motivated and teach skills of independent research and drafting.

Project-based learning is used by some free schools, such as XP School in Doncaster or School 21 in east London. This is what it says on the School 21 website:

'Think back to when you were at school. What work did you produce that made you feel truly proud? It's likely you will struggle to think of many pieces of work you produced at school which had any meaning other than to please a teacher or not get in trouble. At

School 21 we want school work to be beautiful, meaningful and have an impact in the world. We want students to create work that is well above what is usually expected of school children.

Project Based Learning is a series of techniques that produce deep and authentic learning. At its heart pupils immerse themselves in rich subject content or a real world problem and through the application of knowledge and the development of skills and attributes they craft work of real value.

By producing products for an authentic audience and then accounting for them, work is lifted out of an exercise book and given greater meaning and importance. In the classroom, project lessons often look different from traditional lessons.'

The Education Endowment Foundation undertook a study of project-based learning for Year 7 pupils using a randomised controlled trial between September 2014 and April 2016. Twelve schools (2,101 pupils) using project methods were compared to 12 schools (1,973 pupils) who did not.

Their tentative conclusions were that project learning had no clear impact on either literacy or student engagement with school and learning and may have had a negative impact on the literacy attainment of pupils entitled to free school meals. However, project methods may have enhanced pupils' skills including oracy, communication, teamwork, and self-directed study (EEF, 2016).

Drill

'Drill' means repeating tasks until they are committed to memory and become second-nature.

This is the form of teaching Winston Churchill had at Harrow:

'By being so long in the lowest form I gained an immense advantage over the cleverer boys. They all went on to learn Latin and Greek and splendid things like that. But I was taught English. We were considered such dunces that we could learn only English. Mr Somervell – a most delightful man, to whom my debt is great – was charged with the duty of teaching the stupidest boys the most disregarded thing – namely, to write mere English. He knew how to do it. He taught it as no one else has ever taught it.

Mr Somervell had a system of his own. He took a fairly long sentence and broke it up into its components by means of black, red, blue and green inks. Subject, verb, object: each had its colour and its bracket. It was a kind of drill. We did it almost daily. As I remained in the bottom form three times as long as anyone else, I had three times as much of it. I learned it thoroughly.

Thus I got into my bones the essential structure of the ordinary British sentence. And when in after years my school fellows, who had won prizes and distinction for writing such beautiful Latin poetry and pithy Greek epigrams, had to come down again to common English to earn their living, I did not feel myself at any disadvantage.

So naturally I am biased in favour of boys learning English. I would make them all learn English: and then I would let all the clever ones learn Latin as an honour, and Greek as a treat. But the only thing I would whip them for would be for not knowing English. I would whip them hard for that.' (Churchill, 1939).

He went on to win the Nobel Prize for literature.

Nick Gibb MP said in a speech in July 2016:

'One English educationist, now residing at an American university, appeared in the TES in December arguing she would "ban" times table tests, and told the Telegraph that they have nothing to do with mathematics. Earlier last year, Conrad Wolfram wrote in the Financial Times that calculation is an "obsolete skill", thanks to technological advances of the 21st century.

That last comment reminded me of an influential pamphlet about the future of mathematics entitled 'I do, and I understand'. This pamphlet suggests that in the age of the computer and the "simple calculating machine", mental arithmetic has become a thing of the past. It was written in 1967. Such a romantic view was wrong then, and I believe it is wrong today.

Five decades of research into cognitive science, as reviewed by the American psychologists James Royer and Loel Tronsky, shows that there is a positive relationship between computational automaticity and complex mathematical problem-solving skills.'

Drill is a dirty word outside the army and computational automaticity is not much better. But drill is effective and can be enjoyable in the right hands. The crucial thing is to pitch drill at the right level ... not so hard as to be impossible, nor so easy as to be simplistic. It needs to give pupils the satisfying feeling of conquering a tricky problem. And to be fair drill will be much more useful for a primary maths teacher than an A-level English teacher.

In *Cleverlands* (2016) Lucy Crehan explains clearly why it is that drill helps East Asian pupils become creative thinkers and intuitive mathematicians. Drill does not stifle imagination or critical thinking. It just means that the mechanical processes that Western children labour with are automatic to East Asian children, freeing them up to grasp more advanced concepts.

Why are so many people worried about drill? Because it doesn't allow pupils to think for themselves, it doesn't encourage independent learning, it prevents debate, it doesn't do all those things education should do, like develop good character and conduct. All this is true ... which is why drill can only ever be part of the pedagogy.

Digital technology: a mixed blessing

Do computers and tablets help pupils learn better than traditional methods?

A paper by Cambridge International Exams (Elston, 2013) showed that teachers (the people that should know) have confidence in the potential of technology. The vast majority of teachers surveyed believed that technology helps to develop skills that students need in the real world and also that technology creates more confident, engaged and motivated students. They think the main benefit of technology for teachers is access to a wealth of content. In addition, the ability to connect classrooms around the world was an appealing technological outcome.

In 2012 the Education Endowment Foundation in collaboration with Durham University (Higgins, Xiao and Katsipataki, 2012) conducted a meta-analysis synthesising 48 different studies that attempted to quantify the effect of various different technology-based programmes. The different programmes had varying effect sizes ranging from -0.03 to 1.05 (-0.03 being the only negative score which of course means a negative effect). The higher the score the bigger the effect. Eight of the 48 studies had scores above 0.5, meaning the effect was relatively large. The remainder were below 0.5 meaning the effect is quite small. The summary finding was that overall the benefits of technology are positive but there are other types of learning interventions (such as peer tutoring) that enhance learning to a greater degree. *'From the range of impacts identified in this review, it is clear technology alone does not make a difference to learning. Rather, how well the technology is used to support teaching and learning is the key determinant of its impact. There is no doubt that technology engages and motivates young people. However, this benefit is only an advantage for learning if the activity is effectively aligned with clear learning objectives.'*

This finding is reflected in the Education Endowment Foundation Toolkit which concludes: *'Overall, studies consistently find that digital technology is associated with moderate learning gains. However, there is considerable variation in impact. Evidence suggests that technology should be used to supplement other teaching, rather than replace more traditional approaches.'* And computers are pretty expensive.

Recent PISA results (OECD, 2015) suggest that whilst limited use of computers at school may be better than not using computers at all, using them more intensively than the current OECD average tends to be associated with significantly poorer student performance. In addition the report states that students who spend more than six hours online per weekday outside of school are particularly at risk of reporting that they feel lonely at school, and that they often arrived late for school or skipped days of school.

The School Effectiveness and Inequality Initiative in the USA (Carter, Greenberg and Walker, 2016) conducted a study that prohibited computer devices in randomly selected classrooms of an introductory economics course at the United States Military Academy. Average final exam scores among students assigned to classrooms that allowed computers were 18% of a standard deviation lower than exam scores of students in classrooms that prohibited computers. They found that students using a tablet or computer were sometimes surfing the internet, checking email, messaging with friends, or even completing homework for that class or another class.

Mueller and Oppenheimer (2014) found that students required to use computers are not as effective at taking notes as students required to use pen and paper. Students who took their notes by hand tended to understand and remember the lecture better than those who had typed. Mueller suggests that this is because the students who typed mindlessly typed everything without really listening to what was said.

A leading figure in the field of research into the efficacy of computers for learning is Anne Mangen from the Reading Centre at the University of Stavanger in Norway. Her research helps to explain why handwriting is more effective than typing when trying to learn. When writing by hand, our brain receives feedback from our motor actions, together with the sensation of touching a pencil and paper. These kinds of feedback are superior to those we receive when touching and typing on a keyboard.

Mangen (2016) compared two groups of students, one of which was asked to read a story on a Kindle and one of which was asked to read the same story in booklet form. Those who read the story in booklet form were better able to recall and sequence the plot than those who had read the story on the Kindle.

What about Google? Betsy Sparrow *et al* of Columbia University (2011) demonstrated that if people think that they can look up a fact again later, they are far less likely to remember it.

The Center for Research on Education Outcomes at Stanford University published a large-scale study into the effectiveness of online school courses. They found that the results were consistently bad. The online schools relied on students driving their own learning and often determining the pace at which they advanced – things which progressive teachers sometimes see as huge advantages. The biggest problem identified by the researchers was the difficulty in keeping online pupils focused on their work. *'Academic benefits from online schools are currently the exception rather than the rule'* (Woodworth, 2015).

In 2016 the London School of Economics published a study for the Education Endowment Foundation (McNally *et al*) which found that, working with 2241 pupils in 51 primary schools, those following a *paper-based* literacy programme made 50% more progress than those doing an identical course on a computer. The authors believe that the offline course made it easier for the teaching assistant supporting the pupils to be more adaptable and flexible to the children's needs. Computer programs are less flexible than teachers.

So it is difficult to conclude that technology always enhances learning and development. What one can say is that implementation and other practical considerations such as cost are key to ensuring uses of technology in teaching are effective. An EEF report (Higgins *et al*, 2012) suggests several success factors for effective implementation:

- Collaborative use of technology (in pairs or small groups) is usually more effective than individual use.
- Technology can be used very effectively as a short but focused intervention to improve learning. Sustained use over a longer period is usually less effective at improving attainment.
- Remedial and tutorial use of technology can be particularly effective for lower attaining pupils, SEN pupils or pupils from disadvantaged backgrounds.
- Technology is best used as a supplement to normal teaching rather than as a replacement for it.
- Technological benefits in terms of attainment tend to be greatest in mathematics and science (compared with literacy for example).

BESA research (British Educational Suppliers Association, 2015) showed that a lack of suitable bandwidth remains a significant barrier to adoption of mobile technologies. In addition it suggested that 88% of primary schools regard the management and security of tablets as a barrier to adoption. In secondary schools the barriers, in order of significance, were found to be training and support (91%), funding (83%) and management and security (83%).

How to ask questions

Asking pupils questions is a key part of effective teaching. Research has shown that the most effective questioning has certain characteristics:

- Leave enough time for the student to answer your question. The single most effective action you can take after asking a question is

---

to keep quiet. Research suggests that teachers average less than one second of silence before repeating or emphasising material or asking a second question.

- Before leaping in with an answer yourself, ask students to discuss the questions in pairs. Some kind of answer is usually forthcoming.

- Be clear about what your question is aiming to do. Are you simply aiming to see if students can recall a piece of information, are you providing an opportunity for them to clarify their own understanding or to apply or elaborate that understanding?

- Ask a friendly colleague to observe and give feedback on how many and what type of questions you use in a lesson. Are your questions largely closed, requiring a simple recall answer, or are they expansive and open stimulating thought and discussion?

- Encourage deeper responses from students by using 'echoing'. When the student has given their answer repeat back to them a section of what they have said, *eg* "So you are arguing that...?" Then leave a silence.

- Never belittle a question or answer from a student which may seem irrelevant, silly or ignorant. Mistakes are a useful way of learning and students need to feel that their contributions will not be laughed at.

- Be a good listener. Hear what the student response is and use further questions to pinpoint areas where understanding is poor and help develop insight.

- Some students are quiet in a large group situation. Pick them to answer or provide the opportunity for them to speak by using pairs and small group interaction.

- Students do not listen when others are answering a question. So you should, after an answer has been given, ask another pupil whether he agrees with the previous pupil's answer. They will then start to listen.

Treating teachers well

When I went to teach at Holland Park School in the 1990s the first thing I noticed was how badly treated the staff were. The staff room was a ghastly place with broken chairs everywhere, the staff loos were worse, and teachers had to pay for their own coffee at break.

Most schools have now grasped that this sort of behaviour is the road to ruin. Small sums spent on staff welfare, like pastries in the staff room on a Monday, send a signal. It is minor expenditure which will be repaid a thousand times over.

John Tomsett, the head of Huntington School, York, is good on this (Tomsett, 2015): the value of thank you notes, of free tea and coffee, of flowers sent to staff who are ill, the value of a special staff lunches and celebrations. Michaela School (see page 242) has taken steps to review the workload of teachers and limit all those activities which generate limited returns relative to the time they take. If individual teachers matter more than anything else, they need to be looked after.

Schools struggle with performance-related pay, for three reasons:

1. Collegiality. School teachers work in teams and are often good friends. They support each other. They dislike the idea that the head of department (often a department of just two or three staff) will be asked to make judgements about the others which will affect their take-home pay. Because of collegiality such judgements are unlikely to be impartial anyway. The head of department regards it as her duty to defend her staff, not stitch them up.

2. Motivation. As Daniel Pink describes in his book (Pink, 2011), teachers are not motivated by money. They are motivated by the drive for autonomy, mastery and purpose. Autonomy means allowing staff choosing for themselves the best way of achieving targets set by the school. Trying to control people too much lowers motivation. Mastery means doing work which is demanding, which produces complete engagement, which stretches people in a way that produces a sense of focus and satisfaction. Purpose means having a strong sense that what you are doing is worthwhile and important.

3. Bureaucracy. If performance-related pay is to be fair it requires carefully constructed systems, reliable appraisal and a great deal of discussion. What do you do about the teacher who does little outside the classroom but gets great exam results? Or the teacher who got brilliant results with one class, poor with another? PRP is complicated and schools sometimes lack the resources and time to set up appropriate systems.

Things which don't work

Here a few things which I have been told teachers should do but which don't, in my experience, work...

1. Group work

Some teachers make good progress with group work but I never could for three reasons. Firstly, it assumes that children are capable of sitting in a group and seriously discussing something with limited adult supervision (if there are, say, 28 children in groups of four the teacher cannot supervise seven groups simultaneously). Boys in particular do not generally want to do school work – it is something which has to be forced upon them by the personality of the teacher or by pressure. The learning output from group work is always limited for boys.

Secondly, in any group there is quite often one person who is prepared to have a stab at doing the work. As soon as that person is identified and takes a leading role, the rest of the group just copy her. It might be claimed that the great thing about group work is that children learn from each other, but often they don't ... they learn to disengage and then chat or just cheat.

Thirdly, in a group of four sitting in a square one pupil is facing the teacher, wherever she is standing, and the rest are not. One pupil always has his back to the teacher. This makes control and communication much harder.

2. Double desks

One consequence of the need to do group work is that schools buy double desks (two children sit side by side): it is easier to organise group work if you have double desks. One double desk is also cheaper than two single desks. It takes up less space, so classrooms can be smaller. But double desks allow children to see each other's work so they permit copying (cheating). Many less able or lazy children are able to conceal their weakness by copying, especially when the teacher sets tests. This is why it is better to buy single desks and, if you must, push them together.

3. Differentiation and individualised learning

Ofsted used to be keen on differentiation. Teachers were encouraged to plan different types of work and different types of question for different pupils according to their analysis of a child's ability (defined by Key Stage 1 and 2 tests or GCSE results) and special educational needs (nearly a quarter of boys in school are classified as having special educational needs).

The problem with this approach is that it prevents whole-class teaching. It is a throwback to the mixed ability teaching of the 1980s which most people now know does not work. Individualised learning – giving each pupil in a class of 25–30 their own programme of work – is less effective than whole-class teaching.

The second problem is that differentiation generally implies that the teacher expects less of some pupils than others. But all the research into effective schools across the world shows that the distinguishing characteristic of the most successful systems is a belief that EVERY child can do well if they try hard enough. According to the OECD's Teaching and Learning International Survey, differentiated teaching is not common in high-performing south-east Asian countries. This is because it reinforces the performance gap between high and low attaining pupils. Individualised learning and differentiation is one reason why the bottom 30% of boys in England do so badly – less is being expected of them.

4. Independent learning

When I did my PGCE at Cambridge we studied the late 19th century educationalist John Dewey. Dewey became one of the most famous proponents of hands-on learning or experiential education. Many researchers even credit him with the influence of Project Based Learning where students learn by doing their own research.

Dewey not only rethought the way that the learning process should take place, but also the role that the teacher should play within that process. According to Dewey, the teacher should not be one to stand at the front of the room doling out bits of information to be absorbed by passive students. Instead, the teacher's role should be that of facilitator and guide. As Dewey explains it:

'The teacher is not in the school to impose certain ideas or to form certain habits in the child, but is there as a member of the community to select the influences which shall affect the child and to assist him in properly responding to these influences.

Thus the teacher becomes a partner in the learning process, guiding students to independently discover meaning within the subject area.' (Dewey, 1897)

In the past Ofsted has discouraged teachers from talking too much. Well of course a long lecture can be dull and it is hard to maintain discipline if a class is bored. But in fact some of the best teachers are more than capable of delivering high-impact, motivating chalk-and-talk, and more able and motivated children *learn faster* this way (as they do at university).

In the 2015 PISA tests students were assessed on the extent to which their science lessons were enquiry-based. The results correlated negatively with the science test scores. Students learn better with a teacher explaining things well followed by testing on their understanding, they learn worse if they are required to discover things themselves (PISA, 2016).

This is what the PISA report had to say:

'Perhaps surprisingly, in no education system do students who reported that they are frequently exposed to enquiry-based instruction (when they are encouraged to experiment and engage in hands-on activities) score higher in science. After accounting for students' and schools' socio-economic profile, in 56 countries and economies, greater exposure to enquiry-based instruction is associated with lower scores in science.'

The fact that PISA was 'surprised' by this finding illustrates the strangle-hold that child-centred teaching methods have on the mindset of the author.

Independent learning means working on your own. That is a good idea IF you are motivated and have the knowledge-base to work with – which many children don't. Independent learning too often means going through worksheets and not learning very much.

5. Powerpoint

Powerpoint presentations have their place but they suffer from common weaknesses. If every teacher uses them (and many do) the focus is on the screen and not the teacher – and this makes Powerpoint dull. If the Powerpoint is merely a summary of what the teacher is saying (as is often the case) then the pupil switches off and neither the teacher's words nor the words on the screen sink in. The old-fashioned system of writing on a board can be both more creative and more engaging.

Conclusions

The best teachers are liked by their pupils. This tends to mean that they can keep good order, they teach with a sense of drive and ambition, and they are – beneath the surface maybe – kind and approachable.

The best teachers love their subject and have excellent subject knowledge (the two go together). It is the reason that some schools are happy to appoint an excellent graduate in a subject like physics even if they don't have a teaching qualification. They are classified as 'unqualified', even though they may possess the most important qualities needed to teach well. Good subject knowledge matters not only because at the top of the ability range you need to be able to stretch pupils but also because teachers with good knowledge tend to make lessons for younger children more interesting. They have more substance to be interesting about.

Teachers need to have the right personality. Teaching is partly acting and acting ability helps greatly. The Harris Federation gives trainees sessions with a voice and body language coach to help them be a powerful presence in the classroom. Above all you need to be able to control a class, because without good discipline nothing worthwhile can be achieved. So that means good teachers are those whom pupils will respect – and slightly fear if necessary. They are completely in control of what's going on around them. Pupils know the teacher will notice if they are misbehaving or if their work is incomplete or copied from another child and will take action – punish the child, perhaps, or require the work to be redone.

But the best teachers are not disciplinarians. They are a velvet hand in an iron glove. Pupils come to know, over time, that they are warm and generous. But they are not to be messed with. Discipline has to come first.

There are other personality traits that matter too. Good teachers are very hard working, putting a huge effort into preparing lessons, marking work and giving extra time to children who need it. They are generous with their time. They are able to manage stress. They are passionate about their school and their pupils, keen for all to do well. They are driven by the moral imperative of teaching – the opportunity to transform lives.

They are highly organised, because switching in a few seconds from one class to another, keeping track of individuals, remembering which extra duties they are down for, managing record-keeping and databases – all this requires good organisation.

Teachers need to have certain classroom skills. This is why all 'unqualified' teachers need some training, both before they start and throughout their two years of teaching. They need to be shown how to deliver a lesson with pace and interest, how best to ensure good behaviour, how to use digital resources effectively, how to make use of pupil data, how to mark work and record those marks, how to write reports, how best to teach tricky concepts, how to ask questions of pupils in the most effective way, how to identify and teach pupils with special educational needs and disabilities.

Finally, they need to have high expectations of their pupils. This is a characteristic of all the best teachers. They are determined that every pupil will master their subject. This attitude sets the scene for everything which follows. Pupils who produce unsatisfactory work must be made to redo it until they achieve a good level. Pupils will be regularly tested to see whether they have understood and learnt the work; those who do badly will be retested. Excellent teachers believe that it is pupil effort and teaching quality which determine how well a child does, not the ability of the child. The less able children will get there in the end.

There are two caveats to all the above. There are successful teachers who tick few of the boxes above. I was taught A-level history by a man who never left his armchair and who merely lectured to us. He would be condemned by contemporary lesson observation – yet he was most successful. Pupils loved him and worked hard for him. He sent a regular stream of historians to Oxbridge. His personality, subject knowledge and reputation counted for more than his teaching methods.

Secondly, how you teach does depend on the age of your pupils and the subject you are teaching. The challenges of teaching five-year-olds are different from those of 15-year-olds. A secondary maths teacher has more issues with pupil understanding than an English teacher. A good design and technology teacher has different qualities to a French teacher. A PE teacher requires skills that a chemistry teacher may not.

An experiment

Imagine you took the more motivated and able pupils in your school and set out to make them the most knowledgeable pupils in the world about a particular topic.

In 1992 the investor Jim Slater published his book *The Zulu Principle*. He had noticed that his wife, having read an article in *Reader's Digest* magazine about the Zulus, was able to speak with far greater authority about Zulus than most people (after all most people don't know much about much). He reckoned that if she was to read, say, half a dozen books about the Zulus and go to South Africa and live with them for a few weeks, she would know more about Zulus than almost anyone else in the world.

He applied this principle to buying shares and businesses – if you take a narrow field (like zinc, for example, or apricots), you can quite easily become one of the most knowledgeable people in the business and this may give you a competitive advantage when trading.

But there is another reason why children can become experts in a subject and that is that MANY CHILDREN HAVE A GREATER CAPACITY FOR LEARNING THAN WE THINK. Because we find that persuading classes of children to learn much is quite laborious, we forget that individual motivated children can learn a huge amount.

Not long ago I sat on a small panel in the Department for Education rewriting the National Curriculum for Geography. We quickly agreed that it was sensible for geography students to learn the locations of places, something which had inexplicably been missing from the experience of geography students in England for the past 20 years. So we then had to decide how many country locations a pupil should be expected to know by the age of 14 (the age at which he might well drop the subject). There are roughly 200 countries in the world.

Some members of the group thought that learning the location of 20 was enough ... the 20 'most important' countries. So that would be USA, China, Russia, UK, France, Germany, Italy, Canada, India, Brazil, Indonesia ... now it becomes tricky ... but before we got too bogged down in this exercise I suggested that we should require 14-year-olds to know all 200. Of course I was shot down, but to prove them wrong I made a series of short YouTube recordings and set my Year 9 classes to learn one continent a week. Internet-based tests made this fun and my chocolate-based reward system added flavour. Anyway – they all now know all 200 and may well recall most of these for the rest of their lives.

So try teaching your more motivated Key Stage 3 pupils something at A-level standard and see how far you get.

Winston Churchill, a notoriously lazy pupil, learnt 1200 lines of Thomas Macaulay's narrative poems *Lays of Ancient Rome* when he was 14 and recited them to the whole school.

This was part of a competition which taught Harrow boys patience, concentration and stick-at-it-ness. It pulled into the pupils' grasp what they did not know was even within their reach. It taught them the courage to face outsized challenges.

Twelve hundred lines. Could your students do the same with a poem 5% of the length?

> Then out spake brave Horatius,
> The Captain of the Gate:
> "To every man upon this earth
> Death cometh soon or late.
> And how can man die better
> Than facing fearful odds,
> For the ashes of his fathers,
> And the temples of his Gods."

Chapter 3

Successful Pupils?

*This boy is **Ignorance** and this girl is **Want**. Beware them both, and all of their degree, but most of all beware this boy for on his brow I see that written which is Doom, unless the writing be erased.*

Charles Dickens, *A Christmas Carol*, 1843

A PISA survey report in 2013 found that in almost every country in the developed world younger adults performed better than older people, with the biggest gaps seen in South Korea, Finland and Spain. These nations have dramatically improved levels of basic skills over the last few decades.

However, the report said, *'In England and Northern Ireland, the differences in proficiency between younger and older generations are negligible. Although young people in these countries are entering a much more demanding labour market, they are not much better equipped with literacy and numeracy skills than those who are retiring.'*

'In fact, England is the only country where the oldest age group has higher proficiency in both literacy and numeracy than the youngest.' (OECD, 2013)

Looking at 55 to 65-year-olds alone, England was ranked 3rd out of 24 in the developed world for literacy behind only Japan and Slovakia and 11th for numeracy.

But amongst 16–19-year-olds, England was bottom for literacy and nearly bottom for numeracy. In England one-third of those aged 16–19 have low basic skills – weak numeracy and to a lesser extent literacy. Many more young people continue to further and higher education than their parents but they do so with weak basic skills. Many of those who have passed GCSE maths and English still have low levels of numeracy and literacy compared to those obtaining parallel qualifications in other OECD countries.

Percentage of adults with low skills (literacy and/or numeracy below level 2) in different age groups

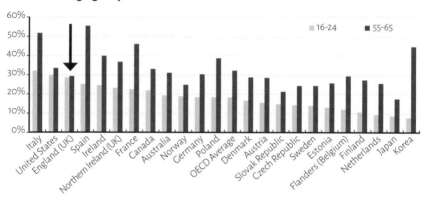

Source: OECD Survey of Adult Skills, 2012. In this analysis 'below level 2' or 'low skills' means struggling with simple quantitative information, such as a petrol gauge in a car, or inability to read and understand the instructions one might see on a bottle of aspirin.

Percentage of 16–19 year-olds with low literacy and numeracy (below level 2)

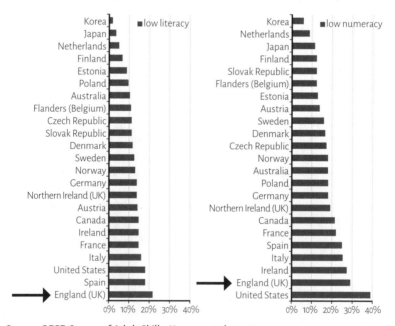

Source: OECD Survey of Adult Skills; Kuczera *et al*, 2016

The main reason for the bad performance of England is schooling. Although the best pupils do well, the tail of low achievers is higher than in other countries. The priority is therefore to improve the basic standard of schooling for less motivated or less able students.

Also shocking was the finding that one in ten university graduates in England have numeracy or literacy levels below level 2. Universities assume that entrants have reasonable numeracy and literacy acquired at school, but this is an error and they do little to improve the situation.

University entrance has expanded but more and more of the extra students have weak numeracy and/or literacy. The increase in higher education participation between 1998 and 2015 was driven primarily by rising student numbers in institutions with medium and low entry requirements, not by improved secondary education.

Distribution of numeracy (chart on the right) and literacy (chart on the left) skills among current university students 16–34 year-olds

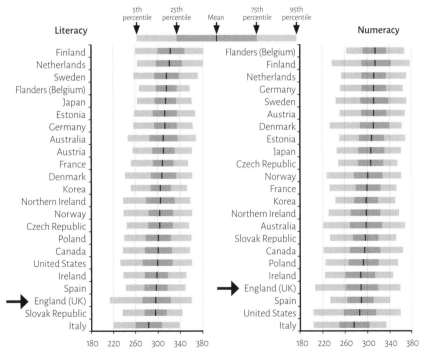

Source: OECD Survey of Adult Skills; Kuczera *et al*, 2016

So England has more students going to university than many countries but more of those students have a low level of numeracy and/or literacy:

20–34 year-olds with university qualifications
low skills = low literacy and/or numeracy

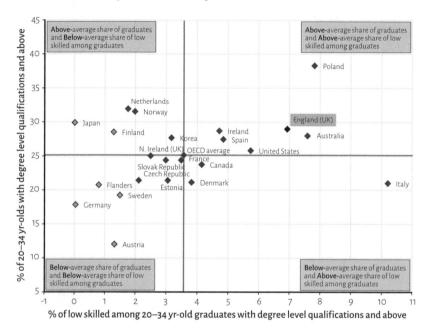

Source: OECD Survey of Adult Skills; Kuczera et al, 2016

Kuczera *et al* (2016) in their OECD report recommend that: *'Those with low basic skills should not normally enter three-year undergraduate programmes, which are both costly and unsuited to the educational needs of those involved, while graduates with poor basic skills undermine the currency of an English university degree. These potential entrants should be diverted into more suitable provision that meets their needs.'*

If the performance of many young people in England is so modest, you can be sure that there are sub-groups doing appallingly. This chapter looks at these sub-groups – attainment gaps related to socio-economic status, ethnicity and gender.

All educational effectiveness research (EER) shows that some groups do better in school than others and that pupils' progress is influenced by their parents, their neighbourhood and their peers as well as by their school.

Research also shows that the **effect of schools** is greatest for disadvantaged students, both positively and negatively. A good school can hugely improve the prospects for pupils with a poor background. Pupils from more prosperous homes tend to do quite well regardless of the quality of their school (Coleman, 1966). The Coleman Differential Effect can be summarised as *school quality affects disadvantaged children twice as much as advantaged children*.

Stranded in the attainment gap

In his 2010 study Professor Steve Strand looked at how well different schools achieved pupil progress age 7 to 11 in relation to prior attainment, ethnicity, free school meals (FSM) and gender using an English national dataset of 530,000 pupils attending over 14,200 primary schools.

He found that no school appeared to eliminate or reverse the typical within-school attainment gaps in relation to FSM pupils or Black Caribbean or White British pupils. Some schools were much better than others in terms of the results achieved on average by all pupils but **the gap remained the same whatever the school.**

Strand concludes that the same schools that are most effective for white British pupils, boys or pupils on FSM are also the most effective for black Caribbean pupils, girls and those not on FSM. In short, there was no evidence of differential school effectiveness for different pupil types.

In a 2016 study Steve Strand analysed the national test results at age 7 and 11 of over 6000 pupils attending 57 mainstream primary schools over three successive years in a socially and ethnically diverse inner London borough. The pupil groups with the poorest progress were white British pupils on free school meals (FSM) and black Caribbean pupils, both those entitled and those not entitled to FSMs. Differences between schools in average pupil progress were large, but there was no evidence of differential school effectiveness in relation to closing gaps relating to FSM, ethnicity or gender. All pupil groupings benefitted from attending the more effective schools to a broadly similar extent.

So more effective schools 'raised the bar' but did not 'close the gap', suggesting that differences between schools in 'quality' plays little role in equity gaps.

Why is it that attainment gaps between rich and poor, black and white, boy or girl remain the same whether the school gets good results or bad results? The answer may be that the attainment gap has little to do with the school. It is a product of the family background. Or the answer may be that schools do things which limit their ability to close the gaps, like setting – which places the more disadvantaged children in lower sets and that reduces motivation.

Whatever the reasons, the conclusion is that if we want to close attainment gaps we need to focus on within-school systems just as much as type of school. 'Failing schools' are not responsible for the attainment gaps.

Free School Meals: who gets them?

In England in January 2016, children in state-funded schools were entitled to receive free schools meals if a parent or carer were in receipt of any of the following benefits:

Income Support

Income-based Jobseekers Allowance

Income-related Employment and Support Allowance

Support under Part VI of the Immigration and Asylum Act 1999

The guaranteed element of State Pension Credit

Child Tax Credit

Working Tax Credit

During the initial roll out of the benefit, Universal Credit.

Ethnicity

Ethnicity and attainment

According to the latest census (2011), about 80.5% of the UK population is white British, 2.2% is mixed, 7.5% is Asian and 3.3% is black. Of the 6.7 million pupils aged 5–16 in England, 27% were from ethnic minorities. The figure was 82% in inner London, 92.8% in Newham.

On the 2016 GCSEs Progress 8 measure in England, Chinese pupils scored +0.68, Black pupils+ 0.17, White pupils -0.09 (the average of all pupils is 0.0)

In 2015 the Department for Education published another research report by Professor Strand – *Ethnicity, deprivation and educational achievement at age 16 in England: trends over time.* This looks at GCSE results in terms of ethnic group, entitlement to free schools meals and gender. He showed that achievement gaps between different ethnic groups have narrowed substantially over the past 20 years. They have narrowed much more than gaps based on FSMs or gender.

In 2004 the average gap between ethnic minority students and white British (based on proportion gaining five GCSEs grade A*–C including English and maths) was 18% compared to a 7.7% gap between girls and boys and a 28% gap based on FSMs. By 2013 the ethnicity gap had fallen to 7.2%, the gender gap had risen to 10.1%, the FSMs gap was 26.7%.

Looking at individual ethnic groups, since 2004, based on five GCSEs A*–C including English and maths:

- Indian and Chinese students have moved way ahead of white British.
- Bangladeshi students have moved from well below to above white British despite being amongst the most socio-economically deprived.
- Black African students have moved from below white British to being better.
- Black Caribbean and Pakistani students nearly caught up and are now quite similar to white British, a bit below for those not on FSMs, a bit above for those on FSMs.
- **If you just look at pupils entitled to FSMs,** all ethnic groups do better than white British and the gap is growing. This true with both the Key Stage 2 results at age 11 and GCSE results at age 16.

Attainment in threshold measures by major ethnic group
England, state-finded schools, 2016

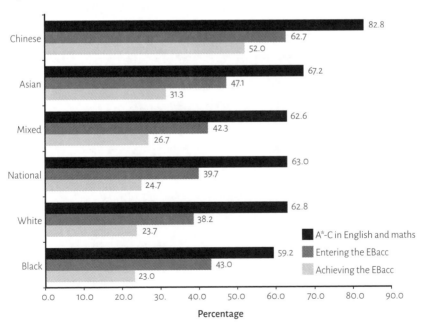

Source: Department for Education, Key stage 4 attainment data

Several studies have shown that ethnic minority parents are more engaged in their children's education than their white British peers. Professor Strand found that Indian students are much more likely to complete homework five evenings a week compared to those from White British backgrounds and Indian parents are more likely to have a home computer or pay for private lessons (Strand 2011).

Cullinane and Kirby (2016) analysed 2015 GCSE results for pupils on free school meals. In 2015, Chinese FSM pupils achieved the highest proportion of five or more GCSEs at A*–C including English and maths at 74%, followed by Asian (48.2%), black (41.2%), mixed (37.5%) and white (28.3%). Excluding only traveller and Gypsy/Roma communities, white British pupils had the poorest performance with 27.9%.

White British FSM boys achieved the lowest grades at GCSE of any main ethnic group, with just 24% achieving 5 A*–C grades at GCSE including English and maths in 2015. White British FSM girls were also the lowest performing main female ethnic group, with 32% achieving the same measure. The figures for 2016 Attainment 8 (normally the best eight GCSEs taken) are shown below:

Average Attainment 8 scores, state-funded schools in England, 2016

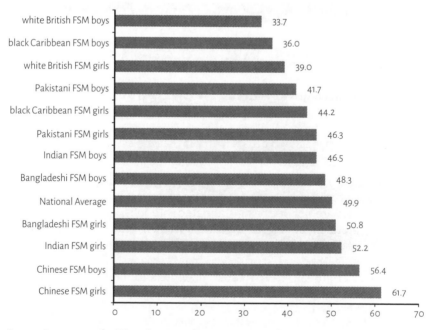

Source: Department for Education, Key stage 4 attainment data

Shaw *et al* (2016) for the Social Mobility Commission found that white British and white 'other' children from low income homes are the worst performing groups at primary school. White British pupils then make the least progress throughout secondary school resulting in a worsening in performance by Key Stage 4. Lower income young people from white British backgrounds are the least likely to access Higher Education, with only 1 in 10 attending university, compared to 3 in 10 for low income black Caribbean children, 5 in 10 for low income Bangladeshis and nearly 7 in 10 amongst low income Chinese students.

In London, there are stark differences between the performance of white FSM eligible pupils by borough. In 2015 in Westminster, 50% achieved 5 A*–C grades at GCSE including English and maths while in Newham the figure was 25.5%.

Allen *et al* (2016) looked at educational choices made at age 16 by pupils who sat GCSEs in summer 2010 and found white British pupils are less likely to go to a school sixth form or sixth form college than ethnic minority groups *with the same GCSE results and living in the same areas.*

Every ethnic minority group apart from Gypsy/Roma attends university at a higher rate than white British. In 2016 only 28.7% of white 18-year-olds from state schools went to university in the UK compared to 42.9% of British Asians and 57.9% of British Chinese (UCAS, 2016).

Black children, especially boys, also underperform. Shaw *et al* (2016) found that, despite starting school with performance largely in line with national averages, Black children fail to maintain this in later years. They are the ethnic group most likely to fail their maths GCSE, most likely to be excluded from school. Black boys do substantially less well than their female peers particularly at Key Stage 4. At Key Stage 5, black pupils are the ethnic group with the lowest outcomes. At university black students are less than half as likely to get a First as their white counterparts and 1 in 10 drop out in their first year.

Asian Muslims do less well than they should do in terms of employment. Young people from Pakistani and Bangladeshi backgrounds are more likely than ever to succeed in education and go on to university, especially girls. Yet these outcomes are not yet being translated into jobs, with unemployment particularly prevalent amongst Bangladeshi women. Both Pakistani men and women are relatively unlikely to secure managerial or professional occupations (Shaw *et al*, 2016). Niven *et al* (2013) found that Bangladeshi families were more likely that other groups to expect their daughters to marry young and have children, reflecting their origins in the rural and socially conservative Sylhet district of Bangladesh.

Ethnicity and school segregation

We know from the 2011 Census that 19% of the UK population were from an ethnic minority background. But the Department for Education's 2016 census found that 31% of primary pupils, and 28% of secondary pupils came from ethnic minority origins. The Casey Review states that in 2013 more than 50% of ethnic minority students were in schools where ethnic minorities were the majority (Casey, 2016).

Demos and Policy Exchange looked at segregation between white British pupils and all other ethnic groups using the Index of Dissimilarity. This measures the percentage of white British or ethnic minority pupils in an area who would have to move schools in order for the ethnic make-up of each school in the area to represent the overall population of pupils in the area. Blackburn (page 259) came top with an index of 63.6% (Policy Exchange Integration Hub, 2016).

The Casey Review (2016) made the point:

'Taken together, high ethnic minority concentration in residential areas and in schools increases the likelihood of children growing up without meeting or better understanding people from different backgrounds. One striking illustration of such segregation came from a non-faith state secondary school we visited where, in a survey they had conducted, pupils believed the population of Britain to be between 50% and 90% Asian, such had been their experience up to that point.' (Casey, 2016)

Shaw *et al* (2016) conclude that where ethnic minorities are clustered in a small number of schools in an area rather than being spread across all schools in that area this may lower attainment for these groups, especially at Key Stage 2.

Chinese pupils

I recruited and taught quite a number of boys from Hong Kong and mainland China and learnt a lot from them.

They were two to three years ahead of English boys at maths. In 2005 I decided that, rather than requiring Hong Kong 16-year-olds to come to England to take an entrance exam, they should sit my normal sixth form entry scholarship exam in a centre in Hong Kong itself. This exam was supposed to sort out the sheep from the goats but in the first year we used it every candidate got 100%. From then on we had to write a different, tougher exam, just for pupils from East Asia.

Secondly, people in England would sometimes say 'the Chinese are great at rote learning but they cannot think'. This turned out to be the opposite of the truth. My Chinese mathematicians did brilliantly in the UK Mathematical Olympiad and were much better at thinking through complex problems than the best of their English counterparts. The reason they were so good is that they had been taught mathematics using mastery methods (page 130): they study a limited range of topics in great depth, they practise a huge amount and develop an instinctive grasp of mathematical concepts.

Some colleagues also said 'the Chinese are good at maths because when they were young they had to learn 4000 Chinese symbols (rather than 26 letters of an English alphabet) and this taught them to think in the abstract'. This explanation, which comes close to saying that all Chinese have a natural ability at maths, is also wrong. The Chinese are good at maths because they have worked harder.

They worked much harder than English students. When I asked Hong Kong pupils what their plans were for the holidays they often replied by saying 'I will have a tutor'. At first I was offended by this, as school teachers in England would be. But eventually I understood that this was the norm for most teenagers in Hong Kong.

Many of my Hong Kong and Chinese pupils were brilliant at one or more musical instruments, usually violin, cello or piano. Several were grade 8 by age 13; it is extremely rare to find an English pupil who is grade 8 by the age of 13. To find out why Chinese children are so good at musical instruments one need only read Amy Chua's account of the pressure she put her daughters under to learn instruments (Chua, 2011). Chinese parents believe in the value of learning to play an instrument and they enforce the discipline required to practise every day. These children find it tough, but once they have reached a good level of proficiency they become self-motivated. Chinese musicians at my school would practise more than English pupils with no encouragement from adults.

Again, some people would say 'they may know how to play the notes, but do they have real musicality?' The answer to this question was 'yes', they had great musicality and several went on to the Royal Academy for Music ... they were on the way to being professional musicians.

So why did these pupils come to English schools? The main reasons were to gain easier access to top UK universities and to learn English. But there were two other things we gave them. We taught them to challenge the teacher and express their opinions more than they would normally do in Hong Kong or China, and we required them to participate in cocurricular activities like sport and drama to an extent that would be unusual in China.

In *The Learning Gap*, Stevenson and Stigler explain the key difference between East Asian and American children. In East Asia it is assumed that all children can do well if they work hard enough. In America (and Britain) it is assumed that either you have ability in an academic subject or you don't. So in East Asia, if a pupil falls behind, the teacher AND THE PUPIL believe that the situation can be recovered by the teacher and pupil trying harder (Stevenson and Stigler, 1992). Of course there are clever and less clever children in China, but the less clever ones simply have to work harder.

In America and Britain, if you are doing badly at a school subject and you believe that this is because of a genetic disability which can never be overcome, you give up.

If you believe that all pupils can do well you will tend to avoid setting by ability because that might end up cementing children in separate pathways, the less advanced moving more slowly down a road called 'self-fulfilling prophecy'.

Chinese pupils are also more motivated than English children by a desire to do well for the sake of their family. They feel that a failure to do well brings shame on the family. Their family loses face if they do not gain good grades.

Lucy Crehan (2016) spells out brilliantly why Chinese pupils do well. Confucian philosophy, which is reinforced by parents and grandparents, states that working hard and persisting with difficult tasks is important because these are things that make you a moral and virtuous person. What is more, failure is something which should spur you on to try harder rather than provide an excuse to give up.

All the evidence tells us that hard work matters just as much as intelligence. In 2016 the Legatum Institute published proposals to create super-selective grammar schools for the top 1–2% of cognitive ability (O'Shaughnessy, 2016). Such a suggestion completely misses the point that all experienced teachers will immediately recognise – that the children who go on to be brilliant adults are not often those who can be identified in an intelligence test when they are 10 or 11 or even 16. Those who do best are those who COMBINE a level of inherited intelligence with the capacity for hard work.

Socio-economic status

Children from disadvantaged homes start school well behind more advantaged pupils.

University of Kansas researchers Betty Hart and Todd Risley (1995) entered the homes of 42 families from various socio-economic backgrounds to assess the ways in which daily exchanges between a parent and child shape language and vocabulary development. Monthly hour-long observations of each family were conducted from the time the child was seven months until age three. They found that children from high-income families were exposed to 30 million more words than children from families on welfare over the four years.

According to the research summarised by Hirsch (2016) the best way of overcoming this huge initial disadvantage is to focus on vocabulary taught through traditional school subjects and a content-rich curriculum, what he calls the Core Knowledge Sequence. Core Knowledge schools in America and England have shown they can make substantial progress with disadvantaged children if the focus is on committing knowledge to memory.

Shaw *et al* (2016) show that gaps in attainment between FSM-eligible and non-eligible pupils are consistently larger at secondary than primary level in England. Disadvantaged children fall further behind at secondary school rather than catching up. In the 2016 GCSEs pupils on FSMs scored -0.46 on Progress 8 compared to +0.04 for those not of FSMs.

They also conclude that setting pupils by ability tends to entrench disadvantage. While those in top sets benefit from a positive peer-group effect, setting by ability widens gaps between those in top sets and those in middle or bottom sets. This impacts social mobility because children from low income backgrounds, some ethnic minorities and boys are more likely to be placed in the low ability groups

Waldfogel, J., and Reardon, S. (2016), *International Inequalities*, Sutton Trust

By comparing data on cohorts of five-year-old children in the US, UK, Canada and Australia, Waldfogel and Reardon found the difference in reading attainment between the richest and poorest to be biggest in the US, where disadvantaged pupils are behind by about a year before they start school. The reading gap is slightly smaller in the UK, at about eight months. Educational inequality before school starts is much less pronounced in Australia and Canada, where children of the least educated lag behind their more advantaged classmates by an estimated six months.

The researchers also found that the attainment gaps in both the US and UK are much bigger today than they were for children born 40–60 years ago. In both countries these gaps have started to narrow slightly in the past decade, but they are still much larger than they were in the past.

Hutchinson, J. and Dunford, J. (2016), *Divergent Pathways: the disadvantage gap, accountability and the pupil premium*, Education Policy Institute

Previous research by the EPI had showed that by the age of 16 the attainment gap between advantaged and disadvantaged children equated to 19 months (two school years) of teaching. The gap at age 16 can be broken down as follows:

- Two-fifths of the gap was already present by the age of five. This suggests that more needs to be done before formal schooling in order to address educational inequality.

- One-fifth develops during the course of primary school.
- Two-fifths develops during the course of secondary school.

In all schools gaps are closing over time but much faster in those schools with the largest numbers of disadvantaged pupils. This may be because they received more pupil premium money (in 2016 this was given for pupils who had qualified for free school meals at any point in the past six years or had been adopted or in care).

John Dunford quotes the National Foundation for Education Research (NFER) research into what constitutes effective use of the pupil premium – the seven 'building blocks of success':

- The school promotes an ethos of attainment for all pupils, rather than stereotyping disadvantaged pupils as a group with less potential to succeed.
- The school has an individualised approach to addressing barriers to learning and emotional support, at an early stage, rather than providing access to generic support and focusing on pupils nearing their end-of-key-stage assessments.
- The school focusses on high quality teaching first rather than on bolt-on strategies and activities outside school hours.
- The school focusses on outcomes for individual pupils rather than on providing strategies.
- The school deploys the best staff to support disadvantaged pupils; develops skills and roles of teachers and teaching assistants rather than using additional staff who do not know the pupils well.
- The school makes decisions based on data and responds to evidence, using frequent assessments.
- The school has clear, responsive leadership setting ever higher aspirations and devolving responsibility for raising attainment to all staff, rather than accepting low aspirations and variable performance.

Bright but poor

Jerrim, J. (2017), *Global gaps: comparing socio-economic gaps in the performance of highly able UK pupils internationally*, Sutton Trust

Jerrim used the 2015 PISA tests to assess how well the UK's schools are doing for the top 10% of pupils. He found that bright but poor pupils lag behind their bright but better-off classmates by around two years and eight months in maths, science and reading, the gap being even bigger for bright lower income girls than for bright but poor boys.

Sammons, P., Toth, K. and Sylva, K. (2015), *Subject to Background: what promotes better achievement for bright but disadvantaged students?* **University of Oxford Department of Education**

This study tracked the progress of 349 bright children (those who had achieved Level 5+ in Key Stage 2 tests) from disadvantaged families. Key Stage 2 tests were taken at age 11 and the 'expected' level was 4. Pupils reaching Level 5 achieved the standard expected of an average 14-year-old.

So these 349 children did very well at age 11. Why?

They were three times more likely than other disadvantaged children to have a mother with a university degree. They were twice as likely to have experienced a good home environment. They were twice as likely to have enjoyed a reasonable number of enrichment activities such as visits to libraries and playing sports. They were twice as likely to have read books at home. They were twice as likely to have attended a pre-school and more than twice as likely to have gone to a good primary school with high value-added in English.

Those who went on to get significantly the best GCSE results had certain characteristics. They were the ones who engaged in school enrichment activities such as outings and who read at home. They attended secondary schools which they liked because there was an emphasis on learning, the students were valued, the headteacher was involved in school activities, and the relationships between students and teachers were good. There was a high level of teacher monitoring of their work. Time spent on homework was also a good predictor of success.

These pupils were significantly more likely to gain three or more good A-levels where they attended a secondary school rated outstanding by Ofsted for the quality of pupil learning and where they experienced academic enrichment at home. Time spent on homework was still a good predictor of success: completing 2–3 hours of homework a night rather than none increased the likelihood of getting three A-levels nine times.

Facilitating A-level subjects are those listed by the Russell Group of top universities as those which 'keep most options open' for entry to their universities. Nearly twice as many 'bright+advantaged' as 'bright+disadvantaged' students took one or more facilitating subject at A-level.

So the study concludes that bright children from disadvantaged homes greatly benefit from:

- going to a pre-school
- encouragement to read at home
- school trips and other enriching activities
- homework
- frequent teacher feedback on their work
- encouragement to take facilitating subjects at A-level

House of Commons Education Committee (2014), *Underachievement in education by white working class children*

The Education Select Committee undertook a survey to establish the reasons that white working-class children have fallen behind other groups. In 2013 only 31% of white British children eligible for free school meals gained five GCSEs graded C or better including English and maths. PISA data shows that the relationship between social class and exam results is stronger in England than in most countries.

The gap is already wide by the age of four measured by the Government's 17 early learning goals. The gap is wider at Key Stage 2 (age 11) and wider still at GCSE. Other ethnic groups on FSMs are doing better. White working-class girls do better than white working-class boys but the gap in achievement between FSM and non-FSM girls is just as wide as with the same boy groups, so this is not a 'boy' problem.

Twice the proportion of poor children attending an Ofsted-graded outstanding school will leave with five good GCSEs when compared with the lowest rated schools, but the gap exists in most schools.

What did the report suggest causes this underperformance?

1. *Lack of aspiration in white working-class homes.* Some witnesses suggested that it was not lack of aspiration which was the problem but lack of confidence – if, for a variety of reasons, a pupil does not succeed in the early years at school they feel that there is little point in trying.

2. *Social capital.* Parents who did not themselves succeed at school lack the knowledge to help their children and give them good advice. Parental engagement with the school and with schoolwork is important and often low amongst white working-class families.

3. *Parenting skills.* Children without stable and secure homes are less likely to succeed at school. Many parents have a much more limited vocabulary and this is passed on to their children. They are less likely to own books, less likely to read to their children.

4. White working-class children have high rates of absenteeism.

5. *Culture.* Based on a two-year research project on working-class families in Bermondsey, South London, Gillian Evans's book *Educational Failure and Working Class White Children in Britain* argues that white working-class boys are often pressured to uphold a stereotypical tough 'street' reputation which is linked to concepts of masculinity. This leads to poor behaviour and a failure to work at school.

6. *Employment prospects.* The exam results of white working-class children are worst in those parts of the country with high unemployment. In some areas the link between success at school and getting a job may be broken.

7. *Genetics.* Professor Robert Plomin (Professor of Behavioural Genetics, Kings College London) concluded that 50% of the variations in children's individual educational *achievement* were the result of genetic factors.

8. *School quality.* The proportion of Ofsted good and outstanding schools is lower in those parts of Britain with more white working-class children.

Jonathan Clifton, Will Cook (2012), *A long division: closing the attainment gap in England's secondary schools,* IPPR

This excellent report for the Institute for Public Policy Research explored the role that schools can play in tackling the link between educational achievement and family income. They noted that academic studies generally had found that about 20% of variability in a pupil's achievement is attributable to school-level factors, with around 80% attributable to pupil-level factors (Rasbash *et al*, 2010).

They found that pupils from deprived areas in England are more likely to attend a school rated 'requires improvement' or 'inadequate' and pupils from wealthier areas are more likely to attend a school rated 'outstanding'. **But even if every pupil in the country attended an outstanding school, the achievement gap between the poorest and wealthiest pupils would only be cut by a fifth.** If the education gap between advantaged and disadvantaged pupils is to be closed we need more focus on interventions such as one-to-one tuition and preschool programmes.

The report examines how the education system in England compares with other countries, including Finland, Canada and South Korea. It finds that a large number of very low achievers is holding England back from becoming a world class system. In the world's leading systems 1 in 10 pupils fail to reach basic proficiency in reading. In England that figure is twice as high.

Social Mobility and Child Poverty Commission (2015), *Downward Mobility, Opportunity Hoarding and the Glass Floor*

In June 2015 the Social Mobility and Child Poverty Commission published research by Dr Abigail McKnight from the Centre for Analysis of Social Exclusion at the London School of Economics suggesting that middle-class parents support their children so that even less intelligent middle-class children do quite well in life.

Seventeen thousand children born in a week in 1970 took an intelligence test when they were five (British Cohort Study). When they were aged 42 their income was recorded. Less intelligent middle-class adults were earning more than the more intelligent adults who had grown up in low income homes.

In the post-war period the number of good white collar jobs grew faster than the size of the middle-class workforce and this enabled working-class children to obtain middle-class jobs. This is no longer happening, so for able working-class children to have upward mobility some middle-class children will have to have downward mobility. The fact that middle-class children do not generally experience downward mobility is the 'glass floor'.

Dr McKnight suggests there are two main pillars supporting the 'glass floor':

More advantaged parents secure educational opportunities to help their children overcome lack of ability by:

- investing time and resources in education to help children showing early signs of low attainment to recover and achieve good qualifications.

- providing good careers advice and guidance – this is likely to be important in explaining why parental education has such a big impact on their children's earnings after controlling for qualifications and schooling.

- placing a high value on polish and 'soft skills' such as self-confidence, decisiveness, leadership and resilience.

- researching and choosing the best schools, with more advantaged parents able to move house to be in the catchment area of a good state school, invest in private tutors to coach their children to pass the 11+ in areas with grammar schools, or give their children a private education.

More advantaged parents secure advantages for their children into the labour market that are unavailable to less well-off parents by:

- helping their children into employment through informal social networks.

- securing informal and unpaid internships.

- investing in their children's 'soft skills' which are highly valued in employment recruitment processes.

Chair of the commission, Alan Milburn, said: *'No one should criticise parents for doing their best for their children. That's what we all want. But Britain is a long way from being a meritocratic society when the less able can do better in life than the more able.*

It has long been recognised that there is a glass ceiling in British society that prevents children with potential progressing to the top. This research reveals there is a glass floor that inhibits social mobility as much as the glass ceiling.'

Social class and university entry

There has been a big increase in the past ten years in the number of pupils from disadvantaged homes going to university in the UK, but mainly to the low tariff universities. The increase has occurred for three reasons. Universities have spent huge sums on outreach activities, persuading school-age pupils to apply. Secondly, all universities have set themselves the target of taking more pupils from disadvantaged homes, and these targets are monitored by the Office of Fair Access. Thirdly, universities are taking more students and this makes it easier for those from the bottom 15% economically (those on free school meals) to find a place.

However, the relatively poor GCSE and A-level results of those from disadvantaged backgrounds make it harder for them to find places at high tariff universities. This is the challenge the nation now faces – better results for able pupils from lower socio-economic groups, not least white boys.

Through the lens of students: how perceptions of higher education influence applicants' choices, UCAS survey 2016

In this survey 6500 people told UCAS why they didn't apply to the higher tariff group of universities. This revealed that a lack of good information was holding back some applicants.

- Nearly half (49%) thought the entry requirements to these universities were too high – more would have applied if they had known they had a chance of getting in. Some students over-estimate the difficulty of gaining places at top universities.

- Forty-one per cent believed none of these universities offered the courses they were interested in – there was a lack of understanding of career pathways from 'academic-sounding' degree courses. Disadvantaged pupils are more likely to believe that a university degree has to have a vocational element.

- Three-quarters said they would have applied to a higher tariff university if they were offered a travel voucher for an open day. Small sums of money can have a big impact.

- A quarter of the least advantaged students who didn't apply to higher tariff universities said they felt the cost of living would be too high.

The survey also asked what students felt about the relationship between their higher education choices and employment. The least advantaged were 30% more likely to think the degree **subject studied** was key to employment while more advantaged applicants were 50% more likely to think the **university they went to** was more important for securing a job.

According to Bowes *et al* (2015) white disadvantaged young people are more likely than others to *'indicate that the best jobs did not necessarily go to those who had been to university'* and to *'believe that university wasn't for people like them'*.

In a big study Allen *et al* (2016) looked at educational choices made at age 16 by pupils who sat GCSEs in summer 2010 and found:

- more FSM pupils drop out of education than non-FSM pupils with the same GCSE grades.

- more FSM pupils study lower level qualifications post-16 than non-FSM pupils with the same GCSE grades.

- fewer FSM pupils go on to Russell Group universities than non-FSM pupils with the same GCSE grades.

Gender

In 2016 52% of boys in England gained five grade A*–C GCSEs including English and maths compared to 62% of girls. **The Progress 8 score for boys was -0.17, for girls +0.11.** Only 26% of white British boys on free school meals gained five good GCSEs.

According to a recent OECD report boys in the UK spend less time reading for enjoyment: 51% of boys and 70% of girls read for enjoyment. Boys in the UK spend over one hour less per week on homework than girls (5.5 hours versus 4.2 hours) (OECD, 2015).

At A-level in 2015 the average point score was 213 for boys compared to 218 for girls. There are 65,000 more unemployed males NEETs (Not in Education, Employment or Training) than females.

According to UCAS, in 2016 about 40% of young men applied to university and 36% went, while 53% of young women applied and 47% went. This gap between the sexes is widening year by year and the gap is even wider when one looks at those who come from low income homes, where women are over 50% more likely to go to university. At this rate the last male will enter university in 2085 – and he will then drop out.

This phenomenon is quite recent. After all, the University of Cambridge refused to make women full members of the university until after the Second World War, in 1948. The number of women undergraduates only overtook men in the mid-1990s (Hillman and Robinson, 2016).

The gender gap: There are consistently more women than men applying to university

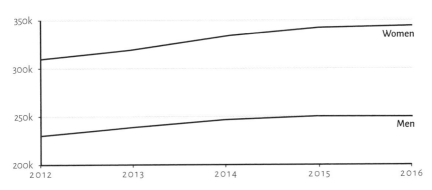

Source: UCAS

The main reason for the university gap is that girls get better GCSE results than boys. Girls mature faster. In the classroom they seem to be keener to please the teacher than boys. They score higher marks in coursework because they work harder and are dissatisfied with themselves if the quality is low. Eight-five per cent of primary teachers are female as are 62% of secondary teachers. If you give boys and girls a test, boys tend to overestimate how well they have done, girls underestimate. So girls will feel the need to work hard more keenly than boys.

The Sutton Trust report *Believing in Better*, in June 2016, showed that one reason so many more girls go to university than boys is that they are much more likely to believe in the importance of a university degree. Even in Year 9 65% of girls said it was important to go to university compared to 58% of boys. And 15- and 16-year-olds with similar GCSE results were twice as likely to go on to do three A-levels if they saw university as a likely goal for them.

The greater appetite for higher education among women is rational in financial terms because the financial returns from higher education are larger for women than for men. This is not because female graduates earn more than male; in fact, they earn less. It is due to non-graduate women typically earning much less than non-graduate men.

Skilled careers traditionally chosen by women, such as nursing and teaching, did not demand full degrees in the past. When this changed, the number of women in higher education increased dramatically.

Women outperforming men is a worldwide trend. In *Education at a Glance 2015*, the Organisation for Economic Co-operation and Development (OECD) found that women make up the majority of entrants into tertiary education in all OECD countries except Mexico, Saudi Arabia, Switzerland and Turkey. On average across OECD countries, 54% of tertiary education entrants are women.

Around five-sixths of higher education institutions in the UK have more female than male students. Yet, aside from initial teacher training, only two set targets for the recruitment of more male students in their 2016/17 Access Agreements.

Also very interesting is the influence of gender on choice of degree subject; here are some examples:

Degree course acceptances 2015 (selected subjects)

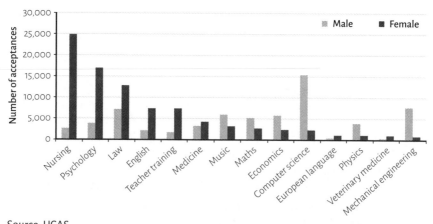

Source: UCAS

Data from the Higher Education Policy Institute also shows that women are securing better degrees than men, are less likely to drop out and are less likely to become unemployed.

Boys are falling behind girls in all parts of the developed world – Europe, the USA and Japan. In America last year four out of five of those achieving the best degrees were women. The 2006 comedy *Failure to Launch* was about a modern phenomenon which is observable across the world – men who prefer life with mum to a serious job and a wife. Young males in the UK were more likely than young females to be living with their parents in 2016. Thirty-one per cent of males aged 20 to 34 were living with their parents compared with 20% of females (ONS).

Moss, G., and Washbrook, E. (2016), *The Lost Boys,* Save the Children

This report is based on a study of Reception year (four and five-year-olds) conducted at the University of Bristol using the Millennium Cohort Study data.

The study found that each year a quarter of boys in England – 80,000 – start Reception, aged four, struggling to speak a single sentence or follow basic instructions. In 2015 24% of boys were below the minimum level in early language and communication expected by the Early Years Foundation Stage programme, as were 14% of girls. So boys make up two-thirds of those who start primary school behind in their communication skills. Even worse, 38% of boys eligible for free school meals were behind. Nor was there any sign of this gender gap closing.

The gap between boys and girls was there irrespective of ethnicity or social class. Boys from wealthier homes reach a higher level but so do the wealthier girls, so the gender gap remains.

Moss and Washbrook found children with lower early language and communication skills at age five:

- performed less well in KS1 reading assessments
- were less attentive
- read less often for pleasure
- enjoyed school less
- liked answering in class less
- tried less hard in school

This is why, once boys fall behind, they struggle to catch up. Children who did not achieve the expected standard of early language and communication at five were found to be over four times more likely to have below Level 4 reading at 11 than those who did. According to Moss and Washbrook two-thirds of the total gender gap in reading at KS2 can be attributed to the fact that boys begin school with poorer language and attention skills than girls.

These boys go on to do badly at GCSE and struggle in life thereafter.

This is not just a British phenomenon. In 2015 girls outperformed boys in reading at the end of secondary school in all 64 countries and economies in the OECD, the average gap being the equivalent to an extra year of schooling.

Moss and Washbrook recommend improving Early Childhood Education and Care (ECEC) provision and increasing the number of 0–5 Early Years teachers.

Boys Adrift

Leonard Sax, an American doctor, has written extensively about the issue of boy underachievement including *Why gender matters* (2005) and *Boys Adrift* (2007).

He claims that research in the past 20 years – made possible by Magnetic Resonance Imaging – has shown that the brains of boys and girls are different from the moment they are born. These genetic differences lead to differences in the ways boys and girls learn. Boys simply cannot learn to read as young as girls, so pushing children to read at a young age establishes male inferiority. Young boys quickly gain a sense of failure at school.

The brains of girls develop quicker than the brains of boys. At 20 months girls have twice the vocabulary of boys. Girls are fully mature by the age of 22, boys at the age of 30, and the differences between the two are greatest when they are about 15, as any experienced parent knows. Girls prefer to read fiction, boys prefer non-fiction. Girls prefer books about characters, boys prefer books about action. Boys respond best to clear rules, deadlines and the threats of punishments. Girls respond best to explanations based on feelings – 'how would you feel if someone did that to you?'.

Another explanation given by Sax is the astonishing fact that the sperm count and testosterone levels of boys are now half that of their grandfathers. This is partly due to residues from plastics absorbed from drinking bottles, bottles which all children use from the earliest age, the chemicals which make your drink taste a bit plasticky. These residues are making girls reach puberty earlier because they mimic female sex hormones. But they also act to reduce testosterone levels and this disproportionately affects boys, because testosterone is what produces motivation in males.

Another factor described by Sax is the emasculation of the male ideal. Men have ceased to be strong role-models as the concept of manliness has withered away. When he was at school the great hero athletes were Eric Liddle (the subject of *Chariots of Fire*) and the man who first ran the four-minute mile, Roger Bannister – academics with great sporting ability. Sport matters to boys, but how many of today's top footballers went to university?

Fifty years ago young men had a strong sense of needing to work hard and get a good job as a duty to their family. Too many boys in Europe and the USA think it is unmasculine to be seen to care about academic work. Douglas Bader has been succeeded by Homer Simpson as the male role model for the modern boy.

Parents seem to find it harder and harder to discipline their children and the impact of this is greatest on boys because boys are born with a greater propensity to take risks and be aggressive. They need discipline. Most of us welcome the fact that the gap between the generations has narrowed – but over the past 50 years authority has been transferred from parents to children and boys are paying the price.

Men are less likely to have done well at school, less likely to go to university, less likely to find a good job, more likely to avoid commitment to a partner. According to Sax all of this can be turned around if boys are treated as boys and taught in ways which are best for them. But meanwhile we have an emerging crisis and one which will ultimately affect women, not least if women aspire to marry a man who is as educated as themselves. Quite soon such creatures will simply not exist.

Mental health

An important new research report by Lessof, C. *et al*, 2016, looked at the mental health of 30,000 14-year-olds in 2014 in Britain, comparing the results with a similar survey in 2005. The two findings were:

- Year 10 students in 2014 were markedly more 'work focused' than their counterparts in 2005

- There were signs that the mental wellbeing of Year 10 students – particularly that of girls – had worsened and that young people felt less control over their own destinies. 37% of teenage girls had three or more symptoms of psychological distress such as feeling unhappy, worthless and unable to concentrate, compared with 15% of boys.

The number of 14-year-olds who said that they were expecting to study A-levels increased from 59% in 2005 to 65% in 2014. And in spite of the increase in tuition fees, the proportion of 14-year-olds expecting to apply to university increased from 60% in 2005 to 71% in 2014. There was similarly positive news in terms of risky behaviours – young people in 2014 were far less likely to drink alcohol, smoke cigarettes or cannabis, engage in graffiti or shoplifting, or to commit vandalism.

But levels of psychological distress increased between 2005 and 2014, especially in girls. Young people from relatively advantaged backgrounds were more likely to exhibit psychological distress than those from less advantaged families.

The research showed that young people in 2014 were more likely to strongly equate hard work with success (believing in the value of working hard at school in order to succeed) but they also had a lower 'locus of control' (the extent to which they believe they can control events affecting them).

The National Study of Health and Wellbeing has been carried out for the NHS every seven years since 1993.

In 1993, 19% of 16 to 24-year-old women surveyed reported symptoms of a common mental disorder such as anxiety and depression compared with 8% of men of the same age. In 2014, 26% of women aged 16–24 reported symptoms of such disorders compared to 9% of men in the same age group. So the gender gap is widening.

Rise in young people reporting self-harm in England

16 to 24-years-olds in 2000, 2007 and 2014 (%)

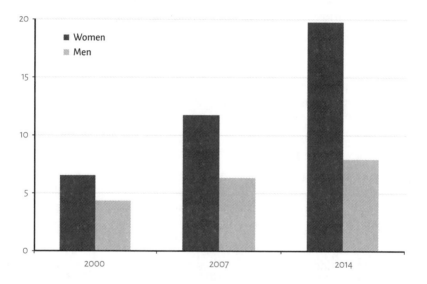

Source: NHS Digital

Stephen Buckley, head of information at the mental health charity Mind, said: *'Young people are coming of working age in times of economic uncertainty. They're more likely to experience issues associated with debt, unemployment and poverty, and they are up against increasing social and environmental pressures, all of which affect well-being.'* (BBC news website). He also said there had been a surge in the use of social media which can negatively affect people's mental health. Girls seem particularly vulnerable to a social media culture which encourages them to compete with apparently perfect lives.

In *Affluenza* the psychologist Oliver James looks at the relationship between 'the affluent society' and mental illness such as depression. He defines affluenza as 'placing a high value on money, possessions, appearances (physical and social) and fame'...all things which generate emotional distress. Younger people, people who live in cities and girls are especially susceptible (James, 2007).

James chronicles the relationship between the growing gap in exam results between boys and girls and the increase in psychological distress amongst girls from high-income families. Pressure on girls is greatest because of their greater tendency to want to please authority – to achieve top grades – and because they often aspire to an unobtainable perfection. Exams have a part to play in this, not because there are more exams these days (there are not) but because society places more weight on them. It doesn't help that so many of the better universities now ask for AAA grades or better at A-level, leaving very little room for slippage. Thirty years ago, because top grades were less common, students gained admission to Oxford and Cambridge with significantly lower grades.

James suggests that societies remove the negative consumerist effects by pursuing real needs over perceived wants, and by defining themselves as having value independent of their material possessions. James strongly urges parents to discourage their daughters from academic prize-hunting and to discourage all children from believing the purpose of education is to launch a career.

Much research suggests that social networking is both highly addictive and damaging to teenagers' wellbeing, a bit like cigarettes (McAfee, 2010, Greenfield, 2014). Mauri *et al* (2011) show why Facebook is addictive: social networking releases dopamine into the brain.

Professor Greenfield shows that social networking is enabling teenagers to create a fantasy image of themselves. Our identity used to be generated internally; now identity is constructed externally as the product of the continuous interaction with 'friends'.

Social networking feeds into the natural narcissism of adolescents (Buffardi *et al*, 2008, Twenge *et al*, 2008) but interestingly, it is also linked to low self-esteem (Tiggemann and Miller, 2010). Social networking helps children to create identities which allow them to be more rude, more sexy, more adventurous and indulge in inappropriate behaviour. Sherry Turkle explains in her book *Alone Together* that the more connected you are online the more isolated you feel (Turkle, 2012). Social media provides an unparalleled platform for social comparison and envy (Krasnova *et al*, 2013). Excessive internet use is also linked to a reduced ability to empathise with people and poor communications skills, including difficulty in interpreting facial expressions (Engleberg *et al*, 2004). At Cornell University Michael Waldman, Sean Nicholson and Nodir Adilov have shown links between screen use and the development of autism (Waldman *et al*, 2006). Cyberbullying is rife (LeBlanc, J, 2012).

In 2016 a UK survey of night-time use of digital devices was carried out by the online safety organisation Digital Awareness UK (DAUK) in partnership with the Headmasters' and Headmistresses' Conference (HMC). It found that children as young as nine are being woken up more than ten times a night by constant message notifications from their phones. Children are so addicted to social media that they cannot bear to turn their devices off at night so they sleep with them in their beds. This is causing sleep deprivation in both primary and secondary school pupils, meaning they are unable to concentrate and work well in class. One in ten youngsters aged 11 to 18 spend more than an hour on their mobile device after going to bed.

So the advice to schools and parents is to remove these things that cause stress in the first place, limiting electronic device use to a few hours a day (page 164).

Stress and mindfulness

There is a distinction between psychological illnesses which can be diagnosed by a psychiatrist and general wellbeing.

Schools are increasingly offering mindfulness lessons. Mindfulness (a form of meditation) has been shown to reduce stress, a bit like smoking used to do. Books explaining mindfulness are pouring out – like *Calm* by Michael Acton Smith. In her review in *The Times* (24 March 2015), Janice Turner wrote:

'Although I feel unkind saying so, Calm *is a beautifully designed little book of the bleeding obvious, the emperor's new yoga trousers. Must we pay £9.99 to be told to go for a walk, take a nap, stare at the sea, have a bath, read a novel, hug someone, plant some seeds or look out of the window? Or to know the importance of a good night's sleep and eating a family meal? Or that good ideas often come to us on train journeys? Don't most people — those of us who are not driven, hyperactive internet entrepreneurs — do these pleasant, everyday things anyway? It feels as if our own lives are being repackaged and sold back to us at a premium.'*

Mindfulness is no doubt a good thing, but as with everything else schools are asked to do (sex education, citizenship, character development, British values and so on) before any school agrees to teach it they must answer the question, 'what subject or activity will be cut to make room for these lessons?' It is always easy to add activities, much harder to subtract.

Suggestible children are being told that they have problems. Pupils are strongly encouraged to put themselves forward as having special needs so that they get extra time in exams. Problems which would in the past have been happily dealt with by classroom teachers are now the province of teams of counsellors.

In the September 2015 issue of *The Atlantic* magazine Lukianoff and Haidt described the destructive impact of the wellbeing army on students in America. They cite a survey by the American College Health Association, in which 54% of college students said they had 'felt overwhelming anxiety' in the past 12 months. But their analysis concludes that this is part of a group-think, fuelled by social media and egged-on by American college leaders anxious to appear PC. They conclude:

'Attempts to shield students from words, ideas, and people that might cause them emotional discomfort are bad for the students.

Rather than trying to protect students from words and ideas that they will inevitably encounter, colleges should do all they can to equip students to thrive in a world full of words and ideas that they cannot control. One of the great truths taught by Buddhism (and Stoicism, Hinduism, and many other traditions) is that you can never achieve happiness by making the world conform to your desires. But you can master your desires and habits of thought.'

Or Mary Wakefield in the *Spectator* (August 29, 2015):

'In my twenties, just as full of self-pity and terror as this new generation, I once dropped in to see a priest, Father Fudge, and poured out my woes, imagining he would be both sympathetic and impressed by my torment. Fr Fudge listened quietly, then said: 'The point of being a Christian is not to feel better, it is so God can use you to serve others.'

Others? They hadn't occurred to me for a while. I said goodbye to Fr Fudge, feeling unaccountably lighter. It wasn't all about me!

I actually laughed with the relief of it.'

At the 2016 Telegraph Festival of Education, the teacher Gareth Sturdy said he believed the focus in schools on pupils' self-esteem allowed them to produce *'all manner of excuses for poor behaviour or achievement'.*

'It's a bit of a mask for children to not focus on the business of learning, that's my experience.

Learning things is hard – it's an affront to your self-esteem and it's difficult to get to grips with.'

In December 2015 the headmaster of Ampleforth made the point that mindfulness is only a temporary solution to stress. *'It doesn't really ask them to find their true personality or to have core values that will guide them through all the problems they will face in their lifetime.'* He said that taking children to see more disadvantaged areas of their community or doing volunteer work is a more effective way of teaching them to cope with stress because it helps them gain perspective. *'Then they can see that maybe their own situation is not as bad as they thought it was.'*

As the head of Ampleforth knows all too well, in the past most children achieved the same effects as those claimed by the mindfulness gurus by attending school chapel and through prayer. Anything which places one's own busy life in some sort of context is a good thing but – quite apart from prayer – there are other ways of reducing stress, like taking children out of the classroom and making them focus on a team game or physical activity.

How bad is stress? We all know the answer to that – some stress is good, too much stress is bad. Some stress is good because it is part and parcel of being motivated. It is hard to imagine boys doing well in an exam if stress hadn't motivated them to revise. Stress is part of life and experiencing stress while at school is preparation for that. Too much stress is bad – it diminishes enjoyment and prevents people from functioning effectively. So we need a balance, as in most things.

Former pupils: the Alumni Associations

Good schools try to appoint a former pupil to teach at the school and to run, with secretarial help, an alumni association. This means making a big effort to retain former students' email and postal addresses, sending them a newsletter once or twice a year and having an alumni party once a year outside the university terms.

Alumni are often the best ambassadors of the school. They should be invited back to speak to current pupils about their universities and careers. They can be great speaking at open days to prospective parents. One day some will become benefactors.

I visited one of the Charter Schools in the Bronx in New York, an unimpressive top floor of a dull building. But the entrance area was packed with lively information about the successes of alumni – their universities and their careers. There could have been no better inspiration for the current pupils.

The London Academy of Excellence (page 263) expects to offer its alumni access to careers advice throughout their whole lives. Both sides gain from this policy.

All good schools have an alumni association.

Conclusions

Attainment gaps based on ethnicity have been greatly reduced in recent years. Gaps based on gender are widening for university entry. Gaps based on socio-economic status are the widest.

Average Attainment 8 scores for state-funded schools in England, 2016 – the average achievement of pupils in up to 8 qualifications, mostly GCSEs

EAL means English as an additional language. Pupils are defined as disadvantaged if they are known to have been eligible for free school meals in the past six years (from Year 6 to Year 11), if they are recorded as having been looked after for at least one day or if they are recorded as having been adopted from care.

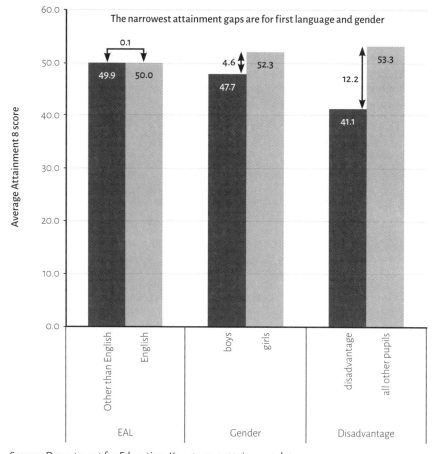

Source: Department for Education, Key stage 4 attainment data

Schools alone will struggle to reduce these gaps because a high proportion of the difference between advantaged and disadvantaged pupils is caused by non-school factors such as poverty or weak parenting. It is a policy mistake to assume that schools alone are capable of creating a more equal society. Something has to be done about income distribution and quality of parenting as well.

Nevertheless, some schools are more successful than others at achieving good results for disadvantaged pupils and more needs to be known about them. Schools whose teachers enforce high expectations and a no-excuses culture seem most successful.

Most of the academic studies described above are based on published test and exam data. But there is more to producing successful pupils than exam results. Many of my most academically disastrous pupils have had stellar careers. Others who were famously brilliant at school have made less of a mark. So schools need to pay attention to those qualities which are not measured by exams, such as imagination, initiative and the ability to lead teams. This is why team sports, the Duke of Edinburgh Award Scheme, talks by inspirational role models and school societies are so important.

Chapter 4

Successful Subjects

You don't think of Shakespeare being a child, do you? Shakespeare being seven? He was seven at some point. He was in somebody's English class, wasn't he?

How annoying would that be?

Ken Robinson: *How schools kill creativity*, TED, 2006

Too much of the debate about education is about structures: are academies a good thing or not? What about grammar schools? Are the accountability measures fair? What about the Ofsted inspection regime? These are the things which preoccupy government ministers and the media.

Less is said about the actual content of lessons – what is taught and what we want inside the brains of 11-year-olds, 14-year-olds and 18-year-olds.

But I am interested in what pupils actually know. I am interested in the fact that so many of my A-level students had never heard of Martin Luther, that my religious studies GCSE pupils did not seem to know what was meant by the crucifixion – what it was, what its significance was to Christians – despite the fact that the crucifixion was at the centre of most Europeans' lives before 1945.

In some respects children in this country know less than they used to and that is not an accident – it is the result of decisions taken by people who should know better.

What are schools for? They are there to help students *make a living* after they have left. But they also teach pupils those things which *make life worth living*, like literature, art, music, drama and sport. These subjects will not often lead to a job but they are just as important as those subjects that do.

Most heads think it's a good idea to teach *subjects* because that's the way mankind has classified knowledge and has done so for a reason. Most teachers have taken a degree in a specific subject. It is just a pity that teacher training in England has given so little emphasis to subject knowledge. If you compare teacher training with the training of doctors or lawyers you can immediately see the contrast: with doctors and lawyers there is a huge emphasis on subject knowledge. It could be like that for teachers too.

If you believe in subjects then that leaves two further questions:

1. You can't teach all subjects so which are you going to leave out? For children up the age of 16 the Government has more or less defined the list of subjects which should be taught and that leaves little room for anything else.

   Beyond 16 there is plenty of subject choice within A-levels, Pre-Us, the International Baccalaureate and vocational qualifications like level 3 BTECs (agriculture, health and social care, business, construction, engineering and many others). This diversity of choice post-16 helps motivate students.

2. How much time are you going to spend on each subject? The danger with having too many subjects for pupils is that you spend little time on each. Schools who try to satisfy 11- to 14-year-olds by teaching a long list like French, Spanish, history, geography, RE, art, music, dance, drama, PE, design technology and computing for just one hour or less a week each may not be doing anyone a favour. It is hard to have a sense of momentum on fewer than two periods a week on two different days.

Some successful secondary schools devote much more time than usual to maths and English. They rightly regard these as fundamental academic subjects which have to be mastered before most (not all) other subjects can be handled properly. The reward for their approach is that all their pupils are good at maths and English by the age of 14. The price they pay for spending so much time on maths and English is that some other subjects cannot be taught until Key Stage 4.

In 2013 Cristina Iannelli at Edinburgh University published research which showed that the subjects a child studied at school had a significant effect on their chances of doing well in life. Taking a cohort of people born in one week in 1958, she found that the subjects they studied mattered more than going to a private school or grammar school. People who studied languages, English, maths and science, regardless of school type, were more likely to enter professional and managerial occupations. Subject choice matters greatly.

Wolf alert

In 2010 there was concern that schools and colleges were encouraging pupils to take subjects which were of little value to universities or employees. The 2011 Wolf Report, written by Professor Alison Wolf from King's College London, found that thousands of vocational qualifications taken by young people were a 'negative qualification' – in other words they actually harmed a pupil's prospects of going to university or gaining a job.

In response to her findings the Government removed funding from these courses and reduced the incentives which had encouraged schools to offer vocational alternatives to GCSEs: in government league tables there had been a raft of generous 'equivalences' where, for example, a vocational ICT course was worth the equivalent of four GCSEs. These equivalences were often far easier than the GCSEs they were supposed to be the equivalent of. They were reined back after the Wolf Report.

EBacchanalia

The Russell Group of 24 leading universities produces a guide for schools in which they state that some A-level subjects are more useful than others if you want to keep your options open in terms of admission to Russell Group universities. These so-called *facilitating subjects* are maths, further maths, physics, chemistry, biology, modern and ancient languages, English literature, geography, history, philosophy and ethics.

The Government was concerned that increasing numbers of pupils were studying non-facilitating subjects and this was especially true of pupils from disadvantaged backgrounds. In order to influence this they created a new performance table measure called the English Baccalaureate (EBacc) which gives the proportion of a school's students passing GCSEs in English, maths, sciences, history or geography and a language.

In 2010, just 22% of state school pupils were entered for the EBacc, and only 15% achieved it. GCSE results in 2016 showed those proportions had risen to 39.7% and 24.7% respectively. So this was a remarkable example of a performance table tweak having a huge effect on what was being taught in English schools.

% of pupils entering the EBacc in England

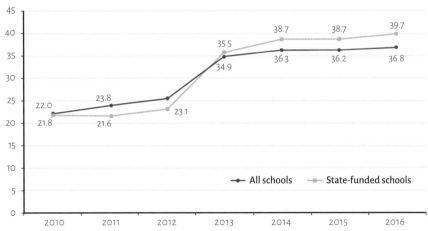

Source: Department for Education, Key stage 4 attainment data

A further measure called Progress 8 was introduced for schools in 2016 based on students' progress measured across eight subjects: English; mathematics; three other EBacc subjects (chosen from sciences, computer science, geography, history and languages); and three further subjects.

The EBacc was given extra punch in 2016 when the *floor standard* (the standard a school had to reach if it was to avoid intervention by the Department for Education) was based on schools' results on the Progress 8 measure. The EBacc performance measure was a nudge. The EBacc element of Progress 8 is really compulsion.

A national curriculum

The 2010–15 and 2015–2020 governments both declared their determination to encourage school-age pupils to study certain subjects rather than others. The 2011 National Curriculum Review stated:

'The National Curriculum should embody rigour and high standards and create coherence in what is taught in schools, ensuring that all children have the opportunity to acquire a core of knowledge in the key subject disciplines.'

For maintained schools the post-2014 National Curriculum subject requirements are as follows:

Key Stage 1 age 5–7
English, maths, sciences, history, geography, religious studies, art, music, computing, design and technology, physical education.

Key Stage 2 age 7–11
The same but add foreign language (ancient or modern).

Key Stage 3 age 11–14
Add citizenship, sex education. Languages must now be modern.

Key Stage 4 age 14–16
English, maths, sciences, computing, citizenship, religious studies, sex and relationships, physical education.

The 2010–15 and 2015–2020 governments implied there was a hierarchy of subjects up to the age of 16 as follows:

Vital: English and maths – double weighting in Progress 8.

Other EBacc subjects: Physics, chemistry, biology, computer science, history, geography, languages ancient or modern.

Others: art, music, design technology, PE, RE, dance, media, sociology, business *etc.*

English and maths are subjects which are helpful for the study of other subjects and for most jobs. Employers represented by the CBI have consistently bemoaned the lack of basic literacy and numeracy of school leavers and graduates.

Mathematics has had particular emphasis. This is because the PISA tests show that British schools are well behind schools in East Asia in numeracy. Not only has the content of the compulsory maths GCSE been increased but extra maths has been added to the syllabus of other subjects such as the sciences, design and technology and geography.

Ministers in the DfE have been keen to see students continue with maths in the sixth form. A new course called Core Maths, the equivalent to an AS-level, has been introduced for those who are competent at maths but not good enough to take the full A-level.

In the case of the other EBacc subjects, these are those which, according to the Russell Group of good universities, keep most options open in terms of university degree choice. They are also subjects which are perceived as being more demanding than some of the alternatives.

English

At the moment my father, an Anglican vicar, retired from his parish in rural Sussex I got my first teaching job, at Eton. In my first weeks of teaching I became aware of the fact that my pupils were being held back by their poor standard of written English. The school at that time required that most pupils were assessed for entry *before the age of one*, so the ability range was quite wide. They had all been to good junior schools but their spelling, vocabulary, punctuation and other aspects of grammar seemed poor.

Before my father retired my family had employed the services of Betty New as a cleaner. She had been brought up in a local council estate, leaving school with few qualifications. After my parents retired to Wiltshire she wrote them long letters – right up to her death. It was striking that her letters demonstrated much higher standards of literacy, as well as handwriting, than my Etonian pupils. She had gone to a school in the 1940s when teaching was rigorous and there was a great emphasis on reading and writing. This had left her with a literacy toolbox which served her well for the rest of her life.

All teachers of essay-writing A-level subjects struggle with the low level of literacy of their pupils. In 2002 a casual conversation with my good head of English revealed that it was possible to get an A* in English GCSE and still have quite weak literacy. So I required all my Year 12s to take a literacy test (spelling, grammar, punctuation) and if they failed, which most did, they had to attend extra lessons until they reached my level, which was higher than that of the exam boards.

I am not in favour of compulsory subjects in the sixth form, but I do think that pupils who cannot write well must continue with English until they reach an acceptable standard. No school should send a student out into the world without a good grasp of English.

Maths

Maths is a subject which has a chequered history. In 2000 a new maths syllabus was introduced that was so difficult many students failed the AS-level and, for a while, numbers taking the subject plummeted. Over time they recovered to the current high level.

The recent reforms mean the popularity of the subject is being tested again. The reformed GCSE is difficult. It is a subject that benefitted more than any other from being modular at A-level; now it is linear. The decoupling of the AS and move from four to three A-level subjects will discourage more modest mathematicians from choosing maths.

Any decline in numbers choosing maths A-level will be a problem. The country needs more, not fewer, students to do the subject at university. The supply of maths teachers is already poor.

Maths mastery

In 2016 the Government announced that primary schools in England would move towards teaching maths using the 'mastery' principles found in East Asian countries such as Singapore, Japan, South Korea and China. PISA results suggest that by age 15 students from these countries are on average up to three years ahead in maths compared to 15-year-olds in England.

How do they do it? Asian teachers have an expectation that all pupils are capable of achieving high standards in mathematics. Pupils progress through the curriculum content at the same pace, taught together from the front of the class and using textbooks which have been carefully designed. Weaker pupils are supported and more able children are given work to deepen their understanding. But they all move through the course together. Pupils' difficulties or misconceptions are identified by the teacher and addressed – commonly through individual or small group support later the same day.

Teaching is underpinned by methodical curriculum design and supported by carefully crafted lessons and excellent textbooks to foster deep conceptual knowledge. **The course is taught in small steps each of which must be**

mastered before pupils move on to the next stage. Pupils learn times tables at an early stage and are fluent in them.

Practice and consolidation play a central role. Carefully designed variations in questions builds fluency and understanding of mathematical concepts. Teachers use precise questioning in class to test conceptual and procedural knowledge and assess pupils regularly to identify those requiring intervention so that all pupils keep up. So one of the key aspects of maths mastery is taking the syllabus slowly – key concepts have to be practised a great deal before a student can move on. Knowledge has to turn into understanding.

Maths mastery was pioneered by the Ark schools in England and is now becoming widespread.

Hall *et al* (2016) used a randomised control trial involving Oxford University Press's *Inspire Maths* – the mastery textbook and professional development programme based on *My Pals are Here!*, which is used in the majority of Singaporean primary schools. The study involved two groups of children aged five to six – a total of 550 – learning maths in 12 English schools in 2015 to 2016. The first group learned maths as normal, the second group used the *Inspire Maths* text and made better overall progress. Maths mastery works.

Modern languages

Proportion of end of Key Stage 4 pupils sitting a GCSE in a language, England

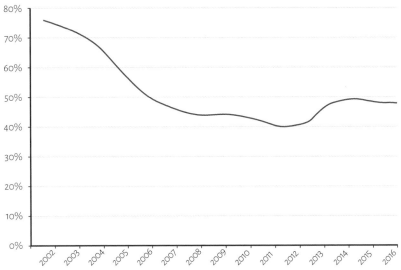

Source: Joint Council for Qualifications

Entries for A-level languages, England

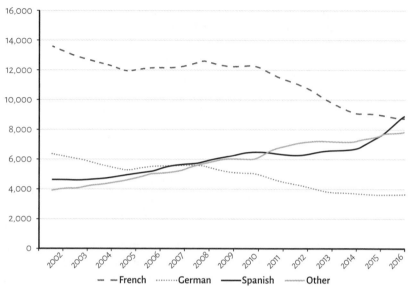

- — French ········· German ——— Spanish ——— Other

Source: Joint Council for Qualifications

Overall numbers taking modern languages have been falling for some years. Spanish numbers have grown but not as much as French and German declined. 31,261 in the UK took A-level French in 1992; despite a huge increase in overall numbers of A-levels taken, the figure in 2016 was only 9,672.

We know that this was partly the result of the decision taken in 2002 to make MFLs optional at GCSE. It is partly because MFLs are harder subjects than some of their competitors (even though standards have fallen further in MFLs than in other subjects since the 1980s. A-level French is about the same standard as the O-level was then).

The arrival of more and more native speakers in the UK has put pressure on the system. They take A-levels in their home language and, because top grades are rationed, this makes it harder for non-native speakers to gain the higher grades. This is especially true of Mandarin.

After 2010 the Government made modern languages an EBacc subject and numbers rose. However, from 2016 modern languages are an optional part of the Progress 8 GCSE measure and may decline again.

There have been problems with the language teaching methods used in schools. Teachers adopted methods used by those teaching English as a foreign language, where the focus is on speed of acquisition and spoken language. Teaching in the target language has been a mistake because it frightens off many pupils and doesn't make use of their knowledge of English. There has been too much focus on 'speaking in a café', too little formal grammar, almost no translation English to French, and far too much rote learning of phrases which gives a false impression of competence.

A-level syllabuses have been boring, with little or no study of literature. Much has been intellectually poor and dull. The ALCAB (A-level Content Advisory Board) report in 2014 spells it out:

The panel identified weaknesses in the current AS and A-level:

(a) The regulatory requirements are of such a general nature that they do not require awarding organisations to prescribe topics which require students' direct engagement with material relating to the society of the countries where the language of study is spoken.

(b) The study of cultural topics is only an A2 option and general topics predominate, some of which are studied and restudied at GCSE, AS and A-level. Despite examples of good practice by awarding organisations and inspiring teaching, this can make the current syllabus rather dull and uninspiring.

Notwithstanding examples of good practice by awarding organisations in this area and of inspired and inspiring teaching, such arrangements have contributed for some students to a repetitive and hence rather dull and uninspiring learning experience, less stimulating than is provided by other related subjects at GCE, such as English, history and classics.

The result of this diminution of content has been an impoverishment of students' curiosity-driven learning. *Cognitive stimulus is largely restricted to practical language learning, together with what teachers may bring to the subject over and above the requirements of the qualification. Hence, the cognitive challenge at GCE in modern languages is met only inconsistently. That challenge is to communicate increasingly complex messages, necessitating the use of more complex structures to connect ideas about increasingly complex material. The panel believes that this weakness makes the qualification less rewarding and less engaging for high-achieving students. That, together with perceptions of severe grading, can discourage students from selecting a modern language A-level.*

(c) The language of study tends to be conceived principally in terms of its immediate practical use and in isolation from the student's competence in other languages. There is therefore no encouragement to develop a more searching understanding of linguistic systems.

Dull, dull, dull. The revised GCSE and A-level syllabuses aim to turn this round but it may be too late. The decoupling of the AS from the A-level is likely to hit MFL more than other subjects because the gap between GCSE and A-level is greater: the AS was a useful stepping stone. Furthermore, the decoupling is encouraging schools to offer just three A-levels in Year 12 rather than four AS-levels. A MLF was often the fourth choice for pupils, so this change might result in further decline.

Arts subjects

The Warwick Commission (2015) report on the state of the arts found that between 2003 and 2013 there was a fall in arts GCSE entries (23% fall in drama for example) despite the fact that the cultural and creative industries make a significant contribution to the British economy. The Gross Value Added of the sector was estimated to be £84bn in 2015 (Creative Learning Alliance), representing 10% of the UK economy and 2.9 million jobs

According to the Government's workforce survey, between November 2011 and November 2015, the number of arts teachers at Key Stage 4 in England's state-funded schools declined by 13.4%. By contrast, the number of Key Stage 4 geography and history teachers increased by 8.5%. The number of taught hours dedicated to Key Stage 4 arts fell by 16.4% in this period, while geography and history saw an increase in teaching time of 22.9% (Fellows, 2017).

The percentage of pupils entering at least one GCSE arts subject was 48% in 2016 (DfE, 2016). So 52% of secondary school students are not taking any arts GCSEs.

It has often been claimed that the EBacc expectations discourage schools from offering arts GCSEs and divert resources away from arts subjects towards EBacc subjects. Some heads have interpreted the EBacc that way, but they are wrong. The new Progress 8 measure leaves plenty of room for creative subjects.

Research by the New Schools Network (Fellows, 2017) found that trends in GCSE entries over the last five years since the introduction of the EBacc showed no decline in the popularity of the arts at GCSE. In fact, the number of arts GCSEs being taken in 2015/16 was higher than in 2011/12 when the EBacc had only just been announced, and the proportion of students taking at least one arts GCSE in this period has increased by 7.4%. Furthermore, schools with higher levels of per-pupil GCSE arts entries got above-average results in the EBacc, Progress 8 and Attainment 8.

A good art or music department can add a great deal to the atmosphere and outcomes of a school.

The outcomes of a successful secondary school music department include:

- Parents of musical pupils apply to the school because of its reputation for music.
- Pupils opt for music GCSE and A-level and achieve good results.
- Many pupils learn a musical instrument, moving up a grade a year.
- Many pupils are in a choir.
- Many pupils are in an orchestra or ensemble.
- There are singing or instrumental performances in the school every week.
- Pupils enter music competitions.

How can this be achieved?

1. In Year 7 all pupils might be required to learn a musical instrument free of charge. This requires investment by the school in instruments, secure storage cabinets and instrumental teachers. They learn to read music. King Solomon's Academy in Marylebone requires every pupil to learn a musical instrument. These pupils are thereby given a skill and an interest many will carry throughout their lives.

    After Year 7, pupils who choose to continue with their instrument might take lessons on a means-tested basis.

2. Timetabled music lessons focus on preparation for performance, both singing and instrumental.

3. The teachers are great teachers and generous with their time. They are ready to put on as many as one performance a week.

4. Pupils are exposed to great live music through their own performances and performers invited to the school.

I like the statement on the website of Michaela School, Wembley:

'At Michaela, we believe that being able to read music, being exposed to a broad and detailed history of music, and understanding the theory of music is what makes a music education, and those are the things we teach in our compulsory music lessons. We drill pupils in reading music. We explicitly teach them music theory – up to grade 4 by the end of Year 9. We don't make music accessible by lowering expectations; instead we make music truly accessible by actually teaching every one of our students a rigorous and academic curriculum.'

Computer Science

Computer science is the fastest growing GCSE subject and is backed by the

Government through the Progress 8 measure because of concern about the lack of skills in the digital economy.

The 2014 reform to the National Curriculum incorporated coding into the syllabus for the first time. The aims of the revised National Curriculum are spelt out:

The National Curriculum for computing aims to ensure that all pupils:

- *can understand and apply the fundamental principles and concepts of computer science, including abstraction, logic, algorithms and data representation.*

- *can analyse problems in computational terms, and have repeated practical experience of writing computer programs in order to solve such problems.*

- *can evaluate and apply information technology, including new or unfamiliar technologies, analytically to solve problems.*

- *are responsible, competent, confident and creative users of information and communication technology.*

The previous ICT curriculum was withdrawn and replaced by 'the more rigorous' computer science curriculum.

With the strong push given to computer science by its inclusion in the EBacc, the upward swing of computer science is set to continue. It is just a pity that so few girls opt for it at GCSE or A-level.

The Key Stage 3 computing syllabus is as follows:

Pupils should be taught to:

- *design, use and evaluate computational abstractions that model the state and behaviour of real-world problems and physical systems.*

- *understand several key algorithms that reflect computational thinking [for example, ones for sorting and searching]; use logical reasoning to compare the utility of alternative algorithms for the same problem.*

- *use 2 or more programming languages, at least one of which is textual, to solve a variety of computational problems; make appropriate use of data structures [for example, lists, tables or arrays]; design and develop modular programs that use procedures or functions.*

- *understand simple Boolean logic [for example, AND, OR and NOT] and some of its uses in circuits and programming; understand how numbers can be represented in binary, and be able to carry out simple operations on binary numbers [for example, binary addition, and conversion between binary and decimal].*

- understand the hardware and software components that make up computer systems, and how they communicate with one another and with other systems.

- understand how instructions are stored and executed within a computer system; understand how data of various types (including text, sounds and pictures) can be represented and manipulated digitally, in the form of binary digits.

- undertake creative projects that involve selecting, using, and combining multiple applications, preferably across a range of devices, to achieve challenging goals, including collecting and analysing data and meeting the needs of known users.

- create, reuse, revise and repurpose digital artefacts for a given audience, with attention to trustworthiness, design and usability.

- understand a range of ways to use technology safely, respectfully, responsibly and securely, including protecting their online identity and privacy; recognise inappropriate content, contact and conduct, and know how to report concerns.

Design and technology

In terms of status, design and technology has come and gone over the past 30 years. The numbers taking DT GCSE in 2003 were 440,000; in 2016 the figure was 185,000. In July 2016 87 MPs wrote a letter to the Prime Minister:

'The UK face a number of challenges:

An annual shortage of 69,000 trained engineers

Only 6% of the UK's engineering workforce is female

We believe that the answer lies in the recently improved, scientific and academic Design Technology GCSE.

As you will be aware, the content for the new Design and Technology GCSE has recently been finalised, ready for September 2017. The new curriculum is a vast improvement on the previous qualification, having been designed over years in partnership with businesses; it is a robust, science-based, academic, valuable option for GCSE.

Secondary schools are judged on pupil's GCSE grades in EBacc subjects. Its exclusion from this important qualification is reducing the incentive for Design and Technology teaching.

As a result of schools being judged on their EBacc results, many of them are pushing their students – particularly 'academic' students – to do as many EBacc subjects as possible; more than the minimum five. The result is that D&T is being squeezed into a single or double option box, to compete with subjects like Photography and Dance for a single place among student options. This is a problem in any case but would be *tragic for the new D&T GCSE – which is academically rigorous and sits comfortably alongside the EBacc subjects.'*

They were quite right to mention photography and dance because in the end it is all about space in the timetable. DT is a great subject, but it is being crowded out.

The EPQ: an original piece of work

The Extended Project Qualification is growing quite fast in English sixth forms. It is based on the International Baccalaureate dissertation – the idea that students choose a topic of their own, receive instruction from a teacher into research methods and how to present a report, and research their chosen topic independently. The report may be in words (5000) or in the form of film or other artefacts.

The EPQ is worth half an A-level in terms of UCAS points but its value goes well beyond that. The EPQ is an opportunity to do some original work, a chance to show a university that you are capable of independent research, and is a way of demonstrating enthusiasm for and knowledge of a degree subject that is not taught at school, like medicine or astronomy.

Having completed the EPQ the student is required to present their research to an audience, so ensuring that oral skills are connected to knowledge.

Sport

Sport is important and worthwhile for all young people so it needs to be compulsory. Most teenagers would rather do nothing than do physical exercise so it just has to be compulsory – with close scrutiny of any child who claims to be 'off-sick'.

Quite apart from keeping pupils fit and healthy and developing a lifelong interest in sport, sport develops them in other ways. Look at the RGS High Wycombe website – *the seven secrets of sporting success:*

1.   *Think confidently – practice turning negative self-talk into positive self-talk.*
2.   *Act confidently even if it is acting.*
3.   *Visualise positive outcomes.*
4.   *Be physically fit.*
5.   *Have a game plan.*
6.   *Expect difficulties.*
7.   *Have the courage to fail.*

These are all qualities which will be transferable to life beyond the rugby pitch.

Some schools require pupils to do PE for an hour. This is a bit of a waste of time because once they have changed and changed back there is not enough left for worthwhile activity. Sport needs to occupy a two-hour slot if possible, with after-school time for team training and fixtures on a Saturday.

Schools have to decide if they can afford to recruit and employ academic teaching staff to take sports teams. It is great if they can because no set of PE teachers can staff enough sports teams in an ambitious school.

Schools have three different levels of sporting activity: elite sport for school teams, inter-House or inter-Form sports competitions, and recreational sports such as climbing and table tennis. It is better to do a limited number of sports well than try to offer too many.

16–19 vocational courses

The size of the English technical education sector is extremely small by international standards. Partly because of this our workforce is under skilled and productivity is up to 36% below that of France and Germany.

There are three strands of vocational courses in England:

1. **Applied General** qualifications are vocational courses that **represent an alternative to A-levels as a route to higher education.** They are regulated by Ofqual and include BTECs, Diplomas and level 3 Certificates. About a quarter of students going to university have BTECs.

2. **Functional skills** are alternatives to GCSEs (level 1 and 2 courses) in English, maths and ICT for students who cannot achieve a good grade in a GCSE.

3. **Technical education** comprises two-year college courses or employment-based apprenticeships (a mixture of paid work, training and assessment). The 2016 Sainsbury Review of post-16 vocational education established that the existing 22,000 technical courses will be replaced by just 15 courses devised and managed by an employer-led Institute for Apprenticeships and Technical Education, to start in 2019.

   The 15, the basis of new T-level qualifications, are:

   - agriculture, environmental and animal care
   - business and administrative
   - catering and hospitality
   - childcare and education

- construction
- creative and design
- digital
- engineering and manufacturing
- hair and beauty
- health and science
- legal, finance and accounting
- protective services
- sales, marketing and procurement
- social care
- transport and logistics

All courses will include elements of English, maths and digital skills. There are some obvious areas of employment such as retail missing from the list but this was because, according to Lord Sainsbury, the skills and knowledge of the retail industry are 'almost all company-specific'. In such cases there is no need for an external technical course – the employers can do the training. The areas where you need technical education are where there are transferable skills applicable to many employers.

The plan is that 16-year-olds will be required to make a choice between academic courses (A-levels), an apprenticeship with an employee which involves training for a job (such as a chef), a technical course at a college, or work-based learning where you get a job and have a shorter period of training (in a shop for example).

There is some trade-off between apprenticeships and college-based courses. When the economy is booming and employers need more staff, apprenticeships grow. In a recession they shrink and college-based technical courses might grow to compensate.

If the Sainsbury proposals can be funded, if teachers can be found to teach the courses, and if schools can be required to promote post-16 technical and vocational education, this will be the most important educational reform of the 2015–2020 government.

Teaching skills in the academic curriculum

Benjamin Bloom, who died in 1999, was an American educational psychologist who made contributions to the classification of educational objectives. In 1956, Bloom edited the first volume of *Taxonomy of educational objectives: the classification of educational goals*, which outlined a classification of learning objectives that has come to be known as Bloom's Taxonomy:

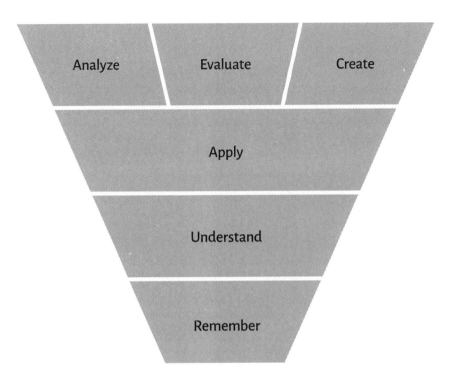

Bloom's taxonomy suggests that remembering something is a low order skill, while analysing and evaluating are higher order skills. This in turn suggests that skills are somehow separate from knowledge and that knowledge is less worthy or important. It encouraged people to think you could skip the lower level bit and jump up to the high order parts, that what we want is not facts but pupils who are able to reason, be creative and imaginative, to learn collaboratively. This was the basis of the idea that schools should teach skills not knowledge.

In England the National Curriculum was introduced in 1988 and maintained schools were required by law to teach it. There was, over time, a gradual reduction in the subject content and its replacement by skills and experiences. For example, the 2007 Key Stage 3 history curriculum prescribed less knowledge than a list of skills:

Pupils should be able to:

A. *identify and investigate, individually and as part of a team, specific historical questions or issues, making and testing hypotheses.*

B. *reflect critically on historical questions or issues.*

C. *identify, select and use a range of historical sources, including textual, visual and oral sources, artefacts and the historic environment.*

D. *evaluate the sources in order to reach reasoned conclusions.*

The Royal Society of Arts has developed a new secondary curriculum for the 21st century called *Opening Minds* which concluded that there were five essential skills which should be the basis of the school curriculum:

- Citizenship
- Learning
- Managing information
- Relating to people
- Managing situations

'*These competences are broad areas of capability, developed in classrooms through a mixture of instruction and practical experience: children plan their work, organise their own time and explore their own ways of learning.*

Subject boundaries are less defined than in traditional curriculum teaching, with schools often integrating the teaching of several subjects together into modules or topics, where competences can be developed through the exploration of common themes.' (RSA website)

In the schools which have adopted this approach, the focus of the curriculum is projects, not subjects. Take the UCL Academy in Camden. In 2013 I went to visit this hugely expensive new school, run by one of the UK's top universities. The online prospectus stated:

'*The first year in the Academy is a year in which students adapt to the unique learning environment which the Academy offers, and prepare themselves to take on the responsibilities for developing their own programme of study in the years ahead. Students develop a wide variety of skills essential for effective learning.*

Students study the International Middle Years Curriculum at the Academy as a model of learning which encourages cross-curricular learning through Big Ideas, an international focus and book ended by Entry and Exit Points, where Big Ideas and concepts are introduced and reviewed.'

The school had its first Ofsted in 2014 and was graded 'requires improvement'.

I taught an A-level called Critical Thinking. I did it because I thought that critical thinking sounded like a good skill that all educated people ought to have. But I soon realised that this subject was in fact completely bogus. There were a set of rules which one learnt and then applied to the information provided in the exam questions. These were not rules that could be generally applied outside this specific exam.

What this told me was that it was very hard to teach thinking skills outside the context of a subject. If we teach pupils to think critically about, for example, the causes of the Second World War, this does not mean they can think critically about climate change or alternative energy options. Critical thinking processes are tied to background knowledge. Martin Robinson makes this point: *'In order to be critical and creative kids need to know stuff, to have a good grasp of the basics... only then can they become creative, critical citizens...'* (Robinson, 2013).

Or Dan Willingham (2007): *'Critical thinking (as well as scientific thinking and other domain-based thinking) is not a skill. There is not a set of critical thinking skills that can be acquired and deployed regardless of context.*

Thus, if you remind a student to "look at an issue from multiple perspectives" often enough, he will learn that he ought to do so, but if he doesn't know much about an issue, he can't think about it from multiple perspectives.'

Adults with good thinking skills have developed them by knowing a lot... not by learning thinking skills. The most reliable basis for 21st century skills is possession of wide-ranging knowledge across many subjects.

Time spent on teaching thinking skills or competencies rather than subjects carries a high opportunity cost – the pupils are not doing something completely useless, but nor are they using the time as well as they could. Time spent on activities supposed to promote 'transferable skills' is time not spent learning knowledge that would really build transferable skills.

The alternative approach – teaching knowledge

E. D. Hirsch was born 1928 and is now retired; he was previously the Professor of Education and Humanities at the University of Virginia. During the late 1970s, while giving tests to measure how quickly students grasped ideas from written texts, he discovered that while the readability of a text was an important factor in determining speed of comprehension, an even more important consideration was the reader's possession – or lack – of relevant background knowledge.

He found that students at the University of Virginia were able to understand a passage about Ulysses S. Grant and Robert E. Lee, while students at a Richmond community college struggled with the same passage, because they lacked a basic understanding of the American Civil War. This led Hirsch to formulate the concept of *cultural literacy* — the idea that reading comprehension requires not just the skill of decoding letters and words but also wide-ranging cultural background knowledge. He concluded that schools should not be neutral about what is taught but should teach a highly specific curriculum that would allow children to know things that writers tend to take for granted.

His book on the subject, *Cultural Literacy: What Every American Needs To Know*, was published in 1987. Beginning in the 1990s Hirsch began publishing the *Core Knowledge Series* where each book focuses on the precise knowledge that should be taught to children at each age. You can read about schools which agree with Hirsch on pages 220, 233, 242 and 259.

Teaching character

Soft skills like good manners, how to speak well, determination, initiative, leadership, teamwork, kindness, optimism and self-motivation are all crucially important to a person's prospects in work. But on the whole these can be taught through normal lessons and the cocurricular programme. There is no need to have a separate curriculum just for them.

I have worked in schools that purported to teach character – boarding schools as well as large urban day schools. Such schools have talked about teaching character for hundreds of years. It is not a new idea.

In 2015–16 we had a Secretary of State for Education telling us that her 'priority' was to teach character. '*We know that children need certain character traits to excel academically,*' she said in a 2015 speech, '*The kind of traits that should be embedded through a whole-school approach to character education, helping children and young people become decent, happy, well-balanced citizens.*' The DfE provided millions of pounds in grants for schools to develop character projects.

The University of Birmingham School promotes itself specifically on the basis of character development. Their website states: '*Character Education is about acquiring and strengthening virtues – traits that sustain a well-rounded life and a thriving society; values such as compassion, humility, sensitivity, creativity, curiosity, determination and resilience.*' They aim to achieve this through enrichment activities such as sport and by encouraging teachers to refer to the values and virtues whenever possible through the academic curriculum.

There is some evidence for the value of character education. Durlak *et al* conducted a meta-analysis of 213 school-based social and emotional learning programmes involving 270,034 kindergarten to secondary school students. Compared to controls, the programme participants demonstrated significantly improved social and emotional skills, attitudes, behaviour and academic performance (Durlak, 2011).

But there is little other evidence that specifically teaching 'character' works. One reason is that a proportion of a person's character is determined by their genes, including things like grit and resilience. The King's College London Twins Early Development study suggests that genes determine between a third and a half of any given characteristic in the population.

In his books *How children succeed: grit, curiosity and the hidden power of character*, and *Helping children succeed: what works and why*, Paul Tough's analysis of the research leads him to believe that character is best developed not by having character lessons in school but by parents and teachers modelling the sort of behaviour they identify as important. It is the day-to-day living environment that matters.

My generation had endless lectures at school about the damage to our lungs caused by smoking but none of it worked. Teenagers don't respond to theory. What they do respond to is encouragement and compulsion, especially teenage boys. The most effective measure to cut smoking has been to make it illegal to smoke in public places. Similarly, the most effective way to make boys work hard is to force them to work hard – by threatening them, if necessary, with punishments which outweigh the pain of hard work. But once they have learnt that hard work pays off (which they do) then the penny drops.

The London Academy of Excellence does not give character 'lessons' but does require all pupils to take part in activities, such as sport, debating and academic work, which allow them to demonstrate positive character traits. The grid they have to complete is helpful because it makes them reflect on these character traits – called 'core values' in the grid:

London Academy of Excellence Diploma

Skill	Core Value	Standard	Self Assessment	Tutor	Teacher	Average Score
Self-confidence	Resilience	Believed that effort would improve his/her future				
		When bad things happened, s/he thought about things they could do to make it better next time				
		Stayed motivated, even when things didn't go well				
Self-discipline	Independence	Finished whatever s/he began				
		Tried very hard even after experiencing faliure				
		Kept working hard even when s/he felt like quitting				
Communication	Respect	Exemplified mutual respect and tolerance of those with different faiths and beliefs				
		Understands the values of democracy, rule of law and individual liberty				
		Delivered a presentation to a group of people				
		Influenced and motivated others to achieve a successful outcome				

Team work	Humility	Allowed others to speak without interrupting				
		Was able to find solutions during conflicts with others				
		Showed that s/he cared about the feelings of others				
Leadership	Excellence	Exemplified the core values				
		Keeps commitments to others				
		Lead a team or group of people				
Service	Kindness	Helped others				
		Supported a charity				

1 = Almost Never 2 = Very Rarely 3 = Rarely 4 = Sometimes 5 = Often 6 = Very Often 7 = Almost Always

Another example is teaching good manners. It is all very well suggesting that pupils write a thank-you letter after a school trip but lazy students never take the hint. But if you force them to write the letter, *ie* get it checked by a teacher who then posts it, they learn how to do it, it seems less painful than they imagined, they will have more confidence next time and are more likely to do it unbidden.

Another example: being organised. If they are to be successful pupils need to bring the right books to the right lessons, they need to do homework on time, they need to bring the completed homework to the right lesson, they need to keep their files in good order. All these things can be taught to the disorganised pupil, lesson by lesson, teacher by teacher, insisting on the highest standards, using sticks and carrots.

Schools can talk about the theory – the Stanford marshmallow experiment, Matthew Syed's *Bounce*, Carol Dweck's growth mindset – but this is not as good as pupils actually trying out the form of behaviour we are trying to get them to adopt. Try something, fail, try again, succeed – prove you can do it. Pupils have to model the behaviour you are trying to teach. Once they have been impelled to try it for themselves, attitudes change. They can see for themselves that hard work is not as painful as they thought and it produces results. They can see that a thank-you letter produces a great response from the teacher being thanked.

When Michael Wilshaw required his pupils at Mossbourne Academy to chant at the beginning of every lesson, '*I aspire to maintain an inquiring mind, a calm disposition and an attentive ear so that in this class and in all classes I can fulfil my true potential*', he did not assume that his pupils would automatically believe this. He reckoned that over time, if they said it often enough, the penny might drop.

Perhaps talking about 'teaching character' is the wrong way of putting it. Often what one is doing is putting in place expectations and opportunities which allow pupils to learn, from the school and from their own experience, that certain forms of behaviour are both possible and worthwhile.

The cocurricular programme (enrichment)

The cocurricular programme is essential because it teaches things conventional school subjects don't and because it often provides a pupil with the one interest that makes school worthwhile for them. Because pupils need a broad, holistic education, at Harrow I developed a diploma which developed into a qualification accredited by Edexcel. It was a way of making a point and nudging the pupils to get involved.

DIPLOMA

AWARDED TO THOSE IN YEAR 13 WHO HAVE SHOWN PARTICULAR COMMITMENT TO AN ALL-ROUND EDUCATION

Minimum requirement

1. *Academic results:* 9 GCSEs A*–C/9–4

2. *Cultural activity: one of*

GCSE Art or Music or AS Photography

Grade 5 on an instrument or singing

Speaking part in a play or significant non-speaking contribution to a play

Sing in a choir or played in an orchestra for a term at least

3. *Physical activity: two of*

School sports team for 5 terms (can be more than) one sport)

Duke of Edinburgh Silver completed

Military Drill Competition competitor

Endurance Event Competition competitor:

run 10 miles, 200 lengths swimming or 10,000 metres rowing

4. *Communication: two of*

Pass Year 12 literacy course

Debating team

House Public Speaking team

Article or creative writing in School magazine

Read lesson in Chapel

Helped do a House Chapel Service or *Thought for the Day*

Helped to write House website

A finalist in a school lecture competition

5. *Service to others: two of*

Community Service: one term minimum

Conservation work: one term

House Monitor

Raised £100 for charity

In charge of a society or activity for at least one term

Hold Bishop's licence to administer Communion

Tour Guide for prospective parents

Another type of service recognised by House Master

6. Developing a skill: two of

Young Enterprise team member

AS Critical Thinking

Worked on school farm for a year

Contributed to an art exhibition

First Aid course

Life Saving course

Cookery course

Canoeing course

Duke of Edinburgh Silver

Engineering Education Scheme

Extended Project

Cadet Force for two years

Pass Driving test

7. Work experience for at least 5 days

For many pupils the co-curriculum turned out to be rather more important than the exam-driven academic curriculum. It was important for all those hundreds of boys I taught who went into the army on the basis of a successful experience in the cadet force. And those who went into acting or script-writing on the back of school plays. Those who became professional musicians, classical or rock (an average of two a year from Harrow). Those who spent much of their adult lives singing in a choir or playing the church organ. The boys who became vets because they enjoyed the school farm (just a few cows). Professional sportsmen or just those who developed a lifelong love of sport. Professional artists and photographers inspired not by exams but by the spirit of the Harrow Art Department. Nicholas Coleridge, author and managing director of Condé Nast in Britain, is adamant that his career success was forged from his experiences editing a school magazine and running a school contemporary arts society.

Private Business: learning for learning's sake

At Eton it is called Private Business, at Winchester it is called 'Div' – a time when students meet in small groups with one teacher for a tutorial and discussion. This is what the Winchester website says about Div:

Every boy meets in his Division for one period every day. His Div Don therefore sees more of him than any other of his teachers, and it is the Div Don who takes him through courses which are designed to foster in him a love and respect for learning for its own sake. Thus for the first three years Div follows a chronological structure which encompasses History and English Literature (which are not offered for GCSE), Ancient History, History of Art, History of Science and Religious Studies.

In Sixth Book (the sixth form), Div can lead almost anywhere, according to the interests of the boys in the group and the Div Don himself, covering an extremely wide range of history and literature, from Ancient Egypt to the Gulf War, from Plato to Shakespeare, from the history of Cricket or Mathematics or Science to the fugues of Bach or the plays of Tom Stoppard. Opportunities to deepen aspects of the broad knowledge he acquires through Div are afforded through the Task Time, when under the supervision of his Div Don, he will write regular essays based on private interest and research. He will often be asked to offer a presentation to his Div.

Div is the hallmark of a Winchester education.

So these tutorials are an opportunity to teach without the burden of exams. Their success depends on the ability of the tutor to capture the interest and imagination of the tutees and this is often possible because the tutor will select topics they are themselves interested in. It is not a million miles from general studies, which many schools had before AS-levels intervened, but the differences are the small group size and the fact that the tutor is personally responsible for the general progress of his or her tutor group – the tutor and tutees have a different relationship from that of a normal teacher and his class.

Cultural capital

Children from disadvantaged backgrounds may miss out because their parents are less likely to take them to museums, theatres and art galleries, less likely to have books in the home. The best schools make an effort to fill the gap. The best teach pupils what they are going to see before they go and expect them to write about what they have learnt afterwards.

Leaders of Tomorrow is an enrichment mentoring programme designed to raise the academic achievement of children and young people, particularly those of African and Caribbean heritage, in south London. Lindsay Johns, a volunteer, describes it as follows:

'Our mission is to help young people achieve their academic and social potential, to broaden their cultural horizons beyond the limiting confines of SE15 and to try and help them develop a fully-functioning moral compass.

With a weekly vocab slot, a focus on reading aloud and the importance of good communication, inspirational guest speakers from all walks of life, regular trips to the National Theatre, the Young Vic theatre, the British Museum, the Tate, the Globe theatre and other cultural arenas, along with visits to Oxford and Cambridge and to empowering leadership conferences in America, we aim to get our young people out of the debilitating spiral of the poverty of aspiration which can afflict so many in inner-city environments.'

Lindsay believes that efforts to make education more 'relevant' to black people can be both patronising and harmful. The western literary canon should be taught to everyone. Several of the good schools I have visited make a point of requiring all pupils to take part regularly in a Shakespeare play.

Gender and subject choice

It is remarkable, given that almost all children are taught in mixed-sex schools, that gender stereotypes still influence subject choice in the way they do. For example, look at UK A-level entries in 2016:

	Male	Female
Physics	27,699	7645
Computing	5633	609
Economics	19,895	9490
French	3093	6579
English	22,980	61,730
Psychology	14,085	45,384
Sociology	7848	26,132

Source : Joint Council for Qualifications

Only geography and chemistry seem to avoid the gender bias. The graph on page 114 illustrates the same phenomenon at university level.

For a range of subjects there is a very clear sense that they are 'female' or 'male'. Schools need specific policies to overcome the negative effects of gender bias on subject choice.

Conclusions

Which matters more: teacher quality or the content of the syllabus being taught? Research by Hirsch (2016) suggests that the content of what is being taught determines a high proportion of the impact of the course. In other words, an outstanding teacher teaching poor quality content is no better than a poor teacher teaching high quality content.

One of the arguments used by those who are cynical about the importance of learning subject knowledge at school is that by the time you are an adult you will have forgotten much of it and the knowledge have become out of date. Well that has not been my experience nor that of my former pupils, many now in their 40s. I can still remember poems learnt at school. I recall most of the maths, history, design technology and science I studied years ago and all of it is still relevant. Indeed I can remember individual lessons and their content and my former pupils can remember individual lessons I taught them. Things learnt in school are *not* soon forgotten.

I like the idea that people have knowledge in their heads rather than in a computer. Deep learning and creative thinking come from the firm assimilation of existing knowledge. You cannot think about things if you don't have information in your brain to think about.

Is it not better to have a poem in your head rather than on a screen?

Skills should be taught through existing disciplines. Teamwork is best taught through playing sport or debating. If you want to teach students to think analytically, why not do that through teaching history?

We should teach maths and English to a higher level at the top end than we have been achieving in recent years. Have a focus on these two important subjects. All should be taught the basics of functional maths and English – useful maths and good standards of writing ability. Key Stage 3 and 4 pupils must be forced to read one decent novel a fortnight and to learn ten poems a year.

Pupils must be taught how to speak well. I raised this point in a governors' meeting at an inner London state school. The parent governor – an African-Caribbean mother – agreed, saying that her son spoke in text-speak and she couldn't understand a word of it. But the staff were not so easily convinced: they were worried about appearing racist and felt that promoting Received Pronunciation was discriminatory.

We should teach physics, chemistry, biology, British history and world geography as defined by the new National Curriculum.

We should teach Big History as explained in David Christian's book (2013) and website – how the universe evolved, how planets developed, how life evolved on Earth, how agriculture and then cities and civilisations evolved.

Pupils need a good grasp of Christianity – Bible stories including the parables, the essential vocabulary of church buildings and worship – as well as other religions.

And a good knowledge of a few European composers and their work.

Pupils should be taught either French or Spanish to a higher level than we are reaching now.

Pupils should be taught how to draw and paint ... from life. Abstract painting can be banned because it is too easy or too difficult for a teenager, depending on your point of view. As Winston Churchill said:

'Art done properly is a tough discipline which teaches concentration ... When I get to heaven I intend to spend a considerable portion of the first million years in painting and so get to the bottom of the subject.'

Design and technology is important including how to use tools like a saw, a hammer and a screwdriver, as well as computer-aided design.

So is how to use a computer, touch type and code.

So is physical fitness, how to swim, the enjoyment of sport and the skills of team sports such as cricket and netball.

So is PSHE as defined by the National Curriculum.

It is hard to fit much else in, even in Key Stage 3. Of course pupils should be taught life skills, such as being organised, good time keeping, resilience, an understanding of the fact that hard work usually produces results, being nice to others, moral values – but with good teachers in good schools these will come as a by-product of good classroom teaching and extracurricular activity.

Above all, we must acknowledge that the curriculum is already full. If people want to add something to the timetable, like citizenship, then point out that children will have less time for something else, like history or English or maths. If you add something, something has to be taken away.

We only have so many hours in the day. We should teach established subjects, teach them well and teach them to a more advanced level than we have been.

Chapter 5

Successful Parents

"'Where are we going?" asks Susan.
"Nowhere" says Mummy, *"the journey is the goal."*

From: *We Go Out* by Elia, M. and Elia, E.

We know that the quality of parenting makes a huge difference to the educational outcomes of children. Parents who do not talk to or read to their children produce five-year-olds who on arrival at school can barely talk in sentences and have no knowledge of the alphabet. Such children rarely catch up.

Should the State train parents to be 'good' parents? If your aim is social mobility or equality of opportunity the answer is 'yes'. Good schools like John Perryn Primary (page 212) teach their parents how to play with their small children, how to read themselves, then how read to their children. Schools like King Solomon (page 220) are prepared to confiscate games consoles from pupils' homes. In Singapore parents sign legal contracts with schools which include things like compulsory attendance at 'help with homework' courses and parents are fined if they do not attend.

In 2016 Greasley Beauvale primary school in Nottinghamshire was praised by inspectors for grading all parents A to D based on their involvement with their children's education. Parents are told what impact their lack of engagement is having on the life chances of their children and are thus encouraged to attend school events and help their children with schoolwork at home.

All good schools provide training or advice for parents in such areas as internet safety, awareness of drugs, speaking to a difficult teenager and university application procedures.

What parents can do to improve the education their children are getting

There is an organisation devoted to giving such information to parents: *Parents and Teachers for Excellence.*

Parents need to work out if their child's school is doing a good job or not.

For primary schools look up 'DfE *Compare school and college performance*' on the internet. Put in the name of the school you are interested in.

You can immediately see how well the school does at Key Stage 2 and progress made since Key Stage 1. The meaning of these two sets of data has to be interpreted carefully because a school that puts a lot of effort into Key Stage 1 will find that the 'progress since Key Stage 1' score is depressed. A school in a middle-class area would expect to get significantly better results at Key Stage 2 than a school in a working-class area.

Nevertheless, this is useful data.

Next, look up the school's last Ofsted report on the Ofsted website ('Find an inspection report') or on the school's own website. This should clearly state all the strengths and weaknesses of the school. For independent schools who are members of the Independent Schools Council, see the Independent Schools Inspectorate website.

For secondary schools you need to get the following information:

1. Look up 'DfE *Compare school and college performance*' on the internet.

    GCSE progress measures look at the average GCSE grade achieved by each child compared to all those other children in England who scored a similar Key Stage 2 SATs score when they were aged 11. Progress 8 measures the progress in eight GCSEs. If the school has a score of zero then it is average for the country; less than zero is worse, more than zero is better. The reason the progress score is so important is that the raw GCSE results (what proportion got a grade 5 or what proportion got a grade 7 *etc*) are very much influenced by the ability of the pupils on entry. Some schools admit a much higher proportion of able or high-achieving pupils than others. **PROGRESS measures are a better measure of the quality of a school's teaching than raw results.**

    Here is an example.

    I go into the Department for Education's *online school performance checker*.

    I put in the name of a school: 'Chelsea Academy'. I look for 'Progress 8 score'. The score in 2016 is +0.38. This is a good result which puts the school in the top 30% in the country. On average pupils got 0.38 of a GCSE grade higher in each of the eight subjects than the average of all other pupils in England with similar Key Stage 2 results.

    Next I look at 'Similar schools'. The table shows how Chelsea Academy's performance compares with all schools whose pupils had a similar achievement profile at Key Stage 2. On a list of 55 schools it comes sixth based on the Progress 8 score – very good.

There is plenty of other data given, some of which adds to the picture. I don't take too much notice of the English Baccalaureate data because the score a school achieves depends in part on the GCSE subject choice policies of the school.

If I was looking up an independent school which puts pupils in for iGCSEs I would have to ignore this part of the website because iGCSEs are not included.

2. Sixth forms

A-level value-added measures are also given. So on the website described above I look up Chelsea Academy, 16–19, A-level performance, progress score. The score is +0.12. This shows how much progress students made between GCSEs and A-levels. The score is shown as a number of A-level grade(s) above or below the national average level of progress for students of similar prior ability. 0.12 is a positive score, albeit not a high one. This tells me that the A-level results are quite good. 0.3 would be excellent.

Some schools get good results at A-level because they demand very good GCSE grades if a student wishes to take A-levels in the first place, and because many students are required to leave at the end of Year 12, half way through the A-level course. So, the A-level results of any school need to be looked at in this light. It is not hard to find out the GCSE requirements for entry to a school sixth form (they tend to range from five C/4 grades to five or six A/7 grades). To find the proportion who leave after Year 12 you can compare the number of pupils in Year 12 with the number in Year 13.

You also need to ask the school to show you DESTINATION data for their pupils who left at the age of 18. Which universities did they go to? Does the school provide extra lessons for those who might apply to Oxford, Cambridge or medical school?

3. Strong and weak subjects

When you are thinking about which GCSEs, A-levels or BTECs your child might take at school, always insist on seeing a grid which shows the number of pupils who got each grade in each subject in the previous year. This will show which subjects are popular and successful. This data is rarely published by schools but you can ask for it.

However, because a subject might only be popular with weak students, it is not enough to look at the raw results. If you ask, most schools will also be able to give you the value-added score for each subject, which tells you how well the pupils did compared to other similar pupils in the country as a whole. Again, such data is rarely published by schools.

4. The curriculum

    You should be able to find out about each school's curriculum by looking at the school websites. Do not be over-impressed by schools which appear to do a vast range of subjects. At Key Stage 3, for example, when pupils are aged 11–14, it may be better to spend a lot of time on maths, English and science as a preparation for GCSE than to spend too much time on things like dance, drama, film, sociology, media, business, art, music, food technology, PE and so on. These are great subjects but are not as valuable as maths and English at this stage and are even less valuable if taught for only one period a week.

    The sixth form curriculum is also important. The key point here is that if you expect your child to go to a good university, some subjects may be more useful than others. The Russell Group of 24 leading universities produces a guide for schools in which they state that some A-level subjects are better than others if you want to keep your options open in terms of admission to their universities. These are maths, further maths, physics, chemistry, biology, modern and ancient languages, English literature, geography, history, philosophy and ethics. Economics is not on this list but should be.

    This is not to say that subjects like art and business are not valuable. Art would support an application to read architecture at university for example. But if your child might want to apply for a top university to read a science subject, then he/she should study chemistry, physics, biology and maths. It is not a criticism of a school if vast numbers do psychology, for example, but psychology does not lead to science courses at top universities.

5. Behaviour

    You need to observe the atmosphere in the school in a normal working day and speak to the parents of existing pupils to satisfy yourself that behaviour is good. Without good behaviour nothing can be achieved.

6. Cocurricular activities

    You may well be interested in activities which occur outside the classroom such as sport, drama and music. It is not enough that a school simply offers these things. You need to determine, by asking current pupils and their parents, how good they are. How many sports teams go out on a Saturday, for example? Is there a school orchestra? How often does it perform? Ditto the choir.

A weaker school will offer these activities but they will be thin on the ground. There will be one football team. There will be two plays a year. A strong school will have 10 football teams and six plays a year.

7. Look up the school's last Ofsted report on the Ofsted website ('Find an inspection report') or on the school's own website. This should clearly state all the strengths and weaknesses of the school. For independent schools see the Independent Schools Inspectorate website.

What do you do if you are unhappy about some aspect of the school's performance?

1. First, you need to double check that your information is correct. The results of some schools change from one year to the next. For other schools the data described above can be misleading (for example, the A-level value-added score for an excellent school will be depressed if that school achieves outstanding GCSE results). So it is important not to go in 'all guns blazing'. You need to check your facts with the school and you need to confer with other parents.

2. Speak to the parent governor of the school.

3. See the headteacher and press him/her for answers.

4. If there is no improvement, get together with other parents and write collectively to the chairman of governors.

Here is a case study...

A parent had a Year 13, 17-year-old daughter at a comprehensive school. She said that she was doing well in two of her three A-levels but that the teacher of economics was 'useless'. Looking at her files of notes showed that, compared to other subjects, her notes were thin and disorganised. Homework was rarely set and tests were rare. She had only two pieces of marked work last term and there had been only one school exam in the whole of Year 12. The pupils had not been issued with a textbook.

The parent asked the Director of Studies at the school for the economics A-level grades from last year. This showed that 16 students had taken the subject and none scored an A* or A, there was one B grade, six Cs, five Ds, and four fails. This was worse than many other subjects.

Economics is a difficult subject, especially as it is not offered at GCSE. However, the daughter had four A grades and five B grades at GCSE and was predicted an A grade and a B grade in her two best A-level subjects. In economics she was predicted a D. ABD are not grades which would provide access to a good university: she needed a B in economics. So this was not a small matter.

In October the mother arranged to see the headteacher. He confirmed that the economics teacher was weak and would be leaving at the end of term. A replacement would be found.

The situation was now critical. The current teacher was weak and the chances that the school could find a good replacement in January (the middle of the school year) were slim.

The parent then contacted the parents of other pupils taking the economics A-level this coming June and they arranged to see the headteacher collectively. Firmly but calmly they insisted that the school find a good economics teacher to lay on extra lessons in the coming Christmas and Easter holidays. This would cost the school unbudgeted money, but this was more important than some of the items of spending which had been budgeted for.

The head said that he would do what he could. This was not a guarantee so the parents wrote to the chairman of governors to describe the problem.

Two weeks' later the chairman and head agreed to find the money and, if the replacement teacher was not good enough, find a retired teacher in the area to lay on the extra lessons.

How can my child get into university?

It is well worth going to university if you are interested in a subject taught at this level or you want a career which requires a university degree. Graduates earn more and have a wider range of jobs to choose from.

On the other hand is really important to appreciate that there is a hierarchy of universities, from excellent to quite bad. You can see such league tables in the websites of *The Guardian* or *Times Higher Education*. Or if you pick up a directory like Brian Heap's *University Degree Course Offers* you will see that some universities are popular and require good A-level grades while others are unpopular. The unpopular universities take students with weak exam grades and many drop out after a few months.

Brittan *et al* (2016) showed that men who studied at any of 23 of the lowest-performing British universities went on to earn less than those who did not enter higher education. The findings have fuelled the debate about the cost to the taxpayer of universities with the worst employment records, because a large proportion of graduates do not repay their student loans.

The research, by the Institute for Fiscal Studies and the universities of Cambridge and Harvard, took several years and required permission to access tax data for the first time. This allowed them to track the earnings of 260,000 students up to ten years after they left university. The data set includes cohorts of graduates who started university in the period 1998–2011 and whose earnings (or lack of earnings) are then observed over a number of tax years.

The study, the first to match tax data with student loan records, also highlighted the big differences in earnings of graduates depending on their choice of degree. Graduates who studied creative arts, such as drama, dance, fine art, design or music, had the lowest earnings and were paid, on average, the same as non-graduates: £17,900 for men and £14,500 for women. Medicine and economics graduates earned most, with big premiums even allowing for higher A-level grades.

There were 23 universities whose male graduates earned, on average, less ten years later than the median for non-graduates. Female graduates from nine universities earned less than the figure for non-graduates. The names of the 23 and nine universities have not been disclosed.

So the bottom line is this. If your child has only modest A-level/BTEC grades and doesn't have a specific vocational course in mind (such as teaching, nursing or social care) then he/she should consider NOT going to university. They may be better off getting an apprenticeship or a job with training. Details of how to find apprenticeships are given on the UCAS website. Going to study a non-vocational course (that is, one that does not lead directly to a career) at a low ranking university is an expensive risk.

However, about 45% of young people go to university these days and the correct way of going about it is as follows; this section is expressed in terms of advice to the students themselves:

1. You need to do the right A-level subjects. For engineering, for example, you should do maths and physics. For medicine you need chemistry and ideally biology and physics. In order to do these A-levels you need to do the right GCSEs – GCSEs which support going on to do these A-levels.

    Some A-level subjects are valued more highly by the best universities than others. You need to check the specific course requirements of any degree you might be interested in. www.russellgroup.ac.uk/informed-choices/ gives information about the recommended A-levels for Russell Group universities – 24 of the most selective universities.

To stand out from other applicants and demonstrate that you are capable of independent study it is a good thing to do an Extended Project in the period between June of Year 12 and October of Year 13.

2. You need to get the right grades. For Oxford and Cambridge universities, for example, you need about eight A*/8 grades at GCSE and be predicted at least A*AA at A-level. Other universities are less demanding and the A-level grades they require can be looked up in Brian Heap's book, *University Degree Course Offers* or on www.whatuni.com. Unifrog is also an excellent website used by many students.

    Some courses are harder to get into than others; amongst the hardest subjects are medicine, veterinary science and law. The *Unistats* website gives the A-level scores of students studying each subject at each university.

3. Some universities are much better than others. In general terms the most popular universities are the best and this is why the rank order of universities given subject by subject in *University Degree Course Offers* is a good indication of their quality.

    Of course there are some slightly less well-known universities that offer amazingly good individual courses, such as the design courses at Northumbria University.

    You also need to realise that some universities have very similar names but are completely different universities: Cardiff University is not the same as Cardiff Metropolitan.

    Some universities offer unconditional places (A-level grades are not needed). These universities are neither better nor worse than universities which do not do this, but it is a marketing strategy so do not be too tempted by an unconditional offer.

4. There are three types of degree course:

    *   Those which lead quite directly to jobs – medicine, fashion design, dentistry and architecture for example.

    *   Those which do not lead directly to employment, like history or English, but if studied at a good university can easily lead to good jobs. Maths and physics quite often lead to jobs in finance for example.

    *   Those which may appear to lead to jobs but don't – such as forensic science, journalism and media studies. If you might want to be a lawyer, accountant, banker, advertising agent or journalist, you do

not need to study these subjects at university. You can be trained after university, whatever subject you studied.

5. If you are applying for Oxford University, Cambridge, or for medicine, veterinary science or dentistry, you must apply by early October a full year before you start. Other universities/courses have a deadline in mid-January but it is best to apply by the end of October in any case because sometimes offers are made to the first good applications received.

    If you get all rejections or change your mind about your course/university you can apply again between February and July through UCAS Extra. If you get better A-level grades than expected you can apply again in August through UCAS Adjustment. If you are holding a firm offer from a university you will not lose it, but you only have five days to do this.

    If you get worse A-level grades than expected and fail to meet the grade offers you hold you can apply again in August through UCAS Clearing.

    It is increasingly the case that universities take students who failed to get the grades asked for.

6. Although you can put down four universities (in the case of medicine, dentistry, veterinary medicine and veterinary science) or five (other courses) on your application form, you should choose only one subject or broadly similar subjects. The reason for this is that you have to write a Personal Statement which supports your application and in this statement you have to explain why you are applying for the chosen course. You will not be able to do this convincingly if you apply for different subjects at different universities.

7. If you want to live at home while you are at university you will need to apply to a university nearby. But most students do not live at home and if you are one of them DO NOT WORRY TOO MUCH ABOUT THE LOCATION OF THE UNIVERSITY. University terms are quite short and you will not come home much during the term, so even if you live in the south of England there is no reason why you should not go to university in Scotland, for example. A four-hour train journey should not be a reason for ignoring a good university.

8. If you are predicted AAA or better at A-level you can apply to four or five top universities. If you are not predicted such grades then you should apply for one university that is aspirational (one grade above your predications), two universities that generally require the grades you are predicted and two others which normally ask for lower grades than this. The reason is that at the end of the process you can only hold two offers

– a first choice offer and an insurance offer. If you are predicted ABB at A-level then ideally you will have a first-choice university that asks for ABB and an insurance offer that asks for, say, BBB, just in case your results are disappointing. There is no value in an insurance offer that is the same as or higher than your first-choice offer.

9. If you are applying for a vocational course like law or medicine or a course which is not taught at school, like archaeology or architecture, you need to demonstrate in your personal statement that you have done more than just sit A-levels. For medicine, especially, you must do relevant work experience over many weeks, ideally that you have organised yourself – working in a hospital, for example, or an old people's home. For archaeology you need to have read a small number of books and visited archaeological sites.

10. Some courses, like medicine, have too many applicants with excellent GCSE grades. Very good applicants can struggle to get one offer. Find out which medical schools are the most popular and only apply to one of them. If you are rejected by all four of those you applied to, apply again after A-level IF you get AAA or better.

11. If you apply to Oxford or Cambridge, try to visit the university on an open day. Find out which colleges attract the largest number of applicants. Do not apply for these colleges – it is very hard to get in to Oxford or Cambridge and you do not want to reduce your chances further by applying for a very demanding college.

   Parents sometimes take their children to university open days – if you do that, leave your teenager to look around on their own.

12. If you are applying for a course that requires you to take a pre-test such as the BMAT or UKCAT then you must do practice papers and you must get all the information about these tests online. If you do badly in these difficult tests, you will not get an offer.

13. If you are applying for a course that requires you to have an interview, it is very important to prepare for the interview. Your school should give you practice interviews.

14. The details of student loans are all on the *Student Loans Company* website. Because the repayment rate of these loans is quite modest and the loans are written-off anyway after 30 years, the student loan should not be regarded as a major barrier to going to university.

How to be a good parent at home

School work for the over-8s

You need to ensure that your older children have a table or desk with a good light where they can do their homework and revision. Even in small flats in Hong Kong and Japan, all children have desks. It is a way the parents can reinforce the importance of homework.

The school should tell you how much time should be spent on homework and it is important to establish a rule in your house that televisions are off and digital devices are not used for social reasons during that time. Have a set time every day when homework is done and enforce it strictly.

Take an interest in your child's homework without being too involved. Congratulate your children for the effort they put in. Constantly remind them that it is effort which generates good results, not brains.

The best schools will give their pupils a note book in which parents can confirm that homework has been done and communicate with the child's form tutor.

In the run-up to important summer exams, like GCSEs, the Easter holiday should be used for revision.

When I was at school there was one boy in the year, Ray, who achieved better results than everyone else and we all assumed he was just brilliant. When we left school a group of us bought a Land Rover and drove to Afghanistan and back. This required a certain amount of planning! One evening I went to visit Ray at his home and mentioned to his mother that Ray had always been top academically in our year. Well, the mum said in a matter of fact way, he has never watched television.

NEVER WATCHED TELEVISION! To a 1970s schoolboy this would be the same as saying, today, he has never been on the internet. Yes, Ray was clever. But he also worked harder than the rest of us.

Behaviour

Children need love. But the best way of showing that love is by giving them a clear structure, rules and discipline in the home. Not by always trying to please them.

Fortunately most children like routine and discipline.

Good schools might recommend guidelines for the home such as:

- Punish your children if they are rude. Be fair, proportionate, consistent and never give up. They have to show respect for their parents. If they persist in being rude or disobedient don't shout at them – try to maintain a dialogue, tell them what effect their rudeness is having on you and punish them in some appropriate way. If you fail, don't give up – you are having an impact even when it doesn't seem like it.

- If your child is in trouble with his or her school, support the school even if you think the school might be wrong. It is important that your child believes the school has your support.

- Encourage your children to develop hobbies but don't fill their spare time too much. Let them have some time when they are 'bored': they need to learn ways of filling that time themselves.

- Buy books for your children, including books which they have chosen.

- For children between the ages of two and eight – read a book to them and with them for 30 minutes every day with no TV in the background. Reading a bedtime story establishes literacy and imagination as well as conversation.

- A child aged 1–3 needs 10–12 hours sleep a night. By the age of 1 get into a pre-bedtime routine by doing the same things, in the same order, at the same time every day – just before going to bed. A routine that lasts 15 to 30 minutes is best.

- Children between the ages of 4 and 11 must get 10 hours sleep a night.

- Children aged 12–16 need 8–9 hours of sleep a night at least.

- TV and computer use are less valuable to a child's development than reading and conversation so room has to be found for the latter. Internet use can be addictive and damaging. It is also very hard to prevent children from accessing damaging material through their computer.

- Eat an evening meal sitting around a table with no TV once a day.

- Eat Sunday lunch sitting around a table with no TV.

- Do not allow your child a TV in the bedroom.

- Do not allow children to use a computer, tablet, iPad, smartphone for more than an hour a day, two hours over the age of 13.

- Do not allow your children these devices in the bedroom until they are 16. Up to that age they should be allowed to use a computer which is positioned in the house in such a way that they can be seen and monitored by you.

- Do not give your child a handheld device which can get internet access until they are 13 and ban use after bedtime. Do not trust your child not to use the device after bedtime – it must be left in a set place outside the bedroom.

- Talk to your children about their online activity. Remind them that any message sent by text or on the internet can be sent on to other people and is not truly private. Remind them that paedophiles go online pretending to be children.

- Whatever their age, check the internet history to see what they have been doing.

- Have filters on all computers in your house. Install apps which remove features like comments and the ability to upload videos and block inappropriate search terms.

- If you need to give your child a mobile phone then the phone record must be accessible by you, the parent, for checking.

- Do not allow a child under the age of 13 to have a Facebook or any other social media account: they are damaging and waste time (page 119).

- Do not allow your children to play unsuitable computer games

- Do not allow a child aged under 18 to attend a party or event during school term time if they cannot achieve 8 hours sleep.

- Do not allow any child under the age of 18 to attend a party which is not supervised by responsible adults.

- Strictly limit the amount of pocket money you give your children: many things you don't want them to do cost money.

- From an early age establish a rota of jobs that they must do in the house to help you. Don't make this excessive but make it a firm requirement ... such as washing up lunch on Sunday, or cleaning the baths and basins once a week. They have to learn that these household chores are to be shared.

- Teach your children to say 'thank you' as much as possible.

- For teenagers, do not be too exercised about things which don't matter much in the overall scheme of things, like tidiness. It is important to try and maintain a good relationship with your children and that won't happen if you are moaning all the time. Most children go through a troublesome phase in their early teens; be patient.

If you are a firm but reasonable parent you will be rewarded with good children who, incidentally, will bring up your grandchildren in a similar way.

Conclusions

With young children parents have to prioritise clear routines, a stable family environment, help with reading and limitations on the use of digital technology.

For teenagers parents must place the emphasis on being strict about the things that matter while being tolerant about the things that don't. Parents of teenagers should try to work together and work with the school. Parents should try to ensure their children choose the right optional subjects at school, have space and quiet to complete homework and revise in the holidays before public exams.

Parents should take an informed interest in their child's university application without hovering over them too much.

Chapter 6

Successful Examinations

You may never know what results come of your action, but if you do
nothing there will be no result.

Mahatma Gandhi

Exams are an essential element of a child's education.

One reason is the tremendous value of committing knowledge and information to the long-term memory. For most children, carrying what they have learnt in school into adult life depends in large measure on them being forced to memorise it. An average 16-year-old boy can reel off 200 or so words in French three months before he sits the GCSE. On the day of the exam that figure has grown to 1000+ – all driven by fear of the exam.

Exams put pressure on children, and that is their great virtue. Girls are more likely to want to please the teacher and are therefore more motivated during the course. Boys do not especially want to please teachers – in my experience of teaching boys, 80% are relatively idle during the term but most make a big effort preparing for exams.

Exams are the essential building block of motivation. Ask any teacher who has had to teach an unexamined course to 15-year-olds, as many schools used to do with religious studies. It was a hapless task, and many now insist pupils take the RS GCSE as a way of improving pupils' attitude in lessons. Anyone who thinks that exams are a bad thing has never taught a class of teenage boys. Exams work because they make pupils work.

The age at which pupils are required to be in education or training in England has risen to 18 so why do we need exams at all at age 16? Because in the English system we typically drop down from ten GCSE subjects to three or four A-levels at that age. On average one of those A-levels is a subject not done at GCSE, so most pupils drop about seven subjects at the age of 16. It is vital that, having studied these seven subjects for up to 12 years, pupils be examined in all of them in order to consolidate what they know and measure their progress.

I have quite often heard people who should know better say 'other countries don't have GCSEs'. They are wrong. If you look at the highest performing countries there is a range of models.

For example, in the lower secondary years in Japan students study Japanese, mathematics, social studies, science, fine arts, foreign languages, health and physical education, moral education, industrial arts and homemaking. In the third year of lower secondary (age 15) they take a national examination in mathematics and Japanese. Their schoolwork across other subjects is formally assessed by teachers in order to be awarded the Lower Secondary School Leaving Certificate. This is their equivalent of GCSEs.

Singaporean students typically take between six and ten subject examinations at either O Level (after five years of secondary schooling) or N Level (after four years).

Exam results are the necessary qualification for moving to the next level. We do not want pupils embarking on A-levels unless they have a GCSE performance which suggests they might achieve something worthwhile. We do not want students embarking on a medical degree if they cannot get an A grade in chemistry – they would be too likely to fail.

The alternative to exams is continuous teacher assessment. In England in recent years we experimented with teacher assessment and it was disastrous. Many teachers hated it because they came under huge pressure to get good marks for all pupils (where do you think grade inflation came from?) and because these 'controlled assessments' were intensely dull. The academic year became dominated by dreary teacher-assessed coursework.

Pupils in successful countries take exams. They force children to place the knowledge they have been presented with into the memory. Once in the memory new things start to happen in the brain – like analytical thinking and the creation of links between different bits of knowledge. Educated people know things and the reason they know things is not simply because 'they have been taught it'. Far too many children are taught things but know nothing. The essential step in the process is commitment to memory.

Of course exams cause anxiety and distress but those who think children should never be challenged in this way are the enemies of good education. Teenagers, and especially boys, have to be driven to succeed. Exams are that driver.

Of course exams are not everything. For many they will not be the most important thing in education. But we should not completely ignore their power to motivate. Nor should we always listen to the voices of teachers from highly selective, academic schools for whom motivation is a lesser concern.

Exam boards

In England we have an unusual state of affairs whereby more than one exam board offers GCSE and A-level exams in each subject. Ministers have been worried about this because the various exam boards compete with each other by offering easier syllabuses, easier questions and more generous grading. Ofqual has to try to stop this happening.

Why have we got multiple exam boards? They arose because in the 19th century schools and universities decided that they wanted external exams. The government wasn't offering to set them up so the universities stepped in to create:

1857: Oxford Board
1858: Cambridge Board
1858: Durham Board
1902: London Board
1903: Manchester, Leeds and Liverpool combined to run the Joint Matriculation Board.

After 1987, exam boards merged and there was a gradual disengagement of the universities; Edexcel, for example, was taken over by Pearson from London University in 2003. Today there are three main exam boards in England: AQA, Edexcel and OCR.

A future government could decide to run all exams itself or might demand that each subject qualification is run by just one exam board. This is opposed by those who fear that the loss of competition might drive out innovation. There would be concerns about politically motivated fiddling with exams by governments; and anyway governments themselves may well balk at the idea of running something as complex and politically sensitive as an exam system.

In 2016 the exam board AQA announced that they were no longer able to offer A-levels in history of art, classical civilisation, archaeology and statistics. They were the last and only exam board offering A-level history of art, a subject which attracted about 800 entries a year. History of art was saved by Edexcel, but this event showed the weakness of relying on private exam boards running the English exam system.

Grade inflation

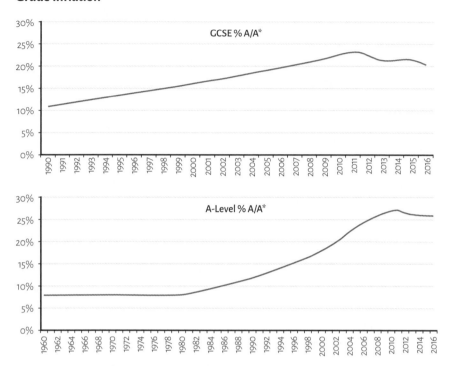

Source: Joint Council for Qualifications

Between 1990 and 2012 there was grade inflation at both GCSE and A-level. This was caused by a number of things. There were several exam boards in competition with each other for customers and, in what was later described as a race to the bottom, they competed by offering ever-easier exams. The exams regulator foolishly introduced a system of *modules* whereby the exam was broken up into parts and each part could be taken at any point and resat as many times as was needed. So whereas the A-level had once been, say, three long papers sat at the end of two years now it was six papers, three of which would probably be sat in Year 12 and resat once or twice in Year 13.

Teacher-assessed coursework was another reason for grade inflation. By 2012 many GCSEs were available where 60% of the marks were for coursework. Coursework is much easier to manage than examinations – the teacher is always able to help candidates gain better marks. A judicial enquiry into the 2012 English GCSE results revealed that a huge proportion of candidates who did badly in the written exam did well in coursework and many did just well enough in the coursework to tip them into a C grade.

And finally, as exams mature they become better resourced and teachers become better at teaching the course.

Nevertheless, there was an element of self-deception about the rise in grades during the Blair-Brown years as the Government talked about the improved grades as evidence of rising standards. But standards were not rising.

Standards in English schools

Between 1918 and 1951, pupils aged 16 took a School Certificate overseen by the Secondary Schools Examinations Council. The School Certificate Examination was usually taken at age 16 with performance in each subject being graded as Fail, Pass, Credit or Distinction. Students were required to gain six passes including English and mathematics in order to obtain the certificate. Some students who passed stayed on at school to take the Higher School Certificate at age 18.

In 1951 these Schools Certificates were replaced by O-levels and A-levels.

Before 1965 only the top 20% of the ability range (those in grammar schools and independent schools) took O-levels and went onto A-levels, the rest (those in secondary modern schools) leaving school without qualifications. In 1965 the more vocational Certificate of Secondary Education was introduced for 16-year-olds; if the O-level was for the top 20–30% of ability, CSEs were for the next 40–50%.

With the advent of all-ability comprehensive schools in the 1970s it became clear that a system which required schools to divide the population into two – O-level or CSE – was unsatisfactory. Forty per cent of those taking O-levels failed and many of those taking CSE could in fact have managed O-levels – so students in both groups were being misclassified by their schools. In 1986 O-levels and CSEs were merged to create the GCSE – the General Certificate of Secondary Education.

The GCSE is designed to be accessible to the bulk of the school population. For this reason some of the questions have to be easy so that the least able can gain some marks and thus a grade. It is not fair to compare the easiest questions in a GCSE with an O-level – they are designed for different groups. However it IS fair to compare the hardest questions at both GCSE and A-level with those set in the past and this can be done by looking in Dropbox at **http://bit.ly/2hDo4sS** and then looking at current past papers on exam board websites such as **www.aqa. org.uk/exams-administration/exams-guidance/find-past-papers-and-mark-schemes**.

Such a comparison shows that some subjects have been dumbed down at both GCSE and A-level, most obviously modern foreign languages and sciences. The hardest questions in a subject like history are not very different. When the first GCSE results came out in 1988 more academically selective schools saw their results shoot up – the GCSE was much easier than O-levels.

The main problem with English schools is the long tail of underachievement. In 2016 57% of pupils in state schools gained five GCSEs grade A*–C including English and maths. 57% is a low figure – after all, a C grade in a GCSE is not a great achievement for many pupils. For those on free school meals the figure was 33%, for white British boys on free school meals the figure was 24%.

In 2016 69.5% of all GCSEs taken by 16-year-olds in the UK were passed at grade C or above but 36% of those who passed only achieved a grade C – a bare pass. So many pupils are scraping by. Even these figures flatter the ability of the students because gaming and teaching to the test push many up to a C grade.

The reformed GCSE maths and English are tough but the comparable outcomes approach to grading (page 183) preserves the numbers who 'pass': the percentage mark required to get a grade 4 (the equivalent to a C in old money) is now quite low. So the true tail of under-achievement in England is longer than we think.

A survey by the Chartered Institute of Management Accountants (CIMA) in 2016 found that eight out of ten British school-leavers 'lack essential business skills' such as numeracy. More than 80% of young people require 'significant training' before being put to work, according to the 4000 finance professionals questioned. The top areas of weakness for new recruits are people skills and business skills, followed by technical skills.

Yet many people in England think our standards are good. This echoes the findings of Stevenson and Stigler (1992): *'we have found little evidence that Americans acknowledge the academic weakness of our nation's children…When they are confronted with data indicating that American children do poorly in academic subjects compared with children in other societies, they dismiss the results…'*

Gaming

After about 2008, schools in England started talking about a private company called PiXL (Partners in Excellence) which perfectly legitimately taught strategies to 'game' the system. For example, they told schools to identify all their Year 10 pupils who were likely to gain a C in maths but a D in English. They then encouraged the schools to cram them for an early sitting in maths. Having passed maths in Year 10 or early in Year 11 they then used the Year 11 maths lessons for extra English. This policy maximised the number of pupils gaining

C grades in both maths and English. This focus on the C/D grade boundary was itself a result of the Government's own 'floor standards' which required schools to get their pupils five GCSEs grade A*–C including English and maths.

Another example of gaming was the discovery by PiXL that lower ability pupils were more likely to pass English if they took the international GCSE rather than the conventional GCSE. One reason for this was that the iGCSE retained coursework and marks for a spoken English test. Following their discovery huge numbers of less able students were transferred to the iGCSE.

Gaming of the sort sponsored by PiXL gives an illusion of progress. I would never blame schools for using their methods – I have done the same – but where gaming works it produces an improvement in pupil's grades without improvement in knowledge or skill.

A final example of gaming was the European Computer Driving Licence, an IT qualification which the Government foolishly agreed should have the same value as a GCSE. It was relatively easy and could be taught, according to some people, in a weekend. For this reason it became immensely popular, with all Year 11s taking it in some schools.

Gaming is the inevitable result of high-stakes accountability – if exam results matter greatly, people will always look for short-cuts to success. But gaming reduces the *validity* of a qualification – you may think that a pupil who scrapes a C/4 (pass) in English is quite literate but you would be wrong.

Gaming is an example of *Campbell's Law*: the more a social indicator is used for social decision making, the more subject it will be to corruption pressures and the more apt it will be to distort and corrupt the social processes it is intended to monitor.

The BTEC

BTEC stands for Business and Technology Education Council, the body which first governed the qualifications (it's now Edexcel). BTECs are vocational qualifications rather than traditional academic courses, with subjects including Business Studies, Travel and Tourism, Engineering and Information Technology – you can't study subjects like history or English at BTEC level.

One of the main differences between BTECs and A-levels is the way they are assessed. A-levels involve two years of study geared towards exams at the end, whereas BTECs are continually assessed via coursework and practical projects.

The BTEC qualification has risen in popularity in recent years and is the route into university for a quarter of undergraduates. In part this increase in popularity has been because of two unhappy developments.

Firstly, UCAS has drawn up a table of tariffs which are designed to permit universities to compare the value of different qualifications. A distinction in level 3 BTECs is worth 56 UCAS points, the same as an A* grade in an A-level.

UCAS has in fact over-valued the BTEC – it is easier to get a given number of UCAS points with the BTEC than A-levels. Tim Gill, a research officer at Cambridge Assessment, found that undergraduates who had taken A-levels were much more likely to get a good degree than BTEC students with the same number of UCAS points. He concludes, '...*given that the UCAS tariff points are meant to be (broadly) equivalent for every qualification, some other method of calculating equivalent points scores might be advisable*' (Gill, 2016).

Quite.

The second issue with the BTEC is grade inflation, as the graph shows. While other qualifications have brought grade inflation to a halt, the BTEC grades are roaring ahead.

Proportions of three-grade A-level, three-grade BTEC and IB Diploma cohorts achieving the 'top grades'

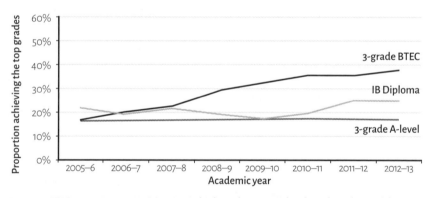

Source: HEFCE, 2015, Young participation in higher education A-levels and similar qualifications

Teaching to the test

In 2010 I was short of a religious studies GCSE teacher in my school so I put myself up to teach the subject, for the first time. An analysis of past papers soon revealed that some topics came up more often than others and certain specific questions came up more often than others. Being short of time and anxious to prove my competence I was therefore encouraged to teach to the test by focusing on those areas. My pupils did well enough, but I knew if they had received a different exam based on other parts of the syllabus, the parts I had deemphasised, their results would have been different.

Just as important was the fact that most questions had to be answered in a very particular way. There were certain key words which had to be used to gain 'the mark'. So much time, too much time, had to be devoted to learning the 'correct' way of phrasing an answer.

Teaching to the test is not good education. It discourages teachers and pupils from straying beyond the syllabus and it conveys a completely false impression of what learning should really be about. This is the danger of highly specific mark schemes and of educational systems focused too sharply on exams.

Teaching to the test may or may not be gaming, but it is something which produces results which can flatter pupils. It gives a false impression of their knowledge across the whole syllabus or domain.

Exam reform in England, 2011–20

Ofqual (the Office of Qualifications and Examinations Regulation) was set up in 2010. In 2011 they announced their hostility to modules (independently graded exam papers): it was impossible to grade fairly if there are many routes to one qualification through modules. In any one year exam boards were being asked to rank students, some of whom had taken all the modules in one sitting, others of whom had spread them out over several years. Some had taken a module once, others had taken it four times.

Then they announced their concern about coursework. Some was never moderated (ie checked by an independent person) including the crucial English GCSE speaking and listening module. Teachers admitted to Ofqual that they had been under pressure to influence their pupils' results.

With exams you normally like to have a range of marks so that everyone doesn't get the same grade. But coursework marks were often bunched at the top end of the scale – which meant that the coursework did not contribute to the necessary range at all.

Further analysis by Ofqual revealed that much coursework didn't measure what it claimed to. For example, fieldwork in geography was supposed to measure the ability to collect and analyse data but in fact it measured little more than an ability to follow instructions given by the teacher.

Coursework in GCSE mathematics and science was also felt by most teachers to be of limited value and burdensome to administer.

At the same time employers and universities were complaining about the quality of their 18-year-old employees and undergraduates: their English and maths were poor, they lacked initiative and they appeared to have gained good exam results by spoon-feeding.

The Department for Education shared this concern about low standards, about the way in which pupils were stacking up marks by taking modules every six months over a two-year period, by sitting and then resitting modules, and by the generally low level of some syllabuses. There was particular concern about A-levels: the content of modules taken in Year 12 was long forgotten by the time the students arrived at university. The modular system meant that at no point did students know the whole syllabus.

So between 2011 and 2015 a number of decisions were taken by the Department for Education and Ofqual that amounted to a radical shake-up of the whole system:

1. They scrapped January exam sittings so halving the number of times a pupil could sit exams.

2. They scrapped modules. The AS-level exam was decoupled from the A-level so that the A-level was now linear – all A-level papers are sat in one go at the end of the course.

3. They told schools that the first sitting of a GCSE would be the only one which would count for performance table measures. This discouraged early and multiple sittings of an exam.

   These three measures have together greatly reduced the burden of exams, something which is rarely acknowledged. The volume of exams has been reduced, as has the amount of time devoted to preparing for exams and actually sitting exams. Most teachers regard this as a good development.

4. In English GCSE the speaking and listening would no longer count towards the main grade (but it would be reported as a separate grade).

5. Coursework was scrapped in all public exams unless it measured something important that could not be measured by an exam. In A-level sciences the only element of practical work now assessed by the teacher is the student's ability to select the right equipment, use that equipment and log the results. At GCSE and A-level the *results and meaning* of the experiments are assessed in the written exam with questions worth 15% of the total marks.

	GCSE %		A-level %	
	Previous coursework weighting	Reformed weighting	Previous coursework weighting	Reformed weighting
English lit.	25	0	40	20
History	25	0	15–20	20
Physics	25	0	20–30	0
French	60	25	30–40	30
Drama	60	60	40–70	60

6. A new National Curriculum including GCSE syllabuses was rewritten by panels of teachers and subject experts under the control of the Department for Education. The focus was on raising standards from a knowledge-light model to the levels of knowledge and understanding being achieved in the highest performing areas such as Singapore. Mathematics GCSE became significantly harder. Subjects such as geography, physics, chemistry, biology and design technology contain more maths.

7. In the past, several GCSE subjects were *tiered* – that is, there were easier papers which could only lead to lower grades or harder papers which allowed candidates to access the full range of grades. The problem was that too many pupils were put in for the wrong tier, including fairly able pupils taking the lower tier. So Ofqual greatly reduced the number of tiered exams.

8. In 2017 England started the process of moving from alphabetical GCSE grades (A^*–G) to numerical grades (9 to 1). They did that because the old alphabetical scale had things wrong with it but it would be hopeless moving from one alphabetical system to a different alphabetical system … that would have been confusing.

   The old alphabetical system was broken for three reasons. First, because of grade inflation too many students were getting A grades. By 'too many' we mean so many that the more selective universities were unable to use GCSE grades to distinguish between applicants. All the many applicants they had to choose from had similar grades.

   Secondly, the introduction of the A^* grade was supposed to allow universities to distinguish the outstanding from the very good, but even this grade had suffered from grade inflation. Anyway A^* is a pretty silly grade.

Finally, the alphabetical grades divided those passing the exam into four: C, B, A and A*. This was not discriminating enough, so the new numerical system divides them into six: 4, 5, 6, 7, 8 and 9.

The alphabetical system divided those failing the exam into four, D, E, F and G, which was too many for relatively few candidates, so this was reduced to three number grades, 3, 2 and 1.

9. All A-level syllabuses were rewritten by panels of university staff so that they were a better preparation for university degree courses. Universities should no longer be able to complain that students came up to university unprepared. The modern linguists produced a syllabus which included more literature and more about the culture of the country whose language was being studied. In maths the syllabus was arranged so that all students took the same papers rather than choosing from options.

    For both A-level and GCSE the reformed specifications were quite detailed. Ofqual ensures that exam board syllabuses faithfully reflect these specifications – if they do not they are sent back to be revised.

Points 1–9 above amount to a long list. Exam reform is of course necessary from time to time. But when it happens it tends to absorb the attention of teachers at the expense of other things they could be usefully doing. There is an *opportunity cost*. So we should avoid further reform until we have some evidence that the 2010–2020 reforms either worked or didn't work.

In 2016 the Sainsbury Review looked at vocational qualifications for pupils aged 16 and above. It recommended that the chaos of 20,000 existing qualifications should be reduced to 15, each run by just one awarding body.

How reliable are public exams in England?

Every year many schools experience some exam results which are obviously wrong and have to be adjusted on appeal.

There are enough errors in any year to make us concerned. In 2016 at GCSE 5.5 million subjects were sat and 51,350 grades lifted on appeal. At AS and A-level 2.2 million subjects were sat and 16,550 grades lifted on appeal – a small number in relative terms, a large number in absolute terms.

In 2014 Ofqual researched the quality of external exam marking and found that it was generally good.

They found that most markers were experienced and well trained. They found that the use of 'item-level' marking (each marker marking just one question) increased accuracy. They found that screen-based marking also increased accuracy because seed answers (standard answers which had been marked by the chief examiner) are injected into the set of answers at regular intervals to check the marker is accurate and consistent.

Many of the problems identified by schools are not in fact about bad marking but **grading.** This was true of the 2015 Cambridge Assessment iGCSE 0500/0522 English. Here there was a sudden increase in the number of candidates, mainly lower ability candidates from state schools. When the cohort taking an exam changes dramatically it is liable to make grading harder because an exam board can no longer rely on the 'comparable outcomes' approach (page 183–184). Relying on examiner judgement, which is what teachers do every day when marking work, is in fact not as reliable as we would like to think it is. All the research shows this: different experienced examiners give the same script different marks. Cambridge Assessment made the problem worse by setting papers which generated a small mark range: the difference between each grade was small so very similar candidates achieved different grades.

In general terms the key to a good exam is the question setting and *the mark scheme.* The questions have to be such that students at each grade identify themselves: easy questions for the less able, very hard for the most able.

The mark scheme has to be clear so that markers know exactly what mark they should be giving. Poor marking is often the result of a poor mark scheme. On the other hand, for subjects like history and politics the mark scheme has to allow for a variety of interpretations. And we need to get away from a system which dictates exactly how answers should be structured – there needs to be a flexibility which allows for creativity. The unexpected, if relevant, should be valued.

In 2016 Ofqual reformed the remarking/appeals system.

Ofqual conducted experiments to test a number of different remarking methods in order to find the most accurate, concluding that the current system of remarking was no better or worse than the alternatives but could be improved further.

They found that remarkers were usually generous, so requesting remarks often yields a result. This is unfair on candidates who do not appeal. From 2016, therefore, exam boards may only raise a mark on appeal if the original mark is not one an experienced examiner could have given – it is an 'unreasonable mark'.

This brings us to the concept of *marking tolerance.* It has long been the case that for *longer answers* there is an accepted range of possible marks. If three good markers marked the same A-level history essay the range of possible marks they gave might be 16, 17 or 18 out of 25. So there is a three-mark tolerance for this type of essay answer.

Remarkers do not necessarily use tolerance when deciding whether in their judgement a mark could reasonably have been given, but the concept is nevertheless relevant to their work.

Differences between different exam boards are a source of unfairness.

Ofqual does a good job trying to ensure that all exam boards are working to the same standard for any given subject. However, it is an imprecise task when one is comparing completely different exam questions. We have been plagued over the years by exam boards competing for market share by 'dumbing down' – easier syllabuses, easier questions, more generous marking, more generous grading. The situation has improved since 2011 as Ofqual has taken a harder line. The situation will improve further as the reformed GCSE, AS and A-level specifications bring exam boards into line and Ofqual makes a big effort to ensure that syllabuses, sample papers and exam papers are all of a similar standard.

None of the above issues may be as profound as the issue of inter-subject comparability.

Some subjects are easier than others. The Centre for Evaluation and Monitoring at the University of Durham has been publishing materials about this for many years. For example, if you look at the average GCSE grade of pupils getting an A grade in an A-level, you find it is lower for some subjects than others. The 'hard' subjects include Latin, maths, further maths, physics, chemistry, modern foreign languages. So pupils taking these subjects get lower grades at A-level than they would have done had they taken the 'easier' subjects. At present there is no requirement for exam boards to align subjects by degree of difficulty (partly because degree of difficulty is so hard to define).

Candidates who get a grade B in English literature at GCSE tend to get a B or C in English literature A-level while those who get a B in physics GCSE get a D in physics A-level (this is called 'comparative progression analysis'). This suggests that physics is harder. Of those who get an A*/A grade (8 or 7) in English literature GCSE, over two-thirds get a C or better in the A-level, while with physics fewer than half do.

The problems with having 'harder' and 'easier' subjects at both GCSE and A-level are:

- Not all users (universities *etc*) will have the knowledge to discriminate between them.

- Performance tables don't discriminate so if some subjects are 'easier' they will become more popular for no very good reason. And then schools which do lots of easy subjects appear better than they are, misleading parents and Ofsted.

- The UCAS tariff doesn't discriminate – all subjects are given the same points score. This is a problem for degree subjects like law where admissions tutors might accept any A-level subjects.

- We don't want to choke off 'difficult' subjects such as modern languages and sciences which the nation needs. We know there has been particular concern about modern languages at A-level in recent years, partly perhaps because of the number of native speakers taking these A-levels. (This is a particular problem with Mandarin where most of the students sitting the A-level in the UK are Chinese.) Science bodies have shown that pupils with any given set of GCSE grades tend to get worse science A-level results than they would in other subjects.

- At school level, teachers of easy subjects might get more pay and promotion than teachers of harder subjects simply because their results look better.

- Pupils kid themselves that they are 'best' at the subjects in which they get the highest grades and make university subject and career decisions on this basis.

There are a number of things which could be done. You could simply publish the inter-subject comparability data to the users (universities etc) and leave them to adjust their offers accordingly. Some countries, such as Hong Kong and Australia, adjust the grades of optional subjects using a formula which relate the scores achieved in compulsory subjects to those achieved in options. Or you could continue as now but publish a SECOND grade which is adjusted. Or you could continue as now but publish a rank as well as the grade.

But the fact will remain it is very difficult to compare the ability required to do well in subjects like art and physics. They require very different skill sets.

Furthermore, one has to take note of what the users of the A-level grades want. Notwithstanding the fact that those who get a B in English A-level and a D in physics A-level might be of the same level of general ability, it might be that at university level a physics degree is not accessible to those only capable of a D in the A-level. It would be unhelpful to move the grade boundaries of the physics A-level so it becomes easier to get a high grade if by doing so you grant access to university physics departments to students who are not able to manage the course. In other words, a B in English literature at GCSE suggests the student might be able to manage a university English degree but the student who gets a B in physics GCSE is not able to cope with a university physics degree. Being more generous with physics A-level grades would make the subject more popular but it might deceive students by making them believe they are better than they really are.

High-stakes tests and exams

The point has been made that tests which are high stakes generate a lot of stress and a degree of manipulation. Different groups are affected in different ways:

There are exams which are high stakes for *pupils*, principally exams taken at age 16 and 18. The results of these exams determine which courses, universities and careers students go on to. Because they are high stakes there is, rightly, a lot of pressure on exam boards to mark scripts accurately and fairly.

There are tests and exams which are high stakes for *schools* but not for pupils, such as primary school Key Stage 2 tests. The results of tests are an important part of the judgements made about primary schools and can determine the fate of headteachers.

There are tests and exams which are high stakes for *individual teachers*. This will depend on individual schools' performance management policies. But many teachers are judged in part on the value-added scores achieved by their pupils in exams. Too much of this leads to 'teaching to the test', teaching whose sole purpose is improving grades.

When an exam is high stakes the pressure on the system to have fair exam questions, accurate marking and fair grading is much higher. Ofqual have often made the point that the expectations placed on the exam system are often greater than that system can ever hope to deliver.

Too much content?

When the Department for Education oversaw the content of reformed GCSEs in 2011 they made one obvious mistake. I was on one of the working parties and observed two others. The subject specialists were asked what they thought should be examined in the qualification. Every member of the group had their own ideas so it was always likely that the content would be much bigger than it would be had just one of the group written it, not least because no consideration was given to the size of the qualification.

The reason this might have been a mistake is the realisation that many of those countries who come top of the PISA league tables study *less content* than we do in England but study it in more depth. As a result their pupils have a better grasp of the subject than we do in England. This is not the place to rehearse the 'breadth versus depth' debate, but one thing I am certain about – next time we rewrite syllabuses, that debate should be had.

Grading by using comparable outcomes

One important objective of Ofqual is to maintain grade standards over time, ensuring that the scripts being graded this year would have got the same grade had they been set, marked and graded last year. They want to stop grade inflation because it undermines confidence in the system.

It is not simply a matter of saying 'over 80% is an A grade', because this year's papers may be slightly harder than last year, in which case the 80% rule would be unfair on this year's candidates. So examiners take a close look at the scripts from last year which were just below and just above each grade boundary and compare them with this year's scripts.

Nor is it simply a matter of saying 'x% of candidates got an A grade last year so we should give the same % an A this year'. After all, the candidates' work this year might be better – over time, teachers become more skilled at teaching a given syllabus, or schools might start diverting weaker students to other subjects where they have a greater chance of success. Or it might be that candidates get worse because schools start putting younger children in for an exam (as some schools did with GCSE in recent years) or because the best students have moved away to other subjects or qualifications (such as the Pre-U, an alternative to A-levels). We know that some bright children found the unreformed GCSEs rather undemanding, which is why independent schools put them in for the iGCSE, instead – so some of the best students were removed from the group taking GCSEs.

Where a new syllabus has been introduced, it is quite possible that it will be slightly easier or slightly harder than the previous syllabus. But because the new syllabus is different from the previous version it is not as easy to simply compare this year's scripts with last year's. Furthermore, experience tells us that results often dip when a new syllabus comes in because teachers are less used to it. This is called the *sawtooth effect* and Ofqual research shows that the effects normally last three years. This is potentially unfair on candidates, so when a new syllabus starts Ofqual asks exam boards to operate on the ASSUMPTION that the grade distribution this year will be very similar to last year if the cohort is similar. **This is comparable outcomes**.

The way they check whether this year's GCSE cohort is similar to last year's is by comparing their Key Stage 2 test scores. If this year's cohort is similar to last year's, Ofqual expects there to be a similar GCSE grade distribution in any given subject. However, it is not a firm requirement – if an exam board can prove to Ofqual that standards really have risen this year, then it can give higher grades. And of course it only applies to the grade distribution for the cohort as a whole, not to individual candidates! A child who did well in KS2 but was lazy for the next five years would still do badly at GCSE.

Of course the use of KS2 data could be criticised as the basis for this comparison – it is five years old and most pupils in independent schools do not take KS2 tests so the data for them is missing. From 2017 onwards Ofqual is running National Reference Tests – tests taken in English and maths by 18,000 children shortly before they sit the GCSE itself. Marks in the National Reference Tests will be aligned to the new GCSE grade boundaries in maths and English Language. The same test will be used every year so it will be possible to see whether standards in maths and English have really risen or not.

So for example, if in 2017 55% of students get grade GCSE 4 or better and in the NRT 55% got 38 marks or better, this means 38 can be set as the minimum paired mark for grade 4. So if in the 2018 NRT 57% got 38, the proportion getting a grade 4 in the GCSE could rise to 57%. In reality, because of the sawtooth effect, the NRT will not be used much before 2020. Furthermore, the results of the NRT will not be used without other evidence to support a rise or fall in the number of higher grades. Examiner judgement and the results of the Key Stage 2 tests for any given cohort will also play a part.

Does the NRT have any bearing on subjects other than maths and English? Yes, because if NRT scores go up and maths/English grades rise, other subjects will need to stay in line. The method by which this happens has to be decided.

Comparable outcomes only works for subjects where there are large groups of students and the make-up of the cohort is similar from one year to the next. It cannot be used for very small subjects or where the cohort has changed, as happens quite often.

Six-hundred-thousand children sit GCSEs every year. In 2016 5.5 million GCSE subjects were sat in England, Wales and Northern Ireland … 11 million exam scripts. Human judgement is central to the grade achieved by every child, but with such huge numbers a statistical framework which acts to ensure fairness from one year to the next is needed.

Good and Cresswell

When judging performance, we are more likely to favour performance against an easier challenge than against a more testing one. This was the conclusion that Good and Cresswell came to when they studied how examiners rated the work of students facing different levels of difficulty in question papers.

Their conclusion was the following:

'The awarders tended to consider fewer candidates to be worthy of any given grade on harder papers or, alternatively, that more candidates reached the required standards on easier papers.' (Good & Cresswell, 1988)

So if judgement alone was used in monitoring the standards of examinations, whenever a hard question paper is set performance will appear to have declined, whereas whenever an easier question paper is set performance will appear to have improved.

Raising the bar

One method used by the DfE since 2010 to raise standards in England is to raise the bar in terms of performance measures (how schools are judged) and floor standards (the minimum acceptable level below which action will be taken). Floor standards have been raised for both primary schools (Key Stage 2 tests) and secondary schools. In 2016, primary schools needed 65% of pupils to have met the national standard in **all of** reading, writing and maths. Floor standards at GCSE are based on the Progress 8 measure. Floor standards post-16 are based on measures of attainment, progress, student retention and student destinations.

Up until 2017 the DfE had regarded grade C/4 as the pass grade for GCSE. From that year the new grade 5 (a high C, low B) may be used in performance tables and designated a 'good pass'.

Successive governments have said that their aim is to improve schools. But expecting all schools to improve is in direct contradiction to the principles of comparable outcomes grading. Comparable outcomes means that the same proportion of pupils nationally will always fall below the pass grade each year. If a school improves it has done so at the expense of another school. This is why the National Reference Test is needed – if standards improve nationally, grades will be allowed to inflate.

What are grade descriptors?

GCSEs and A-levels have *grade descriptors* for each subject. These give 'a general indication of the standards of achievement likely to have been shown by pupils awarded a particular grade'. Here are part of the grade descriptors for Art GCSE:

To achieve grade 8 candidates will be able to:

- demonstrate independent critical investigation and in-depth understanding of sources to develop ideas convincingly
- effectively apply a wide range of creative and technical skills, experimentation and innovation to develop and refine work
- record and use perceptive insights and observations with well-considered influences on ideas
- demonstrate advanced use of visual language, technique, media and contexts to realise personal ideas

To achieve grade 5 candidates will be able to:

- demonstrate competent critical investigation and understanding of sources to develop ideas coherently
- apply a range of creative and technical skills and some experimentation and innovation to develop and refine work
- record and use clear observations to influence ideas
- demonstrate competent use of visual language, technique, media and contexts to realise personal ideas

Until recently these grade descriptors were used for grading exams. If you can imagine applying these to art portfolios, you will see the difficulty with grade descriptors! Everything hinges on the meaning of words such as 'effectively' and 'in-depth'. So now they are merely used to guide teachers as to the approximate meaning of each grade.

If grade descriptors are slightly useless, examples of actual scripts at each grade are incredibly useful for teachers. AQA published examples of EPQ dissertations at A, C and E grades and when I started teaching the EPQ this was the only way of understanding standards. One could easily compare the work of each student with the sample dissertations and this made it clear what grade they were heading for. These are sometimes called *Performance Standards*.

So how are A-level and GCSE exams graded?

Some grade boundaries are defined in part by EXAMINERS' JUDGEMENT. To identify the boundary mark for each of these JUDGEMENT GRADES the procedure followed by the exam boards is as follows:

A-levels

A-levels are graded by establishing the 'correct' mark for the bottom of A and bottom of E and the range between those two is divided equally into four creating the B/C, C/D and D/E boundaries.

The bottom of grades A and E are determined **judgementally** using two elements:

1. 'Comparable outcomes': the proportion of the cohort who achieve an A and E should be similar to the previous year.

2. Examiner judgement: the quality of the scripts at these grade boundaries. They compare scripts from last year that were on a grade boundary with this year's scripts.

   Taking a sample of A-level scripts whose marks are believed to be close to, say, the A/B grade boundary, a group of experienced examiners look at the scripts starting with those with the highest mark and working down. They try to agree on the lowest mark for which there is consensus that the quality of work is worthy of an A rather than a B. This is called the *upper limiting mark*.

   Next, taking scripts which have marks which are a bit worse than the upper limiting mark and working up from the bottom, they identify the highest mark for which there is consensus that the quality of work is not worthy of the higher grade. The mark above this forms the *lower limiting mark*.

   The chair of examiners must then weigh all the available evidence – quantitative and qualitative – and recommend a single mark for the A/B grade boundary, normally within the range of the two limiting marks.

The B/C, C/D and D/E boundaries are determined **arithmetically**.

The chair of examiners makes the recommendation to the officer of the exam board with overall responsibility for the standard of qualifications. That officer may accept or vary the recommendation and will subsequently make a final recommendation to Ofqual. Ofqual may approve it or give reasons why they are not happy with it. In the latter case the exam board must reconsider and produce a final report. Ultimately Ofqual can direct an exam board to prevent it setting what it believes to be unjustifiably high or low grade boundaries.

In the first years of the reformed A-levels (first exam 2017) the A* will be set using the comparable outcomes method: the proportion getting an A* will be roughly the same for each subject every year but can be slightly increased or decreased if the GCSE results of the previous year's cohort suggests it was stronger or weaker than this year's cohort.

Of course if the cohort taking an AS or A-level is very different to that taking it in the previous year, the comparable outcomes method is harder to operate. If a group's GCSE results tell us that they are different from the previous cohort, then examiner judgement (the quality of the scripts) plays a greater role. Similarly, if the cohort size is small statistical predictions are less reliable and examiner judgement plays a bigger role.

GCSEs

For the first award of GCSE grades 1 to 9 and where the size and nature of the candidature in a subject allows, grading will be based primarily on statistical predictions. Examiner judgement will remain as part of the process, but because of the reforms to the content of each subject and the move to a new grading scale, it will be less reliable than in normal years.

Grades 1, 4 and 7 are based on the comparable outcomes method. The bottom of GCSE grades 1, 4 and 7 is aligned with the bottom of the old grades G, C and A. Broadly the same proportion of students achieve a grade 1 and above as previously achieved a grade G and above. Broadly the same proportion of students achieve a grade 4 and above as previously achieved a grade C and above in the subject. Broadly the same proportion of students achieve a grade 7 and above as previously achieved a grade A and above in the subject.

Grades 2, 3, 5 and 6 are awarded arithmetically so that the grade boundaries are equally spaced in terms of marks from neighbouring grades. Grade 5 is positioned in the top third of the marks for an old grade C and the bottom third of the marks for an old grade B.

Grade 8 is awarded arithmetically such that its grade boundary is equally spaced in terms of marks from the grade 7 and 9 boundaries.

Across **all subjects** (as opposed to within each individual subject) close to 20% of those awarded a grade 7 or above will be awarded a grade 9. However, the proportion of grade 9s awarded **in each subject** will vary depending on the overall proportion of grades 7 and above awarded within the subject; a formula will be used to achieve this:

Percentage of those achieving at least grade 7 who should be awarded grade 9 = 7% + 0.5 x percentage of candidates awarded grade 7 or above.

So the award of grades is complex and well thought-through, but has a degree of arbitrariness about it: some grades are determined arithmetically and all are affected by the grade distributions used in previous years.

If grades are a bit arbitrary why do we use them? Because it is easier to make them comparable over time than raw scores. Raw scores will vary from year to year depending in part on the level of difficulty of the papers set. Grades on the other hand are assigned on the basis that a grade B this year should mean something similar to a grade B last year.

The main problem with grades is really the *cliff-edge effect*: the difference between one grade and another is just one mark. But it is also the difference between going to university or not ... so it affects students' lives quite dramatically.

How might the cliff-edge effect be overcome? The answer could be to publish more information. Instead of universities just being given students' grades they should be given details of how close they were to a higher grade boundary or the students' rank in the list of all those taking an exam. Given that all such data is now held digitally, neither of these things would be difficult. Incidentally, the merit of giving ranks is one of the arguments for having just one exam board offering each subject. Ranks are not impossible if you have multiple exam boards, but much more difficult.

The two basic types of grades

Norm-referenced grading simply means that every year you give a fixed proportion of candidates any given grade – 10% get an A, 25% get a B and so on. This method has two great advantages – it tells universities and other people who are selecting the best students where each student is in the rank order, and if the percentages getting each grade are fixed from one year to the next there can be no grade inflation.

We use norm-referencing all the time in our day-to-day lives. For example, my car may get 40 miles to the gallon, but I only know how good that is by comparing it with other cars – some of which are more fuel-efficient, some less. We compare our results with others.

Norm-referencing has detractors because it appears to create winners and losers. You may be a pretty good classicist but if 55% of the other candidates are even better you are 'below average' and however good you are that may make you feel bad.

Another problem with having a fixed % of students getting each grade is that it does not tell you what each student actually knows. After all, half the students taking a subject might be very good at it (as would be the case with GCSE Latin or A-level further maths for example) but under the fixed % system some of these very good students might only get a C grade just because a proportion of the candidates were even better.

So a problem with the fixed % system is that is has the potential to be demotivating. Individual students and indeed whole schools might well feel that there is little point in striving to do better because under this system it is so much harder to achieve improved grades – you can only improve if other people or other schools do relatively worse.

The alternative is called **criteria-referenced grading** where the exam board starts by defining what candidates must know in order to achieve any given grade. Normally there will be an attempt to define this in words and there may also be a minimum mark needed for each grade. This system has the advantage that if all candidates perform very well, all can achieve a high grade. In the case of subjects which are normally only taken by fairly able pupils, such as further maths, Latin or Greek, this seems only fair.

A form of criteria-referenced grading is what we have used for public exams in the UK in recent years, but the system has suffered from grade inflation as candidates have been better and better prepared. If too many students gain a high grade, universities can no longer select the best students using public exam grades – they have been forced to create their own special tests.

Furthermore, it is not easy to define on paper what any given grade should look like – as we have already said, grade descriptors are highly subjective.

Our current system uses both norm-referencing and criteria-referencing. It is based on criteria-referencing to the extent that examiners have to judge the quality of scripts, but the comparable outcomes approach to grading has introduced a greater element of norm-referencing.

Reliability of an assessment

'Reliability' of an assessment is a technical term used by examiners. It means the extent to which the assessment consistently and accurately measures learning. When the results of an assessment are reliable, we can be confident that if we repeated a test with the same or similar pupils tomorrow it would provide similar results. If you weighed yourself on a set of scales you would hope that if you repeated the weighing five minutes later the result would be the same – that is reliability.

Factors which can affect reliability include:

- The length of the assessment – a longer assessment generally produces more reliable results.
- The suitability of the questions or tasks for the students being assessed.
- The phrasing and terminology of the questions.

- The state of mind of the students – for example, a hot afternoon might not be the best time for students to be assessed.
- The design of the mark scheme and the quality of the markers.
- The consistency of the methods used to turn marks into grades.

Measurement error

In fact if a pupil takes the same or very similar exam several times they will not get exactly the same score every time. In 2013 quite significant numbers took both the GCSE and iGCSE in English; one third of them got the same grade in both, one third got a higher grade in the GCSE, one third did better in the iGCSE. Because both qualifications are supposed to work to the same grading standard, all candidates should have obtained the same grade in both. The fact that they didn't was partly due to measurement error, a rarely discussed characteristic of all exams.

The measurement error might have been caused by the fact that the two exam papers contained different questions and students may have been better prepared for one than the other. Or because all students have good and bad days. Or because of slight differences in the harshness or leniency of markers.

In public exams we transform marks into grades. The line between one grade and another (the cut score) is always slightly arbitrary. Many candidates have marks close to a grade boundary. The margin of error certainly means that some candidates who one day got a grade B might on the next day get an A. The use of marking tolerances in long-answer papers like history A-level means that two identical scripts can legitimately be given different marks and thus different grades.

A study by Ofqual (Black and Newton, 2016) looked at the probability of a pupil being awarded the 'definitive' grade for their exam. Ofqual used seeded item questions given a definitive mark by an experienced examiner which were then marked by every examiner during the marking period, to ascertain how often examiners failed to award the correct score. The study found that examiners in physics were 95% likely to agree with the definitive mark per question, compared to 50% in English, 62% in history, and 85% in Spanish and French. The differences in marking accuracy across subjects were inevitable, especially in more subjective essay questions.

The report also showed that the probability of receiving a definitive grade is 'significantly influenced' by the location of grade boundaries. Where boundaries are close together, the marking consistency 'will have a more profound impact' on the definitive grade probability. Therefore the wider the grade boundaries, the greater probability of candidates receiving the definitive grade. The report therefore concluded that the design of tests 'might be as important as marking consistency in securing the "true" grade for candidates'.

Ofqual's research has also shown that double marking (two markers mark each question) increases reliability but not much – and is hugely expensive.

The key point is that it will always be the case that long essay answers will attract different marks even with experienced examiners, so this will always be an issue for candidates close to a grade boundary. It might be thought that markers should be trained better, but unfortunately more training does not impact greatly on the spread of marks given to identical scripts.

The message to exam boards is that the gap between different grades must not be too narrow otherwise this phenomenon will generate even more cases of 'same script, different grade given'.

Another message is to consider giving candidates a scaled score as well as a grade so they can demonstrate how close they were to a higher grade. Or make more use of multiple-choice questions where there is no marker discretion (although that has a big impact on the exam's validity).

The message for pupils is: try to avoid being near a lower grade boundary.

The message for universities and others selecting young people is: try to obtain evidence beyond one set of exam results. Oxford and Cambridge universities are of course the most selective universities in the UK. They typically use a range of measures to select students: GCSE results, AS-level results where they have them, A-level results, pre-test results such as the BMAT test for applicants for medicine, the school reference, the student's own personal statement, a sample of written work submitted by the student, and two interviews. This is sensible, if expensive.

The message for governments is: if you are going to use test and exam results for school accountability purposes, employ an expert in statistics to calculate **the margin of error** so that decisions are not made on the basis of inconclusive data.

Sampling error

> *'I think that, within an acceptable margin of error, he loves me.'*
> Lilith in *Frasier*

Whereas measurement error applies to the mark achieved by individual pupils, sampling error applies to errors that arise from the selection of a *sample* of particular students or schools for the purposes of measurement. For example, the PISA tests *sampled* 20,000 15-year-olds in the UK in 2015.

In the 2015 UK General Election and the 2016 UK referendum about membership of the EU, most polls, even those taken on the day of the vote, were wrong. In 2015 few predicted a Conservative victory. In 2016 most predicted a victory for Remain.

The polls are based on a sample of the voting population, carefully chosen of course but only a sample. The poll results had a known **margin of error** (say plus or minus 2%) which in both cases was fundamental to the outcome as both the General Election and the Referendum results were close. But the British public were not given this data.

Both polls were, incidentally, affected by what is called *social desirability bias* – a tendency for people to give an answer which they felt was more socially acceptable. Many Conservative voters ('shy Tories') felt it was more socially acceptable not to admit to voting Tory as did many EU Brexiters.

In education, sampling error applies where people quote aggregate test scores from a sample of students, such as the PISA tests measuring a sample of 15-year-olds. Sampling error is more likely if the sample is small or, of course, if the sample is unrepresentative of the whole. With PISA this happens when they try to draw conclusions about sub-sets of their sample, such as the performance of different ethnic groups or of private schools: here the sample size is small and much more prone to error.

Sampling error can also apply to conclusions made about individual schools. It is dangerous to draw conclusions about the effectiveness of a school by looking at the exam results gained by just one year group in one particular June because that sample year group may not be typical of all year groups in the school. This is especially a problem for small schools where the very bad performance of just two or three children can distort results.

Validity of an exam

'Validity' is a technical term used in the world of exams which has a specific meaning and should not be confused with the normal use of the word. Validity in exams is not about the exams themselves, it is about *the validity of the inferences* you can make from the exam results. The validity of an assessment **is the extent to which it measures what it was designed to measure.**

For example, a test of mathematics should measure mathematical ability and not the ability to read English so a maths exam with lots of English text will reduce its validity as a test of maths.

In recent years in England university physics departments complained that students coming to them with good grades in A-level physics were not ready to take an undergraduate degree in physics because their maths was too weak. A physics A-level should measure your ability to do physics at a good level. But because of dumbing down much maths had been stripped out so the qualification lacked some validity.

One of the difficulties examiners have is deciding how long a set of exams should be. An exam only samples a pupil's knowledge, but if the sample is too small it is less likely to test all the various domains of subject content. Examiners rather pompously call this *construct under-representation*. It makes the exam less valid.

Another example was the French oral pupils took for GCSE French in recent years. The oral was supposed to test the ability to speak in French but the way it was designed allowed pupils to rote learn a selection of phrases and spout them out to the examiner. The test did not really measure their ability to speak French.

There is a link between reliability and validity. For example, if the purpose of a design technology course is to measure the ability of students to make products out of wood, metal or plastic with technical skill and imagination you are going to have to rely on a good deal of coursework to make the assessment valid. But coursework of this sort, spread over many weeks with the teacher giving greater or lesser degrees of help is a less reliable form of assessment.

On the other hand, insisting on highly consistent assessment conditions to attain high reliability will result in little flexibility, and might therefore limit validity. If all DT students have to make the same product, for example, the assessment would not measure imagination.

Independent Schools: the Common Entrance exam

State school pupils take tests called SATs (no-one knows what this means but it is something like Standard Assessment Tests). SATs are taken in reading, writing and numeracy at the end of Key Stages 1 and 2, that is age 7 and 11.

In the UK, private schools for children aged 2–13 are called preparatory ('prep') schools. They prepare pupils for the entrance exams to 'senior schools' and for most this exam is called Common Entrance taken at the age of 11 or 13. The CE is run by the ISEB – the Independent Schools Examination Board. The CE examines a wide range of subjects – maths, English, physics, chemistry, biology, history, geography, religious studies, modern and ancient languages.

Prep Schools tend to employ subject specialists who teach the CE subjects and others (art, music, computing, sport). CE past papers and teaching materials are a good resource for anyone trying to develop their Key Stage 3.

Conclusions

1. Exam systems are complex and even the teachers whose work will be judged by the system do not always understand them. More needs to be done to educate teachers and the public.

2. Unwarranted grade inflation, which gives the nation as well as teachers and pupils the false impression that all is well, must be contained.

3. GCSE reforms have made these subjects more demanding. This was essential because the standards expected in England have fallen behind other countries (pages 14–15, 93). As Kuczera *et al* (2016) found for the OECD: '*the evidence points to upper secondary programmes in England which require lower levels of basic skills than many other countries.*'

   The comparable outcomes approach to grading GCSEs masks the low level of performance of children by awarding pass grades to students with low marks.

4. High-stakes assessments will always tend to be the victims of gaming.

5. Too much is expected of the exam system by schools, the Government and universities. Exam results cannot be as accurate as people would like. People need to be aware of the danger of making important judgements on the basis of a single test or exam. The Government's accountability system puts more pressure on the testing and exam system than it can bear.

6. Exams are only a subset of the goals of education. If schools are in part designed to prepare children for work and adult life, then the testing of many of those things which matter is limited – how to work as a team, how to speak well, the ability to be imaginative and show initiative. However, because these things are hard to measure, and because exam results are the passport to university and many careers, exams matter more than they should do.

This chapter has been about what is called *summative assessment* – exams which try to measure your grasp of a course, normally leading to a grade which the users of these grades understand. For those interested in *formative assessment* – tests which help the student and teacher understand what they need to do to improve – see Christodoulou (2017).

Chapter 7

Successful Governors

I have been a governor of 12 independent schools and two state schools, have never been paid (of course) and only occasionally thanked. Nevertheless, I have enjoyed being a governor and I know what a difference governors can make.

In recent years the DfE, and Lord Nash in particular, has felt that weak governance was the main problem with many state schools, especially primary schools. Governance is an important issue for all schools.

So this chapter is for governors.

What do governors do?

The four main functions of a school governing body are:

1. They appoint the head and review the head's performance in their capacity as a 'critical friend'. They may well assist with the appointment of deputy heads and the finance director.

   Appointing the head is the most important job of governors. It is always better to not appoint and have an interregnum than appoint the wrong person.

2. They monitor the school's performance and suggest ways of improving it.

   Governors must insist that they receive objective and robust data, collected on a regular basis, about:

   - pupil learning and progress. Governors will receive performance data from a number of different sources such as exam boards, the Department for Education, Fischer Family Trust and ALPs and will need some training to understand it.
   - pupil applications, admissions, attendance and exclusions.
   - staff absence, recruitment, retention, morale and performance.
   - the quality of teaching.

   Governors need to find ways of hearing the views of staff in the school. This can be done formally by having a governor who is elected by the staff as a 'staff liaison governor' and/or informally through events where governors meet staff.

There must be a termly report from the head; governing bodies, not heads, should determine the scope and format of this.

Governors must see examples of lessons, scrutinise pupils' work and find time to speak to pupils and parents. They will receive reports from senior leaders and heads of subject departments.

Governors will know when the school is due to be inspected and will check that the school is ready.

Some governors say 'our job is to support the head', which is true but only half the story. Some abdicate responsibility and say 'we should leave this to the professionals' – also half true. Some go too far – 'we keep a close eye on the head'. None of these feels quite right. They should support the head but also provide reasonable challenge.

3. They give strategic direction to the school and this includes setting the school's ethos. They review the school's strategic plan every year; the plan will include targets with timescales and key performance indicators. In recent years most state schools in England have faced the question of whether or not they should become independent of their local authority, whether they should join a Multi-Academy Trust (MAT) and if so which one? These are huge decisions for governors.

4. For all Academies and independent schools, they manage the school's finances in a prudent way and render an annual report and accounts.

The other functions are:

1. They give expert advice without charge.

2. They support school functions such as Speech Days, concerts and plays.

3. They review school policies on a predetermined timescale. Ofsted expects governors to review policies.

4. They have a special role monitoring health and safety, child protection, appointment of staff procedures and Prevent (radicalisation prevention). These need a governor who has had some recent training. The safeguarding governor(s) have to be able to tell the board every year that they have checked everything is well.

Governors must insist on regular external audits of health and safety by a reliable firm and then check that all recommendations have been implemented. The health and safety governor must see termly minutes of health and safety meetings and follow up on decisions made by the committee.

All governors should have read *Keeping Children Safe in Education*.

5. They hear appeals from the parents of pupils who are being excluded by the school, appeals about admissions and from parents who have a complaint that they feel has not been dealt with satisfactorily by the school. They hear the second stage of staff grievances and disciplinary matters.

6. They appoint the chair and deputy chair of governors. Having the right chair is essential.

7. They plan for their own succession. It is important to have a small group of governors who meet to consider this every year.

8. In independent schools particularly, governors may help market the school. Smaller boarding schools in remoter areas often rely on governors to do this. For example, I know one set of governors carry cards in their wallets summarising the strengths of their school – ready to pass on to a potential customer at a moment's notice. At another school, lists of parents who had visited the school or registered an interest are given out at every governors' meeting so governors knew who to encourage. At a third boarding school, five governors were each given responsibility for a particular area around the school; they then held regional drinks parties for potential parents in order to promote the school.

Things governing bodies need to do and not do

In addition to the functions described there are certain things all governing bodies are expected to do. They are:

1. Avoid managing the school. Governors must not intervene in the running of the school – that is the head's job. This is the single most common cause of tension between heads and governors. If governors have appointed a decent head and finance director then getting involved with management will do more harm than good. For example, governors should manage overall budgets but should not go through budgets line by line.

2. Ensure that the governance operates in the way described in the school's governing documents, including any trust deed or articles relating to the school.

    Academy trustees are charity trustees. As such, they must comply with duties under charity law, ensuring the charity is carrying out its purposes for the public benefit and complies with the charity's governing document and the law.

Most independent schools are charities and governors are trustees. Laws governing the responsibilities of trustees are clear. A full report on the activities of the charity must be prepared each year for the Charity Commission. Governors are responsible for ensuring that the school offers public benefit.

Trustees must comply with their statutory duties as company directors, which are set out in the Companies Act 2006. In practical terms, all trustees need to be familiar with their Academy's articles of association as well as their statutory duties under the Companies Act, which comprise the duties to:

- act within their powers
- promote the success of the company
- exercise independent judgement
- exercise reasonable care, skill and diligence
- avoid conflicts of interest
- not to accept benefits from third parties
- declare any interest in proposed transactions or arrangements.

3. Ensure that the agenda of every meeting is sent out well in advance and good minutes are taken of all meetings by a proper clerk. The clerk can be someone like the finance director or the head's PA but it is better for the clerk to be an independent professional clerk. A good clerk will have been trained to know about legal and regulatory compliance and can give impartial advice.

4. Have a term-by-term plan of regular agenda items so they can be sure that all the key topics are covered and are covered at the right moment. For example:

Autumn Term
Check governors' contact details
Head's Report
Exam results and university admissions
Admissions this year
Admissions criteria for next year
Review the process of performance management of staff over the last round
Review of governance including sub-committee membership
Finance report: budget
Date and times of next meetings

Private Business including head's appraisal report

Spring Term
Head's Report
Lesson observation and teaching quality
Review school development plan; set strategic priorities
Review risk register
Ofsted preparation
Draft budget and pay award
Date and times of next meetings
Private Business

Summer Term
Head's Report
Finalise budget for the coming year
Admissions for the coming year
University applications
Priorities for next academic year
Staff changes
Health and Safety report
Safeguarding report
Complaints report
Future term dates
Plans for Speech Day
Date and times of next meetings
Private Business

5. Have written policies about the role and behaviour of governors.

6. Have training. All governance will be based to some extent on data and governors need training so that they understand this data. Governors of charities must have training which explains their responsibilities as trustees. New governors must have induction. All governors must have some safeguarding training.

7. Note conflicts of interest at the start of every meeting. If a governor possesses skills or contacts that the school wishes to pay for, then it is important that the conflict of interest which arises is considered most carefully.

8. Decide on the sub-committees of the governing body, their membership, the chair of each, the degree to which powers are delegated to the sub-committee. Most schools have sub-committees for finance; many

have sub-committees for education, health and safety and for estates matters. Some have sub-committees looking at remuneration and staff performance review. All need a small Governors' Succession Committee.

9. Governors need to decide how often they are going to appraise the head and they should, if possible, use an external person to do the appraisal. Retired heads often provide this service for a fee. The reason it is important to use an external person is that it is easier to tackle the head's weaknesses if the information has been collected by an impartial person. You do not want the head's appraisal to damage relations between the head and the governors (although it might do that anyway).

10. Have an external review of governance from time to time, often arranged by the clerk.

11. Do a self-review of their governance from time to time, in the knowledge that Ofsted will themselves be inspecting governance. The National Governors' Association has an online self-evaluation package.

12. Schools need to look after existing governors by ensuring they receive good quality papers well in advance of meetings, are invited to school events, are not overloaded and are thanked from time to time.

What a good governing body looks like

Every governor needs to bring something to the table – expertise without cost to the school. The main categories of function or skill are:

Essential

1. Education. Every governing body needs an experienced teacher or head on the board who can help the board form a judgement about whether the school is performing well or not. They will know about performance data, child protection, Ofsted inspections, teachers' pay, staff management, strategic plans. They know what a good school looks like. They know how to run appeals.

2. Pupils with special educational needs and disabilities need particular attention in any school and it is desirable to have one governor with some knowledge of SEND whose job it is to monitor the provision for such pupils. Maintained schools and Academy trusts have legal duties relating to SEND under the Children and Families Act 2014.

3. Finance. As more and more schools have moved from local authority control to Academy status they need governors who can have oversight of the school's finance director and budget from a position of experience

and expertise. All trustees should have an understanding of the statutory and contractual requirements of financial accountability and the principles of good financial management.

4. Representatives of the school sponsors/trustees. So if, for example, the school is sponsored by the Church of England, you will have representatives of the church on the board. Maintained schools will have representatives of the local authority.

Desirable

1. Legal background ... to give legal advice.

2. Local feeder schools ... a head of a local school who can give advice about the competitive position of the school in the local area.

3. For secondary schools, representatives of universities or other institutions the pupils might well go onto.

4. Local authority ... where local authorities retain educational functions, as many do, it is useful to have a representative who make it easy to access these functions, such as training, legal advice and child protection services.

5. Human resources ... to give advice about staff management including appraisal.

6. Buildings and estates.

7. Marketing and fundraising.

Optional or essential, depending on the school

1. Parent governors. Parent governors are desirable because they can spill the beans if something is going wrong at the school. They can be elected to serve by the other parents or simply appointed by the other governors. Obviously there is a danger that they will see the school through the eyes of their one particular child. They might not know as much as one would wish about how a school works so they need to be trained. With a parent in the room it may be hard for other governors to be as critical of the school as they wish. But parent governors can have many advantages.

2. Staff governors. Staff governors are normally elected by the school's staff from amongst their number. They can be useful in that they will present the views of the staff. A good teacher governor can help form a link between the governors and the staff. But with a teacher in the room it may be harder for governors to be critical of the head or those who work at the school.

3. Teacher representative governor. Some schools have a governor who has the specific role of liaising with the school staff but who is not a member of the school staff.

4. It is not a requirement in the DfE model articles that the Principal/CEO of an Academy is a trustee. Members may decide that in line with common practice in the charity sector they want complete separation between the board and its executive.

So governors need to be selected on the basis of their potential to contribute to the school. They should be appointed for a fixed term, say four years but renewable once.

Finding governors

The chairman of governors should have a chart which lists the date when each governor was appointed and the date they retire. Long before a vacancy arises the Governors' Succession Committee will decide what sort of governor needs to be appointed. Each governor will be appointed because of his or her skills and a skills matrix may be a useful tool to help clarify this (below).

The number of governors should be kept to the minimum to do the job. Governing bodies range in size from 6 to 20.

It is important that one eye is kept on the gender and ethnic balance of the governing body, reflecting to some degree the nature of the pupils.

Parent governors can be recruited by asking parents to apply.

Alumni are a good source of potential governors and this is where having a school or college alumni association is useful. But alumni may also be more resistant to change.

There is a Department for Education website where people can express an interest in becoming a school governor – '*Become a school or college governor*'.

SGOSS – Governors for Schools is a free online governor recruitment service for schools in England. Schools can register, and then advertise vacancies on their governing bodies.

Inspiring Governance is a free service that enables you to find appropriately skilled volunteers interested in becoming school governors or trustees in your area.

Academy Ambassadors is a non-profit organisation set up to recruit business leaders to build better Multi-Academy Trust boards.

When a potential governor has been identified he or she should be asked to submit their CV and should be interviewed by the chairman of governors.

If their appointment goes ahead they should be sent an induction pack and receive training.

Skills Audit – Academy Governing Body

Level of experience/skill: 1 =none, 5 = extensive					
A 'D' denotes a skill that is desirable to have in the governing body, and an 'E' denotes a skill that is essential	Desirable or essential?	Governor A	Governor B	Governor C	Governor D
Essential for all governors/trustees					
Commitment to improving education for all pupils	E	5	5	5	5
Ability to work in a team and take collective responsibility for decisions	E	5	5	5	5
Willingness to learn	E	5	5	5	5
Commitment to the school's vision and ethos	E	5	5	5	5
Basic literacy and numeracy skills	E	5	5	5	5
Basic IT skills (ie word processing and email)	E	4	5	5	5
Should exist across the governing body					
Understanding/experience of governance					
Experience of being a board member in another sector or a governor/trustee in another school	D	5	3	4	5
Experience of chairing a board/governing body or committee	D	4	1	5	5
Experience of professional leadership	D	5	4	5	5
Vision and strategic planning		5			
Understanding and experience of strategic planning	E	5	5	5	5
Ability to analyse and review complex issues objectively	E	5	5	5	5
Problem solving skills	E	5	5	5	5
Ability to propose and consider innovative solutions	E	5	5	5	5
Change management (eg overseeing a merger or an organisational restructure, changing careers)	D	4	5	5	5
Understanding of current education policy	E	4	4	4	4
Holding the head to account					
Communication skills, including being able to discuss sensitive issues tactfully	E	5	5	5	5
Ability to analyse data	E	5	5	5	5
Ability to question and challenge	E	5	5	5	5
Experience of project management	D	4	5	5	5
Performance management/appraisal of someone else	D	5	5	5	5

Experience of being performance managed/appraised yourself	D	4	5	5	5
Financial oversight					
Financial planning/management (eg as part of your job)	E	4	2	4	5
Experience of procurement/purchasing	D	3	2	2	3
Experience of premises and facilities management	D	3	1	4	3
Knowing your school and community					
Links with the community	D	3	2	5	4
Links with local businesses	D	2	2	3	4
Knowledge of the local/regional economy	D	3	2	4	5
Working or volunteering with young people (*eg* teaching/ social work/youth work/sports coaching/health services for young people)	D	4	5	5	5
Understanding of special educational needs	D	3	4	3	3

Source: National Governors' Association

Six problems governors face

1. Uncertainty about their powers in relation to the head. Governors give the head advice but what do they do if the head appears to ignore their advice or moves painfully slowly? Governors need to avoid managing the school, but if they do not feel the head is doing a good enough job they may be tempted to do just that.

2. Disenfranchised by a higher power. If you are a local governor of a school in a Multi-Academy Trust, or governor of an independent school which is part of a group of schools, you may not have the final say on anything much. You will feel impotent. Some local governing bodies of MATs have no decision-making powers and would be better renamed 'advisory councils' because everything is decided by the trust board.

3. Uncertainty about their powers in relation to other layers of governance. MATs have tended to introduce layers of governance, and the lack of clarity about what should be done at each level is a problem in many schools.

4. Time commitment. Many governors are members of at least one sub-committee as well as the main board. This will amount to six or more meetings a year. On top of this governors are expected to review policies, visit the school from time to time and support events. There is little point in having governors who do not have the time. The time commitment is especially great for chairs of governors and no-one should agree to be the chair without careful thinking about this fact.

5. Distance from the staff. Staff who work in a school usually don't know what governors do and feel quite distant from them. They may resent the idea that people they rarely see are controlling the strategic direction of the school.

6. Finding good new governors. It is a time-consuming job being a governor and specific skills are required. Primary schools, particularly, find it hard to attract good governors.

General advice

There needs to be a positive relationship between the board and its school leaders, enabling robust and constructive challenge. The chairman has to have a good relationship with the head.

The board needs to establish ways in which it can meet staff. Some schools have 30 minutes of tea and cake at the end of the school day and before the start of the governors' meeting.

The DfE recommends that governors ask the following questions of the head:

- *Which groups of pupils are the highest and lowest performing, and why? Do school leaders have credible plans for addressing underperformance or less-than-expected progress? How will we know that things are improving?*

- *How is the school going to raise standards for all children, including the most and least able, those with special educational needs, those receiving free school meals, boys and girls, those of a particular ethnicity, and any who are currently underachieving?*

- *Which year groups or subjects get the best and worst results and why? How does this relate to the quality of teaching across the school? What is the strategy for improving the areas of weakest performance?*

- *Is the school adequately engaged with the world of work and preparing their pupils for adult life, including knowing where pupils go when they leave?*

- *How is the school ensuring that it keeps pupils safe from, and building their resilience to, the risks of extremism and radicalisation? What arrangements are in place to ensure that staff understand and are implementing the Prevent duty?*

- *Are senior leaders including the finance director getting appropriate continuous professional development?*

- *Does the school have the right staff and the right development and reward arrangements? What is the school's approach to implementation of pay reform and performance related pay?*

- *Have decisions been made with reference to external evidence, for example, has the Education Endowment Foundation (EEF) Toolkit been used to determine Pupil Premium spending decisions?*
- *Are teachers and support staff being used as effectively and efficiently as possible and in line with evidence and guidance?*
- *To what extent is this a happy school with a positive learning culture? What is the school's record on attendance, behaviour and bullying? Are safeguarding procedures securely in place? What is being done to address any current issues, and how will it know if it is working?*
- *How good is the school's wider offer to pupils? Is the school offering a good range of sports, arts and voluntary activities? Is school food healthy and popular?*
- *How effectively does the school listen to the views of pupils and parents?*

(Source: *DfE, Governance Handbook*)

In addition trustees of MATs need to ask themselves:

- *What vision does the Trustee Board have for the size of the Trust and how does the strategy ensure that there is the capacity to support any additional academies well?*
- *Does the Trustee Board have a scheme of delegation of powers, is it published on its website and those of its academies, and does the scheme make clear where the following key governance functions are exercised:*

  Determining each individual Academy's vision, ethos and strategic direction?

  Recruiting each Academy's Principal/Head of school?

  Performance management of each Academy's Principal/Head of school?

  Determination of Human Resources policy and practice?

  Oversight of each Academy's budget?

  Assessment of the risks for each Academy?

(Source: All-Party Parliamentary Group on Education, Governance and Leadership, 2015)

Asking the right questions is equally important in relation to money; appropriate questions might include:

- *Are resources allocated in line with the school's strategic priorities?*
- *Does the school have a clear budget forecast, ideally for the next three years, which identifies spending opportunities and risks and sets how these will be mitigated?*
- *Does the school have sufficient reserves to cover major changes such as restructuring, and any risks identified in the budget forecast?*

- *Is the school making best use of its budget, including in relation to planning and delivery of the curriculum?*

- *Does the school plan its budgets on a bottom up basis driven by curriculum planning (i.e is the school spending its money in accordance with its priorities) or is the budget set by simply making minor adjustments to last year's budget to ensure there is a surplus?*

- *Are the school's assets and financial resources being used efficiently?*

- *How can we make the savings demanded of us by government cuts to our per pupil grant or, in the case of independent schools, our self-imposed restriction on fee rises?*

(Source: DfE, Governance Handbook)

Private business. From time to time governors need to discuss the performance of the head without the head being in the room. Heads don't like this so it is important to establish the principle of private business right from the start of a head's tenure and when things are going well.

The chairman needs to give the head quick feedback on the private business so the head doesn't feel that things are going on behind his back.

Thanking people. Governors will often be the only people who ever thank the head. In addition, they must think of ways of thanking staff if the exam or test results are good, if the budget is being well managed, or if the school receives a good inspection.

Making governance fun. Governors are volunteers and it is important that they enjoy the experience. It is good to have an annual dinner for governors.

Don't just dump governors. I am afraid most schools just ignore governors after their term of office has expired, forgetting the fact that they have given weeks of their lives to the school and are probably keen to know how it is getting on. All schools should have a simple system whereby ex-governors and ex-staff are sent a yearly newsletter. This simple kindness will be repaid.

Sources of data and advice for governors

There are plenty of sources of advice as well as training for governors. If there is a problem then governors should always consider bringing in external advice to help them through it.

Advice

Department for Education Governors' Handbook.

The Academies Financial Handbook: www.gov.uk/government/publications/academies-financial-handbook.

Local Authorities, many of whom still provide advice for governors.

The Education Funding Agency provides information for Academy trusts about the support available to improve efficiency, including a financial benchmarking website.

The National Governors' Association has very good training resources.

AGBIS (the Association of the Governing Bodies of Independent Schools) – provides training and advice and publishes *Guidelines for Governors*.

ISBA (the Independent Schools Bursars Association) – has model contracts and polices.

The website of the National College for Teaching and Leadership (NCTL).

The website of the Department for Education, which gives details of things like curriculum reform and new legislation.

The Key for School Governors – a membership organisation providing information for governors.

Modern Governor – a useful subscription service.

National Minimum Standards in Boarding (for boarding schools).

Boarding Schools Association, *Promoting best practice: Learning Safeguarding Lessons from Recent Serious Case Reviews*, 2016

Ofsted website for inspection frameworks; Independent Schools Inspectorate *Inspection Framework Handbook* and *Regulatory Requirements Handbook*.

Promoting best practice: Learning Safeguarding Lessons from Recent Serious Case Reviews, Boarding Schools Association, 2016

The Charity Commission has excellent information for schools which operate as charities.

Data

Department for Education performance tables.

RAISE (or equivalent) data for your school.

Alps data for Key Stages 4 and 5.

Fischer Family Trust – a non-profit company that provides data and analyses to LAs and schools in England and Wales.

CEM baseline assessments such as Midyis, Yellis and Alis.

Schools without governors

Privately owned schools do not have external governors – they are governed by their owners. But if they are wise they should set up a committee of external advisers and listen to them. Owning and running a school is a huge task and it is difficult to notice changes to things like inspection, health and safety, teachers' pay and the curriculum that they cannot afford to miss.

Conclusions

Governors have a great deal to do but it is interesting and important work. They can make all the difference to a school. They need the support of a good clerk but the essential figure is the chair of governors.

There is little point being a governor if you cannot give the time.

It is important for governors to agree amongst themselves and with the head what their role and responsibilities will be. The danger of governors becoming too involved in the management of the school is an issue which should be addressed head-on.

It is also important for MATs to be clear about the responsibilities of each different level of governance.

Governors should be appointed because of their specific skills.

The Nolan Principles: the seven principles which should apply to all holders of public office including state school governors

1. **Selflessness**
   Holders of public office should act solely in terms of the public interest.

2. **Integrity**
   Holders of public office must avoid placing themselves under any obligation to people or organisations that might try inappropriately to influence them in their work. They should not act or take decisions in order to gain financial or other material benefits for themselves, their family, or their friends. They must declare and resolve any interests and relationships.

3. **Objectivity**
   Holders of public office must act and take decisions impartially, fairly and on merit, using the best evidence and without discrimination or bias.

---

4. **Accountability**
   Holders of public office are accountable to the public for their decisions and actions and must submit themselves to the scrutiny necessary to ensure this.

5. **Openness**
   Holders of public office should act and take decisions in an open and transparent manner. Information should not be withheld from the public unless there are clear and lawful reasons for so doing.

6. **Honesty**
   Holders of public office should be truthful.

7. **Leadership**
   Holders of public office should exhibit these principles in their own behaviour. They should actively promote and robustly support the principles and be willing to challenge poor behaviour wherever it occurs.

Chapter 8

John Perryn Primary School, Acton, London

Disadvantaged pupils making tremendous progress

John Perryn has 440 pupils aged 3–11 (larger than the average primary school) and is a local authority maintained school. For 68% of pupils English is not their first language (the national average is 20%). Forty-one per cent have been on free school meals at some point in the past six years (nationally 25%).

In their Key Stage 2 tests in 2015 86% gained level 4 for maths, reading, and writing (76% was national average). But the reason we visited John Perryn was not the raw results, it was the progress:

2015 SATs two or more levels of progress from KeyStage 1 to 2

	%		
	Reading	Writing	Maths
England	91	94	90
John Perryn	100	100	100
John Perryn disadvantaged pupils	100	97	100
John Perryn low attainers	100	100	100

In 2016 the school was in the top 10% of schools in England for progress in maths.

The school has a difficult pupil intake. 50 of the pupils on the day we visited were Syrian refugees. Eight per cent were the children of travellers. Only 5% of the parents went to university and many were single parents on minimum wage jobs. Many were Somali where their culture limits the amount of reading they might encounter at home. **The average school readiness age of their pupils at the age of 4.5 was 18 months.**

Because of the difficulty of the children the school has found it hard to attract good teachers.

This is what the school has done...

1. A new head, Branwen Hywel, started in 2014 driven by a determination that the low standards and poor reputation of the school could be turned around.

2. The school now has high expectations – no child is allowed to fail.

   After every lesson the teacher writes down which children have not grasped which concept ('misconceptions'). They then have 20-minute catch-ups with specially trained teaching assistants during moments of the day when this is possible ... during lunch or during history/geography/RE/science/PE/art. They select teaching assistants carefully and they are well trained for specific tasks.

   In the classroom the teacher is expected to help all children. The teaching assistant is NOT expected to just focus on the less able as they do in some schools.

   The teaching assistants are trained every six weeks. Each has a specialist area such as writing or reading.

   The school puts pupils in for scholarships to private schools in the area.

3. Training parents to be parents:

   Parents have workshops every term. They receive support for their own reading and in the nursery and reception they are encouraged to 'stay and play' to learn to play with and talk to their children.

   Older siblings are also trained to read to their younger brothers and sisters.

   Parents' meetings are held at *start* of term to spell out what to expect this term.

   Key indicators are written in the back of workbooks and learning targets are sent to parents.

   Many children come with poor quality packed lunches so the school lays on extra fruit and vegetables.

   Now the school has a good reputation, parents are easier to bring into line. They know the head well and she has moral authority.

4. Monitoring teachers:

   Teaching assistants are taught to speak well.

   Regular work scrutiny reveals whether or not high standards are being demanded.

For non-qualified (apprentice) teachers, their lesson planning is monitored weekly, work scrutiny happens weekly and marking is checked weekly.

5. Discipline is excellent:

    There is a hierarchy of responses if a child cannot behave:

    A. warning

    B. table at back

    C. out of room

    D. see phase leader

    E. detention one hour during lunch with the head

    The playground has many staff on duty for which they are paid extra. They keep it calm with strict control of permitted activities.

    There is a smart uniform.

6. Pride in school:

    The head talks about 'the John Perryn way' and staff, parents and pupils are very proud of its achievements.

7. Soft skills:

    The school gives the children cultural breadth. They are taken on trips to Royal Albert Hall, Royal Festival Hall, universities *etc.*

    The children are taught how to have conversations.

    There are specific projects to teach them resilience – to lose but not give up. For example, there is a climbing wall where they are taught to keep going if they fail first time.

    Street language is banned.

8. Retaining staff:

    One of the most important things a school can do is retain good staff so the John Perryn day is not long and the amount of after-school marking is strictly limited.

John Perryn is an outstanding school where pupils from difficult backgrounds make great progress.

Chapter 9

Tollgate Primary School, Newham, London

An outstanding school with tremendous outreach

Tollgate Primary School is in a relatively deprived part of Newham in East London. The pupils are aged 3–11, a two-form entry making 60 new pupils a year, 490 pupils total. It is a local authority school and a Teaching School with 40 partner schools within the Teaching School alliance.

Fifty-one per cent of pupils have been on free school meals at some point in the past six years. In 2016 disadvantaged pupils were in the top 10% in England in terms of performance and progress. For all pupils 92% achieved the 'expected standard' in reading, writing and maths compared to a national average of 53%.

Fifty-five languages are spoken at home and pupils come from 40 countries. Only 10% of the pupils are white, half from Eastern Europe, half from the UK. 78% of pupils' first languages are not English (the national figure is 20%).

The head since 2004 has been Tom Canning. I asked him how he did it and he replied: 'We keep it simple. We have no trendy ideas. We go from A to B in a straight line for maximum impact.' Tom was brought up in the area and the school is driven by his passionate determination to help the community.

This is what that means:

1. They get all pupils up to a high level by the end of Nursery and Reception so they enter Year 1 well ahead of most other children. 'We do that by pushing them from day 1 to read and write well. We reject the old model which said that in Nursery 20% of the teaching time should be adult-led while the other 80% should be a free flow environment in which children learn from play. We do 50/50. Our Nursery pupils become good at phonics and enter Reception with confidence. We do this because our children get little help at home and it is necessary to give them this push. Also, our results speak for themselves.'

    At the end of Reception 92% of pupils are at a good level of development, 40% are better than this. In the Year 1 phonics test, 92% pass. 'What makes us so good is our extraordinary Key Stage 1 progress. This is the secret of our success.' 'Too often the Early Years in other schools is a bastion of play. We reject this.'

Those who arrive in Reception having not been in Nursery education have an immersion programme so they catch up quickly.

2. All teachers are expected to take responsibility for the progress of all their pupils. No child will be left behind. No child will be blamed for lack of progress. So every teacher is observed every six weeks. Every child's books are seen by the SMT every two weeks and checked for progress and marking quality. *'The biggest barrier to a pupil's learning is a teacher's low expectations.'* If a child is behind, the teacher has to explain why ... every six weeks.

If a child is falling behind there are two forms of intervention:

   A. On-call specialist teachers who see children in the afternoon where there have been weaknesses diagnosed in the morning.

   B. Pupils can be withdrawn from lessons for a longer period of extra help ... an intervention support programme.

No class is allowed to be out of kilter; all must keep up.

There are 25 pupils with severe and complex needs such as autism. They, too, will be pushed to succeed.

In Year 6 they have three classes of 20 rather than two of 30 which makes it easier to close any gaps.

In all comprehensive schools there tend to be five sub-groups, from group 1 (the very able) to group 5, those with special needs including those who are new to English. Tom Canning thinks the big issue is group 4 – the slow learners who tend to get stuck for years. He ensures they are under the spotlight and pushed hard. At Tollgate they are not allowed to get stuck.

3. Teachers must follow the 'Tollgate system'. In an hour-long lesson:

The first 20 minutes will be spent teaching and setting out expectations.

The next 30 minutes will be spent on a focused activity for the children – such as writing an extended piece of work.

The final 10 minutes will be spent addressing progress in the lesson and looking ahead to the next steps.

Instructions to the teachers include:

On all work dates and titles must be spelt correctly, underlined with a ruler and have consistent letter size.

Common repeated spelling errors need correcting. Key words must be learnt.

In maths if work is poorly laid out the teacher must rewrite the calculation in the correct model form for children to copy.

Children must have a time within a lesson to correct errors and rehearse spellings/corrections.

Teachers must regularly check work to ensure progression is visible.

Teaching must be engaging, inspiring, with teaching based on good subject knowledge and to the point.

Subject leaders must know the targets for each Key Stage.

Subject leaders must monitor books every week to ensure standards in their subject.

Staff are role models and must have high expectations of themselves and all pupils.

Teachers are expected to impart knowledge accurately and with enthusiasm which generates high levels of enthusiasm from pupils.

4. Pupils spend plenty of time on 'extended assignments'. They all produce five long pieces of English writing a week, five of maths, one for geography and other subjects.

   All pupils do homework including, incredibly, Nursery pupils (age 3) who have homework at the weekend. Older pupils generally do five pieces of homework a week: maths, reading, writing, times tables and spelling. For the Reception this is 15 minutes a night rising to 40 minutes in Year 6.

5. **Teachers:**

   'I won't let agency teachers through the door. In 2004 we were spending £300,000 pa on agency staff.'

   They train their own teachers having set up a SCITT (school-centred initial teacher training); they train 35 teachers *per annum* and cherry-pick the best.

   They remunerate teachers better than other schools by careful management of the non-teaching staff budget. The average salary in 2014–15 was £41,000 compared to the national average of £36,000.

   They promote teachers on merit not age.

   They keep good teachers partly because they offer exceptional CPD – staff go to Singapore, Shanghai, Holland and Finland for CPD.

   'We have staff loos as good as you would find in a five star West End hotel.'

'Our staff are rarely ill ... when they are we have to force them to go home.'

I asked the deputy head what the characteristics are of good teachers. *'Good teachers have to have good subject knowledge. But a big part of it is also your personality – the capacity to dominate a classroom. And part is pedagogy, which can be taught. Good teachers also live an interesting life outside school – it provides them with that bit of jazz.'*

6. **Curriculum:**

    'Our curriculum is tailored to the local community. For example, in geography we use examples from India. Music, art and drama are central to what we do. And we do regular Shakespeare plays.'

    Also: *'Everything starts with oracy.'*

    All do French and Mandarin from Year 3 (age 7) – Mandarin being linked to big Chinese investments in the area.

    The pupils learn chess in Year 4 in order to teach them logic.

7. **Parents:**

    They have a Family Centre with two support workers and one outreach worker who sees the children and families before they join. So they see children aged 0–3 and give advice about child care, health care and school readiness. They also help the parents with issues such as money and visas. In this way parents come to trust the school more.

    They put on parent workshops to help them learn:

    - English
    - phonics
    - maths
    - how to give homework support
    - computing

    'Our parents show us great respect as this is how they would have shown appreciation to their teachers in India and Pakistan.'

    Parents of very disadvantaged or children who are behind are invited to these workshops by letter.

    No child can be withdrawn from any lesson. For sex education lessons parents are shown all the material being used beforehand.

    'If a parent asks 'Can I take my child to Pakistan for three weeks?' I reply 'No... and if you do you will lose your place at this school'.'

8. **Appearance of the school:**

   'The aesthetic environment must be breath-taking. We put the children in an oasis of opportunity.'

   The school is absolutely plastered with pictures, posters and 3D wall sculptures.

   They have a huge and attractive staff room.

9. **Outreach:**

   Their train teachers through their SCITT.

   They support other schools; for example, they took over Cleves primary school and moved it from 'requires improvement' in 2013 to 'outstanding' in 2015.

   They have 40 partner schools. CPD is provided as well as school-to-school support. They have an army of 49 Specialist Leaders of Education who go out to support others elsewhere.

As Tom Canning says: *'Many educationalists would completely disagree with us but for me it's all about pupil outcomes and giving pupils the best start in disadvantaged communities.'*

Chapter 10

Ark King Solomon Academy, Marylebone, London

Outstanding GCSE results for disadvantaged pupils

The school, which opened in 2007, is in an old, quite second-rate building close to the Westway flyover and surrounded by multi-storey Victorian and Edwardian flats. In 2016 60% of their pupils had been on free school meals at some point in the past six years. Seventy-one per cent spoke English as a foreign language (most are from Iraq or Bangladesh). In 2016 95% of their Year 11 got five good GCSEs including English and maths, the best results in England. Their Progress 8 score was 1.07. Forty-four per cent of GCSEs were graded A* or A and 72% got the EBacc.

Distribution of Progress 8 scores, state-funded mainstream schools in England, 2016

Source: Department for Education Key stage 4 attainment data

The school is a Nursery-to-18 through school with 60 pupils in each year group.

When we arrived at 7.45am the deputy head was meeting every pupil at the entrance to the school, shaking their hands, welcoming them by name and expecting them to look at him as they did so. Many pupils had a musical instrument under one arm and a volume of Shakespeare under the other.

How do they do it?

1. The staff have a passionate belief that all pupils can do well. Doing well means going onto a good university regardless of your background. This means they HAVE to get 7 or 8 B grades at GCSE as a minimum, which they do. Every class of pupils is named by the year they will go to university. Classrooms are named after good universities.

2. There is extremely good discipline. Nothing is missed. Before the children start at the school the deputy and head visit every new pupil's house. Each parent has to go line by line through the parent contract with the pupil present. Regardless of religion they have to agree to do music and eat the one-option-per-day food provided. If a parent is difficult the discussion is halted and a private meeting with the parent is arranged later in the week. Eventually agreement is reached.

    If a parent refuses to allow a daughter to go camping, for example, the school will not let the matter rest. They will typically negotiate a deal such as 'she must come for one day out of the five but it will be two days next year'.

    The deputy confiscates games consoles from pupils' homes.

3. **It's all about Key Stage 3 – years 7, 8 and 9.** The aim is to get everyone to a high standard by the end of Year 9. This makes it very likely they will get good GCSEs.

    SO they have a **limited curriculum in KS3** – just English, maths, science, French, music and PE.

    Pupils are taught in mixed ability classes of 30.

    Any pupil who is behind (as many are when they start at age 11) gets extra help BEFORE a lesson is taught (not in the lesson) and is thus ready for the lesson.

	Periods per week	
Key Stage 3 Curriculum	A typical Academy	King Solomon
English	4	8
Maths	4	8
Science	4	6
Art	1	0
Dance	1	0
Drama	1	0
Enrichment	1	0
Humanities	4	0
Computing	1	0
French	2	4
Music	1	2
Personal Development	1	0
PE	2	2
Technology	2	0
Total	**29**	**30**

There are six lessons a day, each 55 minutes.

The school teaches maths using the mastery approach used in Singapore and Shanghai. It encourages deep learning of concepts and pupils do not move on until they have clearly mastered each concept.

The two-year Key Stage 4 is a success because by the age of 14 they are all well ahead in English, maths, science, French – which lead to seven GCSEs. They can easily do three more GCSEs in the two KS4 years (chosen from geography, history, music, art. RE GCSE is compulsory). There are three setted classes for KS4 lessons: size 30, 20, 10. The bottom set always gets the best teacher.

4. There is a long school day: 7.55am-4pm followed by two hours of punishment/missed homework time. Lunch only lasts 30 minutes, break 10 minutes.

They have two hours of homework a night. It has to be handed to the form teacher by 8am. If *any* homework is missing, a text is sent to the parent – the child will have to stay until 6pm that day. Every member of staff is given a work telephone which any parent or child can ring up to 7pm so there are no excuses.

5. The school is small so every pupil is known well.

6. The school is part of the Ark Multi-Academy Trust and the trust provides support when needed.

In addition we noted that...

Pupils take most lessons in the same room as a fixed group. Teachers move, not pupils. So there are no problems on corridors. The school is very quiet.

The same teacher of any given subject teaches ALL classes in that subject in a given year. So for example the Year 7 English teacher teaches nothing else – two hours a day with each of three classes.

Pupils get credits and debits for good and bad things. These are translated into 'pounds' which can be used to buy trips. The idea is to teach the relationship between effort and reward. Pupils without the pounds don't go on the trips – they have lessons at school instead.

All KS3 pupils are lent their own musical instrument which they learn two hours a week. All are in an orchestra. The aim is not to create great musicians but to develop teamwork, concentration, discipline.

All KS3 pupils perform one unabridged Shakespeare play a year.

Pupils need five Bs at GCSE for entry to sixth form but As in some subjects if you are continuing with them.

Pupils are persuaded to go to universities outside London because the school feels, on balance, that living at home while at university will prevent them from developing the experiences and skills they need to be fully integrated into society and able to access top jobs.

Lunch taken as family service is compulsory – six pupils to a table plus a teacher where there will be adult conversation. Food is served at the table.

Ark

The Ark schools are amongst the most successful academies in England. This is what they say about themselves:

'All of our schools have their own ethos, uniform and character. But they all share the same mission: to make sure that every pupil can go to university or into the career of their choice.

To achieve our mission, our schools follow the same set of underlying principles. We call these the Six Pillars:

1. ***Excellent teaching***
    A teacher affects a pupil's achievement more than any other factor. We work side-by-side with teaching staff, supporting them with training and development so

that they can deliver excellent teaching. To make sure that no pupil is left behind, we've developed data management tools which help teachers to monitor progress – this shows when pupils, or indeed teaching staff, need extra support.

2. **High expectations**

   We believe that every child can achieve great things. So we set exceptionally high expectations for all our pupils, and we do whatever it takes to meet them. Our aspirations are no lower for our most vulnerable pupils.

3. **Exemplary behaviour**

   Our schools are characterised by a respectful and orderly environment, where teachers can focus on teaching and pupils can focus on learning. We teach, recognise and reinforce good behaviour, and we don't tolerate poor behaviour. We don't accept any excuses, and we don't make any either.

4. **Knowing every child**

   We organise our schools so that every child knows, and is known well by, every adult in the school. We also recognise that children do best when families and schools work together. We keep parents well informed about children's targets, and we involve families in all aspects of school life.

5. **Depth before breadth**

   When children build firm foundations in English and maths, they find it easier to do well in other subjects too. That's why we prioritise depth in these subjects, giving our pupils the best chance of success.

   We've developed Mathematics Mastery, which aims to improve attainment, enjoyment and confidence in maths. This approach is based on tried and tested methods from around the world, and is also endorsed by Ofsted.

   To nurture a love of reading and develop fluent communication skills, we also dedicate more time to literacy and English. We work with Drive for Literacy to make sure that all of our teachers recognise the barriers that children face in building literacy skills, and we offer tools and expertise to enable teachers to best support students who need more help.

6. **More time for learning**

   To make sure children have enough time both for core subjects and for extracurricular activities, many of our schools run a longer school day. Others are open at weekends and during school holidays, offering masterclasses and revision sessions. Many Ark schools offer residential stays, day trips and summer schools. In every school, no time is wasted – every hour of every day is devoted to children learning.'

Ark schools, and King Solomon's particularly, are outstanding.

Chapter 11

Ark Burlington Danes Academy, Hammersmith, London

An example of rapid turnaround

In 2008 Sally Coates took over as head of Burlington Danes Academy in Hammersmith. By the time she left in 2014 the school had been transformed from one of the worst to one of the highest achieving comprehensive schools with a high proportion of disadvantaged children. Luckily for us she wrote an account of that transformation, *Headstrong* (2015), which describes the steps she took.

In 2016 64% had been on free school meals at some point in the past six years and 47% did not have English as their first language.

Instant actions

Sally had been the head of a successful girls' school in south London which also had large numbers of pupils on free school meals. So she knew what success looked like – a calm, happy, ordered environment with excellent exam results. She decided she had to provide firm leadership from day one. In order to achieve this she researched the problems at Burlington Danes, decided what needed to be done and was clear before she started what changes were needed.

Sally has a forceful personality. As she says in her book, it is possible to help people develop the competencies of headship 'but so much of leadership is about character'. She was confident she could transform the school and she conveyed that confidence to pupils and staff. Classroom teachers are the people who can make most difference but they rely on the headteacher to create the right environment: behaviour, community, tone and ethos. She told the staff that they would double the number of students gaining five or more good GCSEs within two years.

She started with a clear focus on the quality of teaching, asking to check next week's lesson plans for every teacher each Friday. This allowed her to see whether lessons were stretching, whether homework was being set, whether lessons were suitable for both able and less able children. Indeed it allowed to her confirm that lessons were being planned.

In order to establish that things were going to change for the better she made small, inexpensive changes to the physical environment. She installed ten all-weather table tennis tables in the playground, bought carpet for the corridors and put up pot plants and hanging baskets around the site. She got dozens of door stops to encourage teachers to keep their door open while teaching. She introduced a new uniform with a blazer (which was free) and school bag.

Sally asked the senior leadership team who the weak teachers were; they suggested that about a third of teachers were not good enough. These teachers were seen immediately and told that they had been identified as being inadequate and were going to be observed. Twenty-one of them resigned and left that year. *'Such conversations are possible if you always put the interests of the pupils first'.*

Good teachers were encouraged to stay. There were high staff absence rates so rewards were offered to teachers with 100% attendance throughout the term.

She announced that all classes were to be set by ability. Every year group was to be examined at regular points in the year with their results publically displayed as rank orders.

Setting the tone and ethos

In order to convey her messages, especially celebration of achievement, there had to be systems by which this could happen. So:

- She established two assemblies every day
- She had a staff briefing every day
- There was a weekly staff bulletin to highlight good practice
- A student leadership scheme was established
- She established a form period at the end of each day

Behaviour

On her first day as head she gave letters to 73 children who had been identified by the senior teachers as being permanently disruptive. They said that the child should not return to school without their parents. Through these parent interviews she brought the parents onside.

She established with absolute clarity and certainty that rules and punishments will be applied systematically. So if you were late for school you know exactly what would happen – a one-hour detention that day. A classroom teacher will always expect good behaviour. The teacher will notice every example of low-level disruption but will deal with it in a way which does not disrupt the lesson too much. A teacher will always know if homework is late and will always take action. Lazy or disruptive pupils will be kept behind for a two-hour detention on Fridays and there was a daily homework detention.

Heads of Year were appointed with especial responsibility for discipline. They monitored detention lists and worked with students, parents and the school counsellor to improve matters.

She appointed a behaviour manager who patrolled the outside of the school, patrolled corridors, oversaw a room where disruptive pupils are sent and started daily detention.

Specific routines were devised for:

- Corridor behaviour
- Lunch queues
- Lining up outside classrooms
- Entering classrooms ... the teacher greets students at the door. All classes have a seating plan
- Waiting behind desks
- What should be on your desk at the start of a lesson including planner and pencil case
- Taking the register
- Homework ... shown on a slide at the start of the lesson and copied into homework planners
- Distributing materials
- Presenting work
- What to do if you are late
- Answering questions
- Group work
- Handing in work
- Leaving the classroom ... dismissed row by row

Exam results

Teachers have to assume that all their pupils can do well – it is effort, not natural ability, which matters most. What that means is that teachers have to know which pupils are finding the work difficult – so there has to be regular questioning and testing. Then extra help has to be given to pupils who are struggling. They also have to pitch lessons so they are stretching.

She introduced a programme of lesson observations and workbook reviews.

Data was collected on performance of pupils and staff every six weeks.

Rank orders of effort and achievement were published.

Over time she recruited good staff for key positions. She especially believed in the recruitment of subject specialists.

She cut back on temporary and supply staff as well as teaching assistants.

A great deal of effort was made to praise pupils and good work. She saw that it was essential that effort and academic success should be something that pupils admire rather than ridicule.

Right from the start she gave the pupils exam practice: every pupil in every subject they studied. They were taught the procedures of the exam hall – using black ink, complete silence, timing answers carefully. They learnt to see the relationship between effort and results.

She set up an Oxbridge Project to improve the cultural literacy of the more able pupils. Starting in Year 7 they would be exposed to weekly talks and seminars in a range of academic fields.

Part of the process of stretching children was to 'intellectualise the curriculum', not least in the neglected Key Stage 3; for example they would study texts in English which might have conventionally been taught in Key Stage 4.

Pupil performance data was collected and used to:

- Create benchmarks which identify the potential of the pupil.
- Inform parents and students of their current level of work.
- Help with setting pupils. Low ability classes are smaller and have the best teachers. Lower ability classes are smaller than 20, able classes have 30.
- Set individual targets. Every pupil has a sticker in their planner giving their current 'working at' grade and their predicted grade.
- Identify the best and worst teachers.
- Target intervention immediately where there is a mismatch between potential and actual progress.

All pupils were assessed every term in every one of their subjects. Core subjects had exams six times a year. Revision guides were issued before each assessment.

Rank orders were published in public areas after each exam. Rank orders serve, on balance, to motivate pupils. Because of the attention they attract, they serve to emphasise the importance of academic results. Parents understand rank orders more clearly than any other type of data.

For pupils aged 11–14 the school calculated a weighted total of all their subjects, giving a rank of overall academic ability in the year group, from 1 to 180. For pupils aged 14–18 they published progress in relation to their target grades and in the sixth form progress in relation to the grades required by their first-choice university.

The school created a Venn diagram for Year 11 which was put up in the staff room – three circles, one containing the names of pupils NOT on target to get a grade C in maths, one naming pupils not on target to get a C in English and one giving those not on target to get Cs in three other subjects. This served to show up children who were bad at just one subject (so they needed extra help in that subject) and those who were bad at many subjects (so the Head of Year needed to act, calling in the parents, placing them on monitoring report and requiring them to attend extra lessons on a Saturday).

Once every month pupils in years 11 and 13 were given a predicted grade for each subject. Within three days of this event every such pupil had a meeting with a senior member of staff who was their mentor. The mentor will have been given background information by teachers, such as upcoming coursework and specific concerns. The mentor and pupil discussed the monthly predicted grades, comparing them with their target grades. Actions were agreed. These mentor meetings were followed by department meetings that looked at every pupil not on target.

Extra lessons were held after school, on Saturdays and in the holidays. Teachers were paid extra for lessons at weekends and in the holidays. Parents and pupils were provided with clear criteria about what is expected to gain at least a C grade.

Teachers

There is a probationary period within which a teacher can be asked to leave with no further stages.

References employ a numbered scale against which the referee scored the various characteristics of good teachers – which is more reliable than straight prose.

Inset, usually led by Burlington Danes teachers, happened on a day before each of the six half terms of the year. Individual subject departments are vital and so is subject knowledge, so a large part of inset had to be subject-based.

She makes the point that it is easy to become a full-time social worker or police officer so the culture of the school has to constantly direct teachers' attention back to teaching. Every week a vice-principal emailed all staff a list of good web resources and blogs. Every Tuesday a teacher shared a nugget of teaching advice with all staff.

The school offered staff a subsidised Masters in Education from King's College, London.

Supply teachers were scrapped. Existing staff had to do all cover, especially the senior leaders. Every member of staff who was absent had a follow-up meeting. Staff with a 100% attendance over a year were rewarded with bottle of wine or book token.

CPD during the day was limited to avoid cover requests.

As many leadership appointments as possible were made by promoting internally.

On the first day of the autumn term every member of staff received information about how their students from last term performed in public exams compared with those students' other subjects.

Every teacher has three formal lesson observations a year. If a lesson was judged to be inadequate there was a follow-up observation. If a teacher has several inadequate lessons, capability procedures were begun.

Involving parents

Parents were brought onside and made to feel involved by means of:

- Raising expectations of parents by using questionnaires, revision guides and newsletters.
- Having a home-school contract/agreement.
- The head being at the school gate at the end of every day.
- Pursuing parents who fail to attend parents' evenings.
- Sending postcards to parents of successful pupils.
- Offering workshops to parents which teach them how to help their children.
- Explaining performance data to parents.
- Having homework on an internet site so parents and students can see what is set.

Structures

The school day times were changed to start at 8.30am and end at 3.50pm.

The key pastoral unit is the year group broken down into tutor groups. The key academic unit is the subject. Every subject has a departmental base and is encouraged to develop resources which all staff can share. Heads of subject departments are responsible for the performance of their pupils and teachers, the creation of revision guides for every exam, doing lesson observations and analysing GCSE and A-level results. Department meetings are held every three weeks.

All pupils are assigned to one of six houses. Houses are used as the basis for competitions and provide motivation. Pupils are awarded house points for all aspects of school life including work, punctuality and charity events.

After the departure of the super head

Research by Hill *et al* (2016) showed that the sort of measures taken by Sally Coates tend to result in short-term improvements followed by a decline.

This has not happened at Burlington Danes because the new head, Michael Ribton, not only joined the school as Sally Coates's main deputy at the same time as she started but was responsible for many of the measures outlined above.

I asked Michael what the key measures were from his point of view:

1. **A focus on teaching and learning**. This statement will seem platitudinous to non-teachers (what else would a school focus on?) but those who have worked in schools, especially schools with difficult or disadvantaged pupils, will know that there is a temptation to focus on all the issues pupils bring to school with them – family problems, mental health, behaviour. The school deals with these issues but teachers are there to teach, not to be social workers.

   The SMT including the principal each have a group of Year 11s to mentor and they see them five times in the year to push them along.

2. **Maintain good behaviour**. Without good behaviour nothing can be achieved. The school operates a simple four-step disciplinary system: a verbal warning followed by a written warning (the pupil's name is just written on the board) followed by 24 hours in The Consequences Room where pupils work under the close supervision of the no-nonsense discipline manager. Then, as a final resort, five days at home.

3. **Maintain the focus on regular exams and published rank orders**. There are exams every six weeks and pupils change sets based on their results. The reformed GCSEs, with their greater emphasis on end-of-course exams and decreased emphasis on coursework, should suit Burlington Danes. In January of Year 11 they even have a mock exam results day – pupils are given their results in an envelope in order to replicate the experience they will all have in August. They still give pupils a twice-yearly rank in their year group for achievement and progress and the results still go up on the wall.

4. **Support for those falling behind in Year 11**: there is an extra period tacked on to the end of the day Monday to Thursday, for most Year 11s.

5. They aim to create a self-improving school, which means thinking of things every year which can be done better.

6. **Support from Ark**. The Multi-Academy Trust helps in a number of ways. They do not impose a model of how things should be done, allowing individual schools to find their own way.

    - Ark set the school targets which are well above national standards and expect schools to meet them.

    - They send an inspection team in three times a year, two announced and one unannounced.

    - The principal is appraised three times a year.

    - The Ark schools share good practice with each other.

    - They arrange road trips for staff to visit other good schools in the UK and learn from them: this is very valuable.

    - They arrange regular professional development courses for staff.

    - They have subject experts in core subjects who can help a school improve their teaching.

    - They arrange for schools to exchange internal exam papers and check that teachers are marking work at the correct standard.

    - They manage all the human resources work and place adverts for all appointments.

7. **Support from the Church of England**. The school is sponsored by the Church of England as well as Ark. This allows the principal to meet with other CoE headteachers, a different group from the Ark heads.

    The CoE backing allows the school to promote a Christian ethos for all pupils regardless of their home religion. All pupils attend assemblies with a Christian theme, all are members of houses named after one or other of St Paul's letters in the New Testament. The Christian ethos provides pupils with the moral tools they all need.

This is an excellent and popular school which lifted exam results for disadvantaged pupils.

Chapter 12

West London Free School, Hammersmith, London

A pioneering free school

West London Free School (WLFS) was one of the very first free schools, opening in Hammersmith in 2011 and founded by a group of parents including the journalist Toby Young. In 2016 their first GCSE results put them ahead of most state schools with 77% obtaining five or more GCSEs grade A*–C including English and maths, 38% of GCSEs graded A*/A. Their Progress 8 measure was 1.14.

This is a great achievement because in the first year of a free school it is pretty difficult to attract good applicants and hard to find good teachers. Free schools know that they will be judged by their first set of exam results, but it is unfair.

The school had three headteachers in its first five years – not an uncommon issue with free schools. The pool of good people who want to start a school from scratch is small. The ethos and goals of the school have all been determined in advance of opening by the founders and, given the amount of effort it takes to set up a free school, they are bound to be quite demanding.

There are 120 in a year group with a maximum class size of 24. Two-thirds of the 2016 Year 11 stayed on into the sixth form where they were joined by 40 new pupils.

When we visited the school we were struck by a number of quite distinctive characteristics. The website states:

Key Characteristics

- *High aspirations, with a firm emphasis on academic attainment*
- *A classical curriculum, including compulsory Latin up to the age of 14*
- *Strong discipline*
- *Small class sizes*
- *A competitive atmosphere, particularly when it comes to Games*
- *Outstanding pastoral care*

- *Active parental and community involvement*
- *Specialising in Music*
- *A broad range of extracurricular activities*

Objectives

- *Encourage all children to be confident, hard-working and ambitious, regardless of background*
- *Transmit a core body of knowledge to all pupils*
- *100% of pupils pass at least 8 GCSEs at grade C/4 or above, including maths, English, English Literature, at least two Sciences and a Foreign Language*
- *Get as many pupils as possible to stay on in the Sixth Form and do a sufficiently demanding course of Sixth Form study to progress to a good university or embark on a good career*
- *Attract and retain outstanding teachers*

So the key distinctive elements of WLFS are:

1. Classical liberal curriculum

There is a deliberate attempt to copy the curriculum of independent schools with an emphasis on the arts and humanities, especially history. This makes a refreshing change from the huge number of state schools whose declared specialism is science and technology. Latin is compulsory up to age 14.

They call this a 'classical liberal education' and it has several elements:

- academic subjects
- ancient and modern languages
- mathematics
- English literature
- consideration of 'the big questions facing mankind', such as nuclear weapons, radicalisation, ISIS.
- reading books
- music and art

The website explains:

'By a classical liberal education we mean a rigorous and extensive knowledge-based education that draws its material and methods from the best and most important work in both the humanities and the sciences. The aim of such an education is not primarily to prepare pupils for a job or career. It is more to transform their minds so that they are

able to make reasonable and informed judgments and engage fruitfully in conversation and debate – not just about contemporary issues, but also about the universal questions that have been troubling mankind throughout history. We want children to leave our school with the confidence that comes from possessing a store of essential knowledge and the skills to use it. We believe that independence of mind, not compliance with socio-economic expectations, is the goal of a good education.

We believe the main focus of our curriculum should be on that common body of knowledge that, until recently, all schools were expected to teach. This is the background knowledge taken for granted by writers who address the intellectually engaged layman – the shared frames of reference for public discourse in modern liberal democracies. Sometimes referred to as "intellectual capital", at other times as "cultural literacy", this storehouse of general knowledge will enable all our pupils to grow to their full stature. Passing on this knowledge, as well as the ability to use it wisely, is what we mean by a classical liberal education.'

The founders believe that independent schools offer something most state schools don't and part of that is a 'liberal curriculum'. They were especially proud of the fact that for September 2016 12 pupils had chosen medieval history A-level and 14 Latin. At GCSE in 2016 45 took Latin and a remarkable 55 took music. Eight took Ancient Greek as an extra subject.

Music is important to them. They appoint 12 music scholars each year some of whom have no instrumental grades. 40% of the pupils at WLFS learn a musical instrument and there are 24 peripatetic teachers. Fifty-seven per cent of pupils taking music GCSE in 2016 were graded A*or A.

2. Knowledge not skills

Following E D Hirsch (page 143), WLFS believes in traditional teaching methods and the power of simply knowing things – facts rather than 'skills' – because the basis of all understanding is knowing things. You can't speak French unless you know a lot of vocabulary and grammar. You can't appreciate history unless you have a sound grasp of dates, people and events.

Here, for example, is the Key Stage 3 Art syllabus for WLFS:

- *Egyptian Art – Sculpture and Design*
- *Ancient Greece and the Idealized Form, Classical Art – Drawing, Proportion, Colour, Symbolism and Design*
- *Medieval Western Europe – Design, Drawing and Multimedia*
- *James Rizzi, Introduction to Pop Art – Drawing, Designs, Painting, Written Reflection*

- *Gothic Art and Architecture – Design, Drawing, Multimedia*
- *Byzantine Art, Mosaic Design – Design and Multimedia*
- *Jim Dine, Series and Concept Painting – Design, Painting, Observation*
- *Arts and Crafts – Pattern Design, Tessellation – Design*
- *Impressionism and Pointillism, Colour Wheel and Optical Mixing*
- *Post-Impressionism, Rodin – Design and Sculpture*
- *Japan, Carp Kites – Multimedia*
- *Portraits Through the Ages From Holbein*

A central aim of the school is that most pupils will go to a good university.

The syllabus taught at WLFS in each subject is more demanding than that taught in most schools. As the revision booklets are online you can see this for yourself: **www.wlfs.org/docs/YR_8.pdf**

Here is the content of the Year 8 Revision Guide for the summer 2016 exams:

a. *Henry VIII*

    i. *What was the young Henry VIII like as King?*

    ii. *Why did England 'break with Rome' in 1534?*

    iii. *What happened during the 'English Reformation'?*

    iv. *How successful was the reign of Henry VIII?*

b. *Mary I, Elizabeth I and James I*

    i. *Does Mary I deserve to be nicknamed 'Bloody Mary'?*

    ii. *What decisions did Elizabeth I have to make after she became Queen?*

    iii. *Why did England win the Spanish Armada?*

    iv. *Why did the Gunpowder Plotters want to blow up Parliament?*

c. *The English Civil War*

    i. *What mistakes did Charles I make as King?*

    ii. *Why did Civil War break out in 1642?*

    iii. *Why did Parliament win the English Civil War?*

    iv. *Why was Charles I tried for treason and executed?*

d. *The Commonwealth and the Restoration*

    i. *What was life like in Cromwell's Commonwealth?*

    ii. *Should Charles II be remembered as the 'Merry Monarch'?*

    iii. How did the Great Fire of 1666 change London?

    iv. What was life like in Restoration England?

  e. The Georgians

    i. Why was George I made King of England in 1714?

    ii. Was Robert Walpole England's first Prime Minister?

    iii. How were the Jacobites defeated in 1745?

    iv. What was life like in Georgian England?

Chronology

You are not expected to memorise each of these dates, but you should be able to place the events in order of chronology.

1509 Henry VIII crowned King of England

1513 Henry VIII's first invasion of France

1517 Martin Luther's nails his 95 theses to the door in Wittenberg

1520 The Field of the Cloth of Gold

1533 Henry VIII marries Anne Boleyn

1534 The Act of Supremacy starts the English Reformation

1536 The start of the Dissolution of the Monasteries

1547 Edward I becomes King

1553 Mary I becomes Queen

1558 Elizabeth I becomes Queen

1570 A Papal Bull is passed against Elizabeth I by the Pope

1580 Francis Drake returns from circumnavigating the world

1587 Mary Queen of Scots is beheaded

1588 England beats the Spanish Armada

1603 James I becomes King of England and Scotland

1605 The Gunpowder Plot to blow up Parliament is discovered

1625 Charles I becomes King of England

1629 The start of the eleven years tyranny 1

640 Charles I recalls Parliament after war breaks out in Scotland

1642 The English Civil War breaks out 1645 The Battle of Naseby

1646 Charles I surrenders to the Scots

1648 Parliament wins the second Civil War

1649 Trial and execution of Charles I

1650 Oliver Cromwell's Ireland campaign

1653 Cromwell becomes 'Lord Protector'

1658 Death of Oliver Cromwell

1660 The Monarchy is restored and Charles II becomes King

1665 Outbreak of the Great Plague in London.

1666 The Great Fire of London

1670 Charles II agrees to the Treaty of Dover with France

1685 James II becomes King of England 1688 The Glorious Revolution

1714 The Hanoverian Succession

1721 Robert Walpole becomes the 'Prime Minister'

1745 The Final Jacobite Uprising

So you can see that they follow the outlines of the National Curriculum for KS3 but at a more demanding level.

The books they use are stretching and many are written by staff. There are two sets of books for each class – one for the classroom and one for home in years 10 and 11 – and this costs an extra £50,000*pa*.

There is 25 minutes of silent writing in each lesson so the atmosphere is very quiet.

There are frequent tests and exams. All internal exams are externally moderated by experts – the questions set, the marking and the grading.

So the focus is on knowledge, teaching and testing followed by reteaching. There is an emphasis on knowing detail and on extended writing.

3. No one is allowed to fall behind

Pupils are carefully monitored. The motto is 'be tough to be kind'.

Homework must be done and if it is not then the pupil goes straight into detention that same day. Detention is taken by a member of the senior management. This is a good system: all pupils, teachers and parents are clear about the consequences of failure to complete homework and the fact that it does not require the classroom teachers to give up their time is sensible.

If a pupil is struggling they will be given help. The excellent Lindsey Johns was brought in to help motivate black boys.

There are routine low-stakes tests and quizzes.

At the end of term pupils are given a progress and attainment score.

4. Looking after staff

There is a close focus on the quality of lessons with an open door culture. There is an optional Friday breakfast meeting and four-fifths of staff come. New staff receive two and a half hours of training a week. Staff are protected from over-work ... all are gone by 5pm and all cover is done by senior staff.

5. The shape of the curriculum is as follows:

Key Stage 3

Subject	Periods per week
English	4
Maths	4
Science	4
Art	1
Classics	2
Divinity	2
Geography	2
History	2
MFL	4
Music	2
PE	1
Games	2
Total	**30**

Key Stage 4

At Key Stage 4 the subjects are biology, chemistry, physics, English language, English literature, maths, one language, one of history or geography and two others chosen from French, German, Latin, Spanish, history, geography, art, music, classical civilisation, PE, RS.

Sport is taken seriously. On the website it states:

The PE department runs a "No Note" policy. The Department considers that if pupils are fit for school they are fit for sport. Although certain injuries and illnesses may make it impossible for a pupil to fully take part in lessons, all pupils are expected to change for the lesson and will be given suitable activities to do; this could include coaching, umpiring/refereeing, taking part in a limited way or working with a different group on an appropriate activity.

All pupils are grouped into houses for the purposes of competitions, again something taken from independent schools.

Key Stage 5

In Year 12 students choose **four** A-level subjects to study and **one** enrichment option. This gives students greater breadth in Year 12. Towards the end of Year 12 students will decide which three subjects to pursue to A-level; where appropriate students will be able to continue with four A-levels in Year 13.

The following subjects are available as A-level courses:

- Biology
- Chemistry
- Classical Civilisation
- Physics
- Mathematics
- Further Mathematics
- English Literature
- English Language
- French
- Spanish
- Latin
- History
- Geography
- Economics
- Government and Politics
- Religious studies
- Music
- Computer science
- Fine Art
- Physical Education

In addition, students select one of the following subjects as an 'enrichment' option.

- Computing
- German
- Ancient Greek
- Extended Project Qualification
- Pre-U global perspectives
- Mandarin

6. Extracurricular activity

Every pupil becomes a member of one of four houses – Athenians, Corinthians, Olympians and Spartans. Houses are organised vertically and contain pupils from each year group. Each house supports a charity and pupils are encouraged to organise fundraising activities throughout the school year.

The house system motivates pupils to engage in a diverse range of activities including sport, music, drama and art competitions, and engenders a healthy spirit of competition.

West London Free School is a pioneering example of a school focused on a knowledge curriculum, high expectations and great exam results. It copies best practice from independent schools and does so well.

Chapter 13

Michaela Community School, Wembley, London

'Work hard, be kind'

When Michaela School in Wembley, north-west London, opened in September 2014 it was one of the most widely anticipated free schools of the Coalition government. The reason for the excitement was that it had been set up by a state school teacher as a reaction to what she described as generally appalling standards across the state sector.

Katharine Birbalsingh's parents came from the West Indies; she herself went to a state school in Canada and in Leamington Spa then Oxford University where she read French and philosophy. She gained attention as an anonymous blogger writing about her experiences teaching at a London secondary school and came to national prominence after she spoke at the 2010 Conservative Party conference about the state of the British education system. After the speech she was asked not to attend her school 'for the rest of the week while senior teachers and governors discuss her position' and she subsequently resigned after being asked to comply with conditions she could not accept. Birbalsingh's novel, *To Miss with Love*, based on her blog, was published in March 2011 and outlines many of the faults she seeks to eradicate in Michaela.

After searching without success for sites in other parts of London Katharine was eventually given the go ahead to open her own (free) school in a converted office block opposite Wembley Park tube station. The school started in 2014 with 120 Year 7 pupils – four classes of 30. It was named Michaela after a former colleague of Katharine's who had died of cancer.

In 2015–16 58% of pupils had been on free school meals at some point in the previous six years and for half English was their second language. .

The school has a number of distinctive characteristics...

1. The passion of the head

Katharine has a point to prove – she wants her school to show that children are capable of much much more than is achieved in most schools. She is highly critical of Ofsted, highly critical of schools which pander to Ofsted ('you lose your heart and soul'). As their website says:

'Staff at Michaela tend to reject all of the accepted wisdoms of the 21st century. This ranges from the way that we teach, how we deal with SEN pupils, our expectations of parents, our zero-tolerance attitude to bad behaviour and our high expectations of professional dress at all times from both pupils and staff.'

A related feature of the school is the sense of urgency. Children only have a limited number of hours in school. Many are already well behind the progress made by pupils at private schools. So no time can be wasted – not a minute of the day.

2. Discipline

Katharine tells prospective parents *'I am the dragon lady. I will always say no'.* They laugh ... but she means it. She requires parents to support her rules.

On the Michaela website information for prospective teachers they say:

'We believe in zero-tolerance. We do not make exceptions. When we say we have high standards, we mean it. If you think it is mean to give a detention when a pupils doesn't have a pen, Michaela isn't the school for you. We hold parents to account as well and insist that they support their children by supporting our rules. This creates a very orderly school where children are safe. It requires staff who are willing to make mountains out of molehills. You need to know how to act appalled over the little stuff.'

Everything about life at Michaela is highly disciplined. Everything – the way pupils speak, the way they walk, the way they sit, the way they eat, the way they read – everything follows clear rules.

On the walls are posters:

How we are polite: STEPS

Sir or miss
Thank you
Excuse me
Please
Smile

How we discuss things: SHAPE

Sentence
Hands down
Articulate
Project
Eye contact

How we listen: SLANT

Sit up straight
Listen
Answer questions
Never interrupt
Track the teacher (make eye contact)

A demerit is given as a corrective reminder if a pupil makes a bad choice, breaks a school rule, or for:

1. *disrupting or interrupting others in lessons (talking or whispering over instructions, explanations, discussions or silent practice)*

2. *misbehaving in corridors (running, wrong side, chatting)*

3. *persistently not tracking, not SLANT-ing or not concentrating*

4. *incorrect uniform or equipment in lessons (no pen, pencil, ruler; loose tie or shirt untucked etc)*

5. *reacting badly to a demerit or instruction (tutting or rolling eyes)*

Misbehaving pupils are given reflection letters to write, parental phone calls and meetings, and self-control mentoring. Persistently disruptive pupils are positioned in every subject at the back of the room on an individual table. Pupils who persistently fail to complete their evening prep are supported with compulsory IXL club, reading club and self-quizzing after school and in lunch break. Persistently late pupils have phone calls and letters home from tutors and senior team, miss half-termly reward events, and parents are called for meetings with the headmistress.

If a pupil brings a mobile phone (or any electronic device) to school it will be confiscated if it is even seen by a teacher – confiscated for the whole term or, if in the final fortnight of a term, confiscated for the following term as well. There are absolutely no exceptions or excuses. As Katharine says 'it's all about the discipline'.

There are two detentions every evening, managed by senior staff; one at 4pm-4.30pm, one at 4.30pm-5pm.

Pupils walk calmly in single file down one side of a corridor with a line in the middle. 'Silence is golden' in the corridors.

Pupils are banned from going into local shops.

3. Rapid progress

In England the school curriculum is divided into five 'Key Stages'. Key Stage 1 is ages 4–7 (years 1, 2 and 3). Key Stage 2 is ages 7–11 (years 4, 5 and 6). Key Stage 3 is pupils aged 11–14, years 7, 8 and 9. Key Stage 4 is GCSE – ages 14–16, years 10 and 11. Key Stage 5 is A-level, ages 16–18, years 12 and 13.

In many English secondary schools Key Stage 3 is wasted time – pupils and teachers tread water until they get to Year 10 when suddenly the pressure is on with the approach of the Year 11 GCSEs. But at Michaela there is so much emphasis on rapid progress in KS3 that many pupils will be at GCSE level by the end of Year 9.

We asked what will happen in years 10 and 11 to pupils who are already prepared for the GCSE. Answer: they will study a far broader curriculum than that required by GCSE. GCSE will examine a subset of what they know.

Rapid progress is achieved in several ways.

First, the focus is on memorising large amounts of 'factual' knowledge. So where a pupil might typically learn 10 new French words a week, at Michaela they would learn 50.

Secondly, pupils who are behind in maths or English will be taken out of other lessons and given intensive tuition until they have caught up. In Year 7, for example, a weak mathematician may receive 11 hours of maths a week.

They will be taught in sets, but the expectation is that all pupils will reach a good level by the end of each year.

Thirdly, the level of discipline is such that pupils are not allowed to be lazy. If a pupil fails to produce homework of a good level, he will be in detention on that day.

Fourthly, the school day is long – 7.55am to 4pm, open to 5pm for those who wish to do homework at school. There are six one-hour lessons a day.

Finally, by having a curriculum which gives priority to subjects which matter most:

The Key Stage 3 curriculum

	Periods per week	
	A typical Academy	Michaela
English	4	5
Maths	4	5
Science	4	4
Art	1	2
Dance	1	0
Drama	1	0
Humanities	4	5
Computing	1	0
Modern languages	2	2
Music	1	2
Personal development	1	0
PE	2	2
Technology	1	0
Enrichment	1	0
Total	28	29

Katharine correctly understands that subjects taught for one period a week are not worth doing – too little progress can be made. She knows that studying a modern language for only two periods a week is also a hapless task.

4. The Knowledge Curriculum

Michaela's strapline is *'Knowledge is Power'*. Katharine was influenced by the writing of E D Hirsch (page 143) and her experiences in the other schools she worked in (*'I came across a 16-year-old boy who had no idea what the Holocaust was'*).

All subjects at Michaela are taught with acquisition of knowledge (as opposed to 'skills') in mind. This is most apparent in art and music. In art pupils were learning facts about the lives and styles of artists (Year 8 pupils could describe and explain all the stages in the artistic evolution of Picasso for example). They spend some time copying the art of famous artists by gridding copies of a picture and transferring it to a similarly gridded blank piece of drawing paper. Techniques of drawing and shading are demonstrated from the front, casting the picture of what is being shown onto a large screen using a visualiser (a camera).

Every pupil is given the key information they need for each subject in 'knowledge organisers'. The organisers for every subject are put in one file, the 'knowledge book'. This is the basis for their subsequent revision.

Michaela believes that pupils must be able to read music, be exposed to a broad and detailed history of music, and understand the theory of music – pitch, scales, rhythm, chords *etc*. They explicitly drill pupils in reading music. They teach music theory up to grade 4 by the end of Year 9. It is a rigorous academic curriculum.

In England pupils are taught things but know little. I sat through eight years of French lessons and failed the O-level; I knew close to nothing. So simply teaching knowledge is not enough ... you have to ensure pupils learn it. Every pupil at Michaela has two exercise books for each subject. One book contains the knowledge they are expected to learn. The other is the book they write in. They learn material by writing it out and then testing themselves by seeing if they can write answers from memory – self-quizzing. Then there are regular tests in class and exams in January and June.

The emphasis on testing at Michaela is very important. There is no point in having a knowledge curriculum if the information is not secure in the pupils' long-term memory. This can only be achieved by regular revision and retesting. School exams are cumulative year on year so in each exam you must revise everything you have done up to that point.

Because the pupils remember what they have learnt, every teacher knows exactly what every child has in their memory from previous years. This is incredibly helpful because it means they can build on that knowledge with confidence.

5. Very high expectations

Teachers are expected to teach to a high level, especially in terms of knowledge. The Year 8 French class I observed was above GCSE standard (these were 12-year-olds). ALL pupils are expected to do well so there will be no excuses for pupils with labels such as dyslexia. Of course pupils DO have special needs, but these must never be allowed to lower expectations. Weaker pupils simply need more practice and more rigour.

Existing school textbooks are well below the expected standard so every subject has had to write their own texts.

All pupils will do up to two hours' homework a night. Homework is mainly about revision. So that might mean:

- 30 minutes on the IXL website doing maths quizzes or on Quizlet (a free website) for modern languages

- 30 minutes self-quizzing on a set page of the knowledge organiser. This will be followed by a test on that work the following day. There is a printed timetable of self-testing topics so if a child is away from school they know exactly what they have to learn during their absence.
- 30 minutes reading
- 30 minutes of English vocabulary work

Teachers check pupils' practice books and quizzes every week and set a detention if the self-quizzing is not complete.

All pupils are expected to have a library book out at all times.

Pupils are expected to go to university.

6. Teaching methods

'We believe in standing at the front of the class and teaching. We do not believe in learning styles. We do not believe in personalisation or differentiation in the way that most schools do. We do not believe in target-setting or prioritising skills. If you believe in these things, Michaela isn't the school for you.

We believe in feeding back to pupils from the front because pupils tend to make the same mistakes. We believe in rows of desks and learning things by heart. We would never do group work at Michaela.'

New teachers have to be trained in the Michaela way. Katharine prefers teachers who have not been trained previously.'

So all teachers instruct from the front of the class.

No group work is permitted (see page 87).

Powerpoint is banned (see page 89). ICT is felt to be of limited value.

Little work is marked by teachers in the evening because it is felt that this is a misuse of their limited time. Essays are given a mark but no comment. Instead the teacher makes a list of common errors and uses these for teaching in the next lesson. Michaela is right that this is more effective than writing comments – and it frees the teachers up in the evenings.

'So we are guided by a philosophy of simplicity that aims for maximum impact on pupil learning with minimal overload on workload for staff. We reduce burnout applying this effort-to-impact ratio to everything we do. For example, our slimmed-down marking, centralized homework, minimal display policies minimise work. We use oral feedback to reduce workload. Our sky-high standards on strict discipline reduce stressful confrontations.'

Drill is used in all subjects. Discovery-based learning is simply too slow and too ineffective.

Pupils' work is not on display because takes too much of the teachers' time for limited effect.

In the school-made textbooks all lines of text have letters down the margin (A,B,C *etc*) so pupils can be directed quickly to any line. All pupils have a Perspex ruler which they use for reading, running down line by line. If the teacher reads text aloud pupils follow using the ruler. In this way all pupils follow the text closely. If the teacher comes to a difficult word the teacher pauses and says 'I say you say' and then repeats the word followed by the whole class repeating the word. Pupils build up tremendous vocabularies.

Michaela believes in the motivating power of competition. Daily rankings of the pupils' performance in the IXL maths homework are published. League tables are published showing performance in the daily quizzes. Demerits and merit lists are published.

7. 'How we do things': the Michaela way

Pupils have to be taught how to operate the Michaela way of doing things. This is why they have a seven-day bootcamp before the start of Year 7. Teachers have to teach in a particular way at Michaela and so all have to be trained carefully.

Lunchtime lasts exactly 30 minutes. All pupils must eat the school lunch. Children arrive and sit at tables for six pupils and one or two adults ('family lunch'). The pupils are numbered one to six and each has a job. Pupil 1 collects the main course. Pupil 2 clears the main course. Pupil 3 pours water into beakers *etc*. But before the meal begins all will stand and recite a poem or piece of prose that has been learnt beforehand such as Kipling's *If* or William Henley's *Invictus*:

It matters not how strait the gate,
How charged with punishments the scroll,
I am the master of my fate:
I am the captain of my soul

Pupil 1 starts the serving. But a teacher appears and addresses the whole room. All pupils raise their hands and stop speaking. The teacher announces the topic of conversation for the next few minutes ... '*today we are going to try to think of four ways in which we can be kind to other people*' ... the directed discussion then begins. Five minutes later the teacher is there again, announcing the next topic, and so on.

As the meal ends the teacher calls for 'appreciations'. Most pupils raise a hand. One child is chosen ... *'I would like to give an appreciation to Miss Smith for marking my long essay and returning it to me within a day. Appreciation for Miss Smith!'* All the pupils clap twice. Then the next child stands up *'I would like to give an appreciation to Mr Lenon on my table for coming to visit us today. Appreciation for Mr Lenon. Clap clap.'*

So in these ways the pupils are learning how to have conversations, how to be polite, how to express gratitude. They are learning teamwork. Learning how to speak well is a central task of the school.

Pupils from wealthier backgrounds learn from their families how to speak well, how to read around a subject, how to be ambitious. Michaela aims to ensure their pupils have the same advantages and regularly references private schools. The board outside the school spells it out: *'Michaela Community School...Private School Ethos...No Fees.'*

8. Protecting staff time

Michaela expects a lot from its teachers so it takes the trouble to cut out those things which don't work or where the benefits are small: performance-related pay, individual lesson plans, lockers, homework collection and marking, photocopying worksheets, unnecessary ICT.

9. Cultural experience

Pupils are taken to the National Gallery, the Greenwich Observatory, Natural History Museum, British Museum *etc*. The great thing is that they have been taught a lot about what they are going to see before the trip so the level of engagement is much higher.

10. Kindness

Because behaviour is so good bullying is very rare, something the children emphasise as the main difference between Michaela and their previous school. Pupils who cannot speak well are able to make speeches in front of their whole year group without fear of being laughed at or teased.

No physical contact between pupils is allowed during the 30-minute free time they might have at lunch.

So should all schools be like Michaela?

Katharine was influenced by schools which came before Michaela – by charter schools in America, by Mossbourne, Dixons Trinity and King Solomon's Academy. So she is not alone in doing things the way she does. Arguably her very tough approach is most suited to disadvantaged pupils who lack the middle-class cultural background that Michaela is compensating for. The approach will be tested as the school becomes larger and the pupils older, but for the moment it is an example of the benefits of the free school policy.

For more information see: Birbalsingh, K (ed), 2016, *Battle Hymn of the Tiger Teachers; the Michaela Way.*

Chapter 14

St Mary Magdalene Academy, London N7

Incredible progress in a short time

When we visited this secondary school it had 1200 pupils and 67% had been on free school meals at some point in the previous six years. The school is an Academy sponsored by the London Diocese of the Church of England. They say that their sponsor does not drive them in any direction but it helpfully arranges meetings with other Diocese schools to share ideas. It is a light-touch sponsor.

The Academy runs a primary school and a special needs school nearby but we just visited the secondary school.

The proportion gaining five or more GCSEs graded A*–C including both English and maths had risen from 46% in 2012 to 76% in 2016 – making it one of the fastest improving schools in England.

How did this happen?

1. The senior leaders have a strong sense of moral purpose

All things are done on the basis of what is best for the children. For example, they made changes to the curriculum mid-year because they felt this would benefit the pupils even though it meant a lot more work for staff.

2. Keeping it simple

They focus on 'plan-teach-mark'. Plan good lessons, teach well, feed back to the pupils effectively. Cut out all the rest such as enrichment days. The Senior Leadership Team focus on teaching and learning, walking the school three times a day looking at lessons, marking and the quality of exercise books.

Senior and middle leaders had their multiple responsibilities cut so they each have just one clear task.

Teachers are paid £2500 above the norm and the senior leadership team is kept small.

3. Collecting very regular and reliable data on pupil progress

If a department predicts badly then one person in that department has to become an examiner.

The Head of Department has to check the predictions of his staff and then hand a PAPER copy to the head, every month in Year 11. This is psychologically more emphatic than simply entering data on a computer. The evidence for the prediction then has to be given.

4. The Key Stage 4 'pastoral group'

The school identifies the 25 Year 11 pupils who will fail without help but might well pass with help.

These children are required to be in school 7.30am–5pm instead of 8.45–3.30pm. This costs the school £5000 per child each year in extra staff pay. Parents are told 'if you don't do this your child will fail'. This has proved to be true, which gives the scheme credibility. They receive extra careers advice in order to try and generate aspiration. They are taught by the heads of English and maths who give them extra lessons and rigorous testing. In addition they have a learning mentor who pushes them hard.

5. Ensuring good behaviour

The school has a Pupil Referral Unit (the St David's Centre) across the road where pupils who cannot behave are sent. There are three stages:

Stage 1 – Nine weeks intensive care. Very structured. Get them to reflect on the causes of their misbehaviour. Class of 12 for Years 7–8, class of eight for Year 9.

Stage 2 – If no success they have one year, Year 9, in the PRU.

Stage 3 – Permanent exclusion (rare).

The school is quite strict but *'Generally we are not a silent or coercive environment. We want them to choose to behave.'*

6. The Inspire Programme to raise aspirations and challenge the more able

This includes masterclasses, Oxbridge lessons, Mandarin (the school is a Confucius Classroom), Latin, university summer school and competitions.

Deloittes run a great scheme where pupils join in debates and discussions. They read *The Week* magazine and discuss it. They run personality workshops, leadership development schemes, they teach interview skills and CV writing, they give career mentoring and motivational talks.

This is a school with large numbers on free school meals which has made tremendous progress in a short time.

Chapter 15

Dixons Kings Academy, Bradford

Another school showing rapid improvement in a short time

Dixons Kings is another good example of a rapidly improving school. It was started as Kings Science Academy in 2011 in the first wave of free schools; in 2013 it was graded 'requires improvement' by Ofsted and the founding principal was later convicted of fraud. Following this bad start the school was adopted in January 2015 by the Dixons Academy Trust with a new head, Neil Miley.

The Dixons Academies Trust runs eight schools in Bradford. The original sponsor, Lord Kalms, who built the Dixons Stores Group, still takes an interest in the schools, and the MAT retains the name.

Neil Miley came from Dixons Allerton Academy where he taught maths and was vice-principal. In 2016 Kings achieved a GCSE Progress 8 score of 0.47 compared to a Bradford-wide average of 0.15. It moved within 18 months from being a troubled school to one which attracts more than 700 applicants a year for 180 places. In 2017 it was graded 'outstanding' by Ofsted.

How did he do it?

1. Establishing good discipline

This, Neil says, comes first. If discipline is good, teachers can teach. They don't have to waste time dealing with problems in the classroom.

Six simple rules were laid out:

- you must be on time for school and for every lesson
- you must have the right books and equipment for every lesson
- you must complete your homework
- you must be on-task in all lessons
- you must speak politely to people
- you must dress smartly

There are no excuses. If you break one of these six rules you will do a detention for 30 minutes after school that same day. In his first term Neil saw the number of pupils arriving late to school fall from 150 to 7. All staff are trained to enforce the six rules consistently.

Neil has never had to permanently exclude a pupil, even in his first term.

2. The school has high expectations of all pupils

Forty-three per cent have been or are on free school meals and they will need good GCSEs if they are to escape disadvantage. Because the school has a comprehensive intake, the emphasis is on *progress* as opposed to specific GCSE grades. Taking the Key Stage 2 results from their last year at primary school as the baseline, every pupil's progress is measured every six or seven weeks, culminating in a Progress 8 score (see page 48). Pupils wear a lanyard which gives their progress score for each subject based on their last assessment, together with an overall progress measure. This acts as a constant reminder to them of the fact that it is GOOD PROGRESS in each subject that matters.

In addition, around the school are noticeboards on which are the pictures, names and scores of pupils who have made most progress in the previous 12 weeks.

On the doors of classrooms are the pictures and scores of those pupils who left last year with the highest progress scores.

Dixons Kings makes good use of Progress 8!

3. Interventions

Of course not all pupils work hard all the time and may fall behind due to a variety of reasons. Pupils are tested every six weeks and if a pupil is behind in any subject an intervention plan will be produced which summarises the areas of knowledge where the pupil is weak and what the teacher intends to do about it. For some this might just mean addressing the issue in class. For others it will mean extra lessons at the end of the school day.

4. A focus on good teaching.

Teachers are told that they are only expected to do two things – teach well and mark the pupils' books. The senior management team walk the corridors all day long and *every lesson is visited every day*. Photographs of good practice are taken and passed on.

In addition every teacher, including the Principal, has a 'coach' who observes them for 5–10 minutes every week and gives them one piece of advice about something they could do better.

Every class is taught according to detailed schemes of work which are created by the teachers in-house (an account of what is being taught when, what resources are available, how pupils are assessed). This means that if a teacher is absent or a new teacher arrives it is entirely clear what the pupils should know and what they are being taught next.

All lessons follow the same pattern in terms of how they start and how they finish.

Work is marked according to a clear system. Stickers are produced for each piece of work giving tips about how to make answers even better.

Teachers are appraised annually and only move up the pay scale if they reach pre-determined targets.

5. Quality assurance

The school regularly inspects the culture of the place (availability of equipment, presentation of work, classroom environment *etc*) and the quality of learning (work books, progress, the quality of teacher feedback *etc*). They do this by assigning each member of the senior management team to look at a specific area every week, such as 'the culture of Year 8' or 'the quality of learning in music'. This is done according to a detailed plan so no area of school life is missed.

6. A keen sense of competition with other schools

Neil wants his school to be the best (he is on the way to achieving that aim). He wants his pupils to know they are at an excellent school. He wants the parents to trust the school's thoughts about their children. Competition with other schools, motivation to be the best, drives the Academy.

7. Support from the Multi-Academy Trust

The Dixons MAT handles all the human resources and financial aspects of the school. More importantly, they provide support when the school needs it. For example, if the geography department appears weak the school can draw on the expertise of the strongest geography department in the MAT for advice.

All pupils in the Dixons secondary schools take the same end-of-year exams in maths, English and science. This allows them to compare progress with each other.

The Dixons schools work together as a National Training School to train teachers. They award teacher qualifications in partnership with Leeds University.

8. Long school day

The school day starts at 8am and finishes at 3.30pm. There are 28 hour-long taught lessons, more than the national average of 25. This is followed by 2–3 hours of homework a night.

9. Focus on the EBacc

The EBacc performance measure (see page 127) was introduced by the DfE because of concerns that disadvantaged pupils in some schools were taking 'easy' subjects which made it harder for them to gain a place at a good university. Neil Miley completely agrees with this reasoning and many pupils take GCSEs in English, maths, sciences, RE, history or geography, Spanish and three other subjects. In 2016, 43% of pupils gained the EBacc compared to a national average of 22.8%.

10. Simplicity and clarity

Neil believes in clear and simple rules, clear and simple systems: *'if you can't fit something onto one sheet of paper we don't do it'.* Only in this way can every child, every teacher and every parent know exactly what the school expects of them.

11. Using parents

In the week I visited, the Principal had seen every parent of every Year 11 student whose progress was unsatisfactory. In addition the school had run a 'how to help your child revise' course for all Year 11 parents.

This is a great school on an upward curve. Neil summarises the success of the school in three words – *rigour, clarity and determination.*

Chapter 16

Tauheedul Islam Boys' High School, Blackburn

Outstanding progress scores

Blackburn is a town of 105,000 people 20 miles north of Manchester. It grew as a textile manufacturing centre, like many towns in Lancashire. The industry attracted immigrants from Pakistan in the 1960s (over 30% of the population are from ethnic minorities) but textiles collapsed soon after in the wake of international competition.

Given this background it is astonishing that in 2016 Tauheedul Islamic Boys' High School was amongst the highest achieving schools in England in terms of progress from Year 6 to GCSEs in Year 11. Their Progress 8 measure was 1.16 so pupils made more progress than almost any other school in England.

TIBHS is run by the Tauheedul Education Trust which had 14 schools at the time of writing: five in Lancashire, two in Greater Manchester, one in West Yorkshire, three in the West Midlands and three in London. 'Tauheedul' means 'oneness' and refers to both the common purpose of the schools and the notion of one community. Some of these schools are faith-based, some are not, some are primary, some secondary. The trust is run by Mufti Hamid Patel who was once the principal of the Tauheedul Islamic Girls' High School, the first school in the group.

TIBHS is an 11–16 free school and it opened in 2012. All the pupils, 120 a year, are Muslim boys: priority is given to them in the admissions code and formal lessons end at 12 noon on Fridays so that pupils may observe this religious day. On other days the school day is operates 8am to 3pm.

Twenty per cent of the pupils have been on free school meals at some point in the past six years and 80% have English as a second language. No pupils have been permanently excluded in the past three years.

To me the interesting characteristics of this school were:

1. High expectations

All schools say they have high expectations but this school translates the aspiration into firm actions. Every week every middle leader (heads of subjects) comes to a meeting with other middle leaders and the senior management team. They consider the progress of all the pupils they teach relative to the targets set by the Principal – over 90% A*–C/9 to 4 at GCSE. If a head of subject expresses doubt about a group or individual boys an action plan is devised to push them to a higher level. The teachers of those pupils then meet with the Principal (Mubaaruck Ibrahim) *every day* to monitor progress with the plan.

The Principal achieved outstanding standards in the previous schools where he was a head so when a teacher tells him that a group are going to do badly he can say, with good reason, that he knows the target grades *can* be achieved.

If a group needs extra teaching they will be required to come back after school for 2–3 hours or come in on a Friday afternoon, or on Saturday or Sunday for extra lessons in blocks of 2–3 hours; groups as small as five or six can make great progress in these times. *Teachers are not paid more for this extra work.*

If a boy is lazy his parents are called in and parents are taught how they can help their sons.

If homework is not complete a boy will do two hours' detention that same day.

2. Regular testing

All pupils take a formal exam every six weeks in all subjects. The MAT employs subject specialists to set or check the standard of the questions being set and the realism of the grading. It is important, if targets are to be reached, that teachers are not too kind in terms of the questions set or too generous in grading. A commercial company has been employed to assist with setting and marking papers to relieve some of the pressures on teaching staff. Pupils are put in rank orders, out of 120, for each subject.

3. Traditional teaching methods

In some schools, the Principal said, teachers 'sing and dance', have lessons graded 'outstanding', yet pupils learn little. A very good observation. At TIBHS pupils face the teacher in rows, teaching is based on acquisition of subject knowledge, little use is made of ICT. In the Trust's primary schools they teach the UK Core Knowledge Sequence in English, maths, science, history and geography based on the ideas of E D Hirsch (see page 143).

4. Methods geared to boys

Boys require a different approach to girls. Girls tend to want to please the teacher and work hard. Boys tend to be lazy and overly optimistic about the quality of their work. They therefore have to be monitored carefully and work to clear structures and routines. They cannot be trusted to complete coursework in time.

There is also a strong feeling that boys need ways of releasing pent-up energy so in addition to timetabled sport the school runs clubs in such things as boxing, martial arts, fencing and riding. At the weekends boys whose work is good are taken on trips such as go-karting and paintballing.

5. An academic curriculum

The Tauheedul Trust believes in teaching traditional subjects. 90% of the GCSE curriculum is determined by the Trust: maths, English language and literature, sciences, ICT, RE, history or geography, French or Arabic (no, they do not speak Arabic at home). This is why TIBHS does so well in the DfE EBacc measure: 72% of pupils achieved the EBacc in 2016 compared to a national average of 23%. Optional subjects are available in the other 10% of time – art, food tech, business, PE or citizenship.

They do not offer music GCSE.

6. They all take several GCSEs early

Year 10 take 3–5 GCSEs a year early in RE, ICT, core science, French, Arabic. They do not resit. Whether the boys do well or less well, the early sittings means they are motivated to work hard in Year 11.

7. Support from and control by the MAT

The MAT determines the schemes of work for every subject in every school. These are written by subject experts in consultation with the middle leaders, but in the end just one set of schemes of work emerges to apply across all schools.

The MAT provides subject experts to help train and monitor staff.

The MAT runs a Teaching School, the Tauheedul College for Teaching and Leadership, and helps train potential teachers.

The MAT offers professional development opportunities to all the staff, including NPQ training for middle leaders and potential heads. They employ many teaching assistants who are then trained to become teachers with Qualified Teacher status.

All staff are encouraged to take an MA.

There is a 'Trust way' of doing everything.

8. The leadership specialism

Most secondary schools have a specialism like science or the arts. The specialism of all the Tauheedul Education Trust schools is leadership. Part of that is civic leadership and all Year 11s spend an afternoon a week on a placement in an old people's home, primary school or charity shop.

9. A faith school

This is a school for Muslims. The Trust argues that residential segregation means that the school would be largely Muslim in any case, and indeed some of the local Church of England primary schools are 100% Muslim pupils. 70% of Tauheedul's staff are Muslim.

They know they can be criticised for the limited mixing between their pupils and those of other faiths and ethnicities, but of course faith schools are permitted for other religions – Church of England, Catholic and Jewish schools for example.

This school is transforming the prospects for Muslim boys in a disadvantaged area.

Chapter 17

London Academy of Excellence, Newham, London

An outstanding sixth-form Academy

The LAE was the first sixth form free school set up under the 2010–2015 Coalition's free school programme. It has attracted a great deal of media attention, partly because it was the first free school to get public exam results, partly because of its links with Eton.

The idea for the school originated in 2006 on a bus in China. Joan Deslandes, head of Kingsford Community School in Newham, East London, found herself sitting next to Richard Cairns, head of Brighton College – a private school. They were both on a Confucius Schools trip to China for heads of schools keen to teach Mandarin.

Joan's school is an 11–16 comprehensive which gets excellent GCSE results. She told Richard that her best pupils had no really good sixth form to go to in Newham. Richard offered her some sixth form scholarship places at Brighton College – and so the connection began.

In 2010 the Conservative/Lib Dem coalition government was elected and Michael Gove launched the free schools programme, based on the success of free schools in Sweden and similar Charter Schools in the USA. Parents or teachers could apply to the Department for Education for funding to start a new school where one was needed – either because of a local shortage of places or a shortage of schools with good results.

The application for the new school was submitted in 2011 and permission to go ahead was received in November 2011 – for a September 2012 start. The deputy head of Brighton College, Simon Smith, and the bursar of Brighton, Paul Westbrook, were appointed to do the work required to start the Academy.

LAE has a number of distinctive characteristics:

1. It is backed by several independent schools

At the time of writing these were:

Brighton College, which supports the school by providing the services of its bursar and backing for geography and economics A-levels.

Caterham School, which supports modern languages.

Eton College, which supports English, maths, biology and financial management.

Forest School, which supports physics.

Highgate School, which supports chemistry and French.

University College School, Hampstead, which supports history.

Francis Holland, which supports psychology.

Putney High, which supports philosophy and ethics.

The reason the Academy wanted these partnerships was that, in the early years, many of the staff were young and inexperienced. It was obviously good to be able to draw on the resources and experience of successful teachers in other schools.

The degree of involvement of the partner schools has ranged from supplying a full-time teacher paid by the partner school to occasional visits by the partner teachers across the year.

2. A focus on hard subjects

We know that one reason bright pupils do not get into the best universities is that they do A-level subjects which are unattractive to high tariff institutions. The only subjects taught at LAE are maths, chemistry, physics, biology, French, Spanish, Mandarin, geography, history, philosophy and ethics, economics, psychology and the Extended Project Qualification.

3. Academically ambitious

LAE set out from the start to improve the A-level results in the borough and to send many more students to Oxford, Cambridge and Russell Group universities from the area than had been the norm. In the first two years the minimum entry requirement was five B grades at GCSE – a modest level which reflected uncertainty about the number of applicants the Academy might receive. The minimum entry requirement is now five A/7 grades. The school is academically elitist – it aims to help the brightest in the borough achieve their potential. Pupils with five or more A*s/8s at GCSE are awarded an entrance scholarship which gives them status as well as some money.

4. Small size

The Academy takes 220 students a year and has a total size of about 440. This was regarded as the minimum number to support the A-level subjects on offer but the maximum size for a new, untested school.

5. Sponsorship by HSBC

HSBC headquarters are only a short distance from the school, in Canary Wharf. They generously allowed the school to hold open days in their offices before September 2012, when there was no school building. They have provided financial assistance ever since.

How successful has LAE been?

The school opened in September 2012 so at the time of writing has been operating for four years.

1. Demand

In advance of the first year there were 400 applicants for 200 places. This rose to 2100 for the 2015 entry and over 3000 for 2017 entry.

2. Exam results

In the first year of A-level results (2014) 39% of the cohort secured AAB grades or better in at least two facilitating subjects. This achievement put it top of the Sixth Form College League tables on that measure and they won the Sunday Times UK Sixth Form College of the Year Award.

In 2016 A-level pupils gained 86% A*-B grades and a value-added score of 0.56, a figure that made LAE amongst the most successful schools in the country.

3. University entry

In 2012 two students from the whole of Newham went to Oxford and Cambridge. In 2017, 20 pupils at LAE gained offers from Oxford and Cambridge – higher than most other schools in England.

In 2012, the year LAE began, the whole borough of Newham sent 80 pupils to Russell Group universities. In 2016, 165 LAE pupils held at least one Russell Group offer.

4. Outstanding teachers

Over one-third of the teachers have degrees from Oxford and Cambridge. Another third have first class degrees from Russell Group universities.

5. Social mobility

Seventy-five per cent of LAE sixth formers will be the first in their families to go to university. Many speak a language other than English at home. Most pupils come from Newham and Tower Hamlets, two of the most deprived boroughs in England; 93% of the school-age pupils of Newham and 89% in Tower Hamlets come from ethnic minorities. Over half the pupils are classified by the DfE as 'disadvantaged'. The school is an engine of social mobility.

6. Raising standards in Newham

Michael Gove always said that free schools should shake things up, should show-up other local schools and inspire them to do better. Since LAE got its first set of results several other sixth form colleges have opened and some 11–16 schools have opened sixth forms.

In 2012, Newham was ranked 11th out of the 33 London boroughs in the percentage of students securing AAB in any A-level. Thanks in part to LAE and the effect it has had on the borough overall, Newham is now ranked third. Sixth formers used to leave Newham to go to Redbridge for A-level study; that flow has now been reversed.

7. Cocurricular provision

Every pupil does at least one sport and one activity session every week. In addition all sixth formers undertake an outreach programme where they visit local 11–16 or primary schools. LAE's lecture programme has attracted speakers such as Professor Lord Winston, Lord Butler and Matthew Barzun, US Ambassador to the UK. All pupils take the LAE Diploma (page 145) which places extracurricular education within a framework of the school's core values.

8. Inspiring others

Once LAE was underway others came to visit the Academy and learn from its success. Several have copied aspects of the school, not least the King's College Maths School and Harris Westminster Sixth Form (supported by the independent Westminster School). In 2017 a second LAE opened in Tottenham, sponsored by Highgate School and Tottenham Hotspur Football Club.

Problems LAE has faced

1. Financial

The Academy receives £5500 a year per pupil but spends £7000. The shortfall is covered by a generous grant from HSBC. LAE is trying to offer the same level of education as that provided by independent schools but the average independent day school in London charges parents £16,000 a year.

2. The start-up

The school was given the green light only 10 months before it was due to open. In that time they had to find a suitable building and convert it into classrooms. The building they identified was former Newham Council offices close to Stratford tube station but the work was not completed in time, so in the first term some lessons were held in Newham town hall.

Many new schools start with 25 or 50 pupils. Because LAE was a sixth form and had to offer a range of A-levels the minimum viable size in term one was 200. The school had no track record and no building to look at so inevitably the quality of the first cohort was relatively weak.

3. Ofsted

Call them naïve but it wasn't until the end of their first year that the governors and senior leaders realised what an Ofsted inspection required. They had all come from independent schools and had a good grasp of Independent School Inspectorate's requirements. But Ofsted requires things that ISI do not and in particular they want DATA. They expect results to be broken down by pupil gender, by family income, by ethnicity, by ability. The Academy had not been collecting this data (in independent schools there is an assumption that gender, ethnicity *etc* are pretty irrelevant) and so they had to catch up rapidly.

4. Predicting numbers

Students can register to go to several sixth forms but there is no mechanism requiring them to commit to any one. Until the start of the school year you have no idea how many of the pupils to whom offers have been made will turn up. In the first year of operation too few offers were made for the 2013 entry and several very weak students were taken at the last moment to fill the shortfall.

5. Too many medics

Too many of the students come with pretty average GCSE grades but want to be doctors. They have to do physics, chemistry, biology and maths but they are not necessarily suited to any of these subjects.

6. Uneven teacher quality

It is hard to recruit good teachers in London because the cost of living is so high. At first it was hard to attract teachers to a school with no track record and (at the start) no building. It is very hard to find good teachers of chemistry or physics. So, although some of the first cohort of teachers were excellent, some were not.

7. Unwillingness to leave home

Many of the pupils do not want to go away to university. They prefer to live at home, partly because it is cheaper, partly for cultural reasons. This is fine because they live in London and there are plenty of good universities in London, but would be an issue in other areas.

8. Ignorance about the university system

Because their parents had not been to university, the students sometimes suffered from two misconceptions. First, they had no concept of the hierarchy of universities. They did not all know what pupils from the middle-classes know – that universities vary greatly in terms of prestige, facilities and teaching quality.

Secondly, they thought that their university degree should be one which leads directly to a job – medicine, dentistry, law, accountancy. They had not grasped that most jobs do not require a particular degree subject and that a subject which appears 'useless' in a vocational sense, like philosophy, can in fact lead on to wide range of good careers.

Why is LAE successful?

1. Success breeds success – if people get to know about it.

Starting a new free school is a risky business and starting a sixth form Academy is hardest of all. The school is unknown in the local area and other headteachers may be somewhat hostile to it. There is only one thing to do – get good results in year one and shout about them.

2. Good headmasters

The founding headmaster was Robert Wilne who had been Head of Maths at Highgate School in north London. Robert is an inspirational figure. He helped design an exciting school and he persuaded students to apply. He established strong relationships with the feeder schools. He was succeeded by John Weeks, previously the deputy head at Brighton College. He has been brilliant at putting in place routines and systems, has established an ethos of calm determination and has continued to market the school well.

3. The partner schools

The partner schools contributed the advice of experienced and successful teachers. They transferred the high standards of their schools to the LAE.

4. Experienced governors

The governing body includes the head of Brighton College, the head of Kingston Community School (Joan Deslandes) who brings essential local knowledge, the heads of Forest School, of Highgate, of University College School, of Eton, of Caterham, and the former High Master of St Paul's boys' school. No governing body has so many distinguished headteachers. In addition there are the former and current deputy heads of Brighton College, the current bursar of Brighton College, a lawyer, a school parent, a senior executive from HSBC, representatives of Oxford University and University College London, and the tutor for admissions at King's College London. This is a formidably skilled governing body.

5. High expectations

Pupils feel proud to be at LAE, one of the most successful schools in the country. They expect to do well and are expected to do well. They are tested regularly and the school makes it clear if they are not working hard enough. If pupils have grades good enough to apply for Oxbridge they are encouraged to do so.

The school is academically selective. Bright children encourage each other to succeed. All the pupils want to do well and this ambition is infectious.

Another way in which expectations are raised is through the house system. Every pupil is in a house named after a partner private school – Eton, Caterham *etc.* The students visit their partner schools and pupils from the partner schools visit them. Not only does this provide them with insight which comes from meeting children from some of the wealthier families in Britain but it allows some of the high expectations of pupils at top independent schools to rub off.

6. Gold-plated UCAS advice

It is important to have very authoritative UCAS advice. Paul Teulon, a governor, is head of admissions at King's College London and knows as much as anyone about university entry – which A-level subjects to do, which grades you need for which universities. As does Claudia Harrison, the deputy head, who was in charge of university advice at Westminster School which gets as many pupils into Oxford and Cambridge as any school in Britain.

7. Bangladeshi pupils on the rise

The most numerous type of pupil at LAE is a Bangladeshi girl. In 1991 in England only 14% of Bangladeshi pupils achieved five or more GCSEs grades A*–C compared to 37% of white pupils. By 2006 57% of Bangladeshi pupils achieved this benchmark against 58% of white pupils (Strand, 2015). By 2013 the figures were 85% and 82.7% despite the fact that many Bangladeshi pupils still came from the lowest socio-economic group.

If one looks only at pupils on free school meals, in 2013 59.2% of FSM Bangladeshi pupils in England gained five or more GCSEs graded A*–C including English and maths compared to 32.7% of white FSM British pupils (Strand, 2015).

Many Bangladeshis came to London from rural areas In Bangladesh and the first generation typically had very limited English speaking ability. As they have assimilated they have improved academically. The grandparents or parents of LAE students believed in improving their position by moving to England. Their route to success was through migration and hard work; subsequent generations maintain this trajectory through education.

Not all the local schools welcomed the arrival of LAE but in the few years of its existence the school has achieved incredible exam results, including value-added, and the standard of education across the whole borough has risen.

Chapter 18

Brighton College

An improving independent school

The academic hierarchy of independent schools tends to remain fairly consistent across decades, even hundreds of years. It is hard to find schools that have bucked this trend and moved up the pecking order, but Brighton College is one.

Back in 1996 the senior part of the school had 475 pupils, was struggling financially and little-known. It has been fortunate to have two heads who have each contributed to a transformation. Anthony Seldon was the head from 1997 to 2005. Under his care the school numbers rose to 600. Since 2006 the head has been Richard Cairns and there are now 1080 pupils aged 11–18, of which 345 are boarders.

Academically the school has been transformed. The percentage of subjects graded A*/A at GCSE rose from 64% in 2006 to 92% in 2016. The proportion getting A*-B at A-level rose from 78% in 2006 to 97% in 2016. In the latter year 39 pupils received offers from Oxford or Cambridge, amongst the best results of any school in the UK.

Both heads can take credit for this. But how did they do it?

1. Marketing

Both Anthony Seldon and Richard Cairns are known for their aggressive and persistent marketing flair. Both took the trouble to form a good relationship with the national press, making themselves readily available for comment and writing frequent articles. Anthony started a high-profile annual conference for headteachers which continues to this day. Both were quick to claim that their school was, in the early days, 'the best in Sussex' and, more recently, 'the best in the UK', statements which became a self-fulfilling prophecy.

There was a virtuous circle: good marketing = more applicants = the academic ability of the pupils rises = better exam results = marketing benefit.

One should not underestimate the importance of the cult of personality that began under Seldon and has continued under Cairns in a less flamboyant but still determined way. Both have impressed parents hugely. At the start of his time Seldon conducted a survey of parents to discover what they wanted and this led to the decision to scrap lessons on a Saturday morning. He made enormous efforts to meet and know parents and impressed them by remembering everyone's names. He started trips for parents to the battlefields of northern France.

2. Finding the niche

All independent schools, especially those with boarding, need to be distinctive and promote themselves on the basis of that distinctiveness. At one point Brighton was a traditional boarding school. The abolition of Saturday lessons shifted the school to weekly boarding – which has had a big appeal to London-based parents. Girls arrived in the sixth form in 1973 and in Year 9 in 1989, so doubling the number of potential applicants. So the niche is now clear: Brighton is a coeducational day and boarding school with a strong academic focus.

The age structure of admissions has been changed with beneficial results. Up until 2009 the senior school started at age 13. In that year they started taking pupils at age 11 with a highly competitive 11+ exam; this increased the academic quality and had a major impact on results.

3. Focus on teacher quality

There is a **constant focus on good teaching**. Staff appraisal is backed by a regular process of pupil assessment of staff using a confidential online form. Weak staff have been quickly picked out by the pupil survey and moved on (or choose to move on). The staff probation period is implemented rigorously.

It goes further than this through the way Richard talks to the Common Room and through his inherent suspicion of fads, unnecessary technologies and ill-thought-through change. If he is confident that a member of staff is inspiring children he doesn't really care *how* they do it.

Good appointments have been made and there is a focus on teachers' subject knowledge. Cairns is not afraid of taking teachers straight out of university or from a change in profession (nuclear physicists, lawyers etc). He internally promotes anyone with promise; 'if you are good enough you are old enough'.

Heads of department are free to decide how their subject is taught in their department. There is no enforced whole school style of teaching. However the basics of clear explanation, marking and feedback are monitored and enforced centrally.

4. Academic management

Very important are the 'Heads of Section' (*ie* heads of year especially the Head of Middle School for Year 11 and the Head of Sixth Form for Year 13). With Heads of Section there is a degree of year-group-wide monitoring which allows for a consistent approach to be applied for pupils who are failing to perform at the level they could. Heads of Section are members of the SMT and have clout: they put in place action plans and work closely with House Parents and heads of academic departments to come up with bespoke strategies for each child.

They work on the assumption that a C grade or worse at A-level is a fail. They have a very clear grip on each and every possible A-level grade below B and on every Year 13 pupil who is at risk of missing a university offer. They have a plan of action for each pupil that allows departments to work together towards one overall outcome.

The Heads of Section spend about 80% of their time on academic issues, and along with the Heads of Academic Support (who work very closely with pupils in each year group who most need day-to-day guidance), have been responsible for much of the improvement in results.

Heads of Section ensure pupils make the right subject choices and encourage them to give up a subject early on if things are not going well. Heads of subject departments are under pressure to deliver: departmental meetings focus on targets and monitoring.

Richard Cairns has built a highly productive senior management team, getting the roles right, getting the right people in the right roles and ensuring there is a balance of talents and personalities across the whole team. Most SMT who leave go on to headships.

5. Curriculum innovations

In most ways the curriculum at Brighton College is very traditional but there are three good innovations that have been used for maximum marketing effect. First, compulsory Mandarin for all in Year 9. Second, the Years 7–8 *Story of our Land* course tells the story of Britain from the beginning of time until the end of the Georgian era and in doing so combines history, geography, philosophy and religion. Thirdly, there is an excellent focus on entrepreneurship in Year 12.

6. Ethos

A deputy head commented:

'*There is an emphasis of individuality, respect and kindness. This isn't just something that, like almost all other schools, we say. It is something which is deeply engrained in the ethos and day-to-day reality of school life. Every pupil and teacher wears a rubber bracelet reminding them to enact a daily random act of kindness; this is just a way of reminding everyone that this should be central to all that we do. Our embrace of and*

273

celebration of diversity is fundamental to what we are as a school and it is all designed to ensure that all pupils feel comfortable in their own skin, and happy to be at school. I do think that we get as close to achieving that as any school in which I have worked, and — on top of its obvious value as an aim in itself — I am sure that it provides a foundation for pupils to make better progress academically. They are worried less about what others are thinking of them and hence are more able to focus on themselves. If Richard has a motto, it would be "if I try to be him, who will be me?" And it means that the reality of school life is very different from what many of our detractors would suggest (eg in terms of us being an exam factory).'

There is a strong feeling at Brighton that everyone pulls their weight. You don't have lazy staff, either inside or outside the classroom. This means that the Common Room is less cynical than many. Staff work very hard and are often tired at the end of term. But, there is a level playing field, and there is a real sense of collaboration and pulling together in the same direction.

There is a strong commitment to supporting state schools and it was Brighton College which set up the London Academy of Excellence (page 263).

7. Extracurricular life

Brighton College has always had a good reputation for cricket, partly because of a link with Sussex cricket. Seldon and Cairns have improved things further with a big emphasis on results. Rugby is stronger; girls' cricket has been sensational; music, dance, drama and art thrive.

8. Acquisition of feeder prep schools

If you can gain control of viable feeder schools and improve them, as some state schools have done through the creation of MATs, you are going to improve the quality of the intake. Brighton College bought St Christopher's Prep in Hove in 2003; Handcross Park Prep in 2011; and acquired Roedean junior school in 2011 as their pre-prep.

9. Money

Brighton College has opened franchise schools abroad: BC Abu Dhabi (2011), BC Al Ain (2013), BC Bangkok (2016) and others are in the pipeline. The money from these schools is being used to fund ambitious building developments.

In addition, fundraising has been immensely successful in recent years, not least in Russia.

10. Keep it simple

I spoke to Richard Cairns's deputies and all mentioned 'clarity of vision':

'Richard doesn't allow the school to be dragged from its core objective at all, and he will stand up to anything which might get in the way of that. He backs his staff if parents are unreasonable, or are demanding things he doesn't want to prioritise. He articulates the vision very strongly. Everyone who works at the school knows what they are trying to do.'

'I think it is also important to stress that there is a simplicity to Richard's vision – to make sure that every pupil makes the most academic progress they are capable of. That runs through every decision made.'

A really good school which has been marketed brilliantly.

Chapter 19

The social mobility conundrum

Take physic, pomp.
Expose thyself to feel what wretches feel,
That thou mayst shake the superflux to them
And show the heavens more just.

King Lear, Act 3 scene iv

When I helped set up a free school in a low income part of London I was told I was trying to improve social mobility. When I worked for independent schools I was accused of educating my pupils well and so limiting social mobility. What did that mean?

'Social mobility', it transpired, means people moving up or down the social classes – being better off or worse off than their parents. Social mobility matters because if able children from poor backgrounds cannot do well we waste human potential. It is bad for the individuals concerned and it is bad for the country.

It also matters because if people feel that there is social immobility there will be understandable envy of those who have done well. It results in social tension and potential unrest.

It matters politically because meritocracy is today a central creed of all Britain's main political parties. When the Labour peer Michael Young wrote *The Rise of the Meritocracy* in 1958 he was using the term pejoratively ... but today meritocracy is certainly not regarded as anathema. In its more frequently heard formulation, 'equality of opportunity', it is something to which no one dare admit opposition.

On the day that Theresa May became the British Prime Minister in 2016 she addressed the country:

'When it comes to opportunity, we won't entrench the advantages of the fortunate few, we will do everything we can to help anybody, whatever your background, to go as far as your talents will take you.'

That was a call for greater social mobility.

So *IS* there social immobility in the UK?

Sociologists don't agree

There is some evidence that social mobility is lower now than it was in the 1950s, when the economy was changing in a way which produced more middle-class jobs. Jo Blanden and Stephen Machin at the London School of Economics tracked the lives of children born in one week in 1958 and another cohort born in a week in 1970 ... and found the latter exhibited less social mobility. Abigail McKnight (2015) studied 17,000 children born in 1970 whose intelligence was measured when they were five, finding that by age 42 those with low ability from higher income families were earning more than high ability children from low income families.

This led to an academic debate as Blanden and Machin's findings were challenged by several subsequent studies. Goldthorpe and Jackson (2007) found that relative mobility for both men and women remained 'essentially constant' in the post-war era, and when Goldthorpe and Mills (2008) studied data from 1972 and 2005, they again found that social mobility had not declined. Much the same conclusions were drawn by Paterson and Iannelli (2007), Lambert *et al* (2007) and others. Some found that relative mobility had actually improved somewhat, such as Heath and Payne (2000) and Li and Devine (2011). All would agree with John Goldthorpe who stated that '*no decline in mobility, either absolute or relative, occurred in the late 20th century*' (Goldthorpe, 2012).

In his recent text *Social Mobility Myths*, Peter Saunders, professor of sociology at Sussex University, demonstrates that social mobility in the UK is high. '*Four out of five children who grow up in poor households escape poverty in adulthood. Social mobility is the norm in Britain, not the exception.*'

There is plenty of evidence that many people do better than their parents, but few move from low to high income in the course of just one generation. So of those born in 1970, 63% of those with parents in the poorest 25% escaped low income as adults. However, most of this mobility was *short-range* and only one in seven reached the top 25% as adults. This contrasts with those with parents in the richest 25%, almost 45% of whom remained there as adults.

The 2012 and 2015 PISA (Programme for International Student Assessment) analyses showed that the UK has above-average equity in education outcomes compared to other countries. There are countries that are more equal than we are, such as Japan, South Korea, Hong Kong, Finland and Canada. But there are a larger number of less equal countries, including France, Spain and Germany.

The OECD report on the 2015 survey concluded that only 11% of the variation in student performance in science (the main concern of the 2015 survey) is attributable to differences in students' socio-economic status, the OECD average being 13% (OECD, 2016).

But we know that educational attainment gaps remain wide

Over the last 25 years there has been a modest reduction in the differences in educational achievement between children from richer and poorer backgrounds. For example, children eligible for free school meals were 55% as likely as their peers to get five good GCSEs including English and maths in 2013–14 compared to only 39% as likely in 2004–5 (*Department for Education, 2014*).

However the gap is still wide. By age five, 48% of children eligible for free school meals achieve a 'good level of development' (according to the Government's school readiness measure), compared with 67% of other children. By age 11, 60% of children on free school meals achieve the expected level of attainment, compared with 79% of those not on free school meals. In 2015, 33% of children on free school meals gained five A*–C grades at GCSE (including maths and English), compared with 61% of other children.

Proportion of pupils gaining five GCSEs grade A*–C including English and maths, state-funded schools in England, 2015

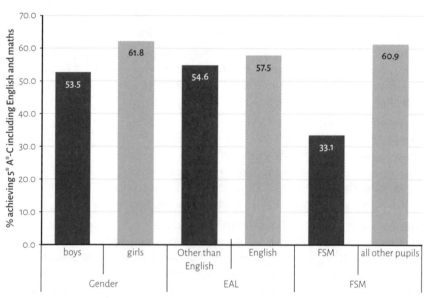

Source: Department for Education, 2015 GCSE results

Poor children not only start school at a lower base, but also make less progress while they are there. The attainment of wealthier children accelerates during their school years, while it stalls for the poorest. This means that wealthier children exceed their educational potential but the poorest do not get near to fulfilling theirs.

Having said all that, the link between poverty and academic outcomes is not as great as is often claimed. Of the bottom 20% of pupils academically at age 16 only a quarter are on free school meals. Of those on free school meals only a third are in the bottom 20%. So the pupil premium, which is designed to raise the academic achievement of poorer pupils, misses two-thirds of those in the bottom 20% academically.

Women are part of the picture

Studies based on 1950s and 1970s data were mainly concerned with men because men constituted a high proportion of the workforce. Since the 1970s the most significant change in the workforce has been the increasing proportion of jobs taken by women.

Social mobility has improved for women due to the general rise in women in work, an increase in middle-class women returning to work following childbirth, and more women attending university, unlocking senior jobs in areas like law and medicine.

Although the massive expansion in university places after 1997 was supposed to provide the ladder of opportunity for the working classes, most of these extra places have been taken by middle-class girls. According to UCAS, in 2016 about 40% of young men applied to university and 36% went, while 53% of young women applied and 47% went.

The expansion of the universities is also part of the reason why the less able children from the higher income families have not moved down socially, as a truly meritocratic model would suggest they should. Less able children of wealthier families go to university in a way they did not before 1997.

The expansion in the numbers of middle-class children going to university also increased assortative mating – the number of graduate women marrying graduate men. And assortative mating is one of the things which can reduce social mobility because the less educated are left to pair off with each other.

Immigration is also part of the picture

All people are members of a socio-economic group (SEG), albeit one which is sometimes quite hard to define. But all people also have a gender and an ethnicity. Social mobility can apply equally to SEG, gender and ethnicity.

An OECD report in 2012 found: '*The socio-economic composition of UK schools poses significant challenges for disadvantaged students as well as students with an immigrant background: 80% of students with an immigrant background attend schools with a high percentage of immigrant students. Even immigrant students with highly-educated mothers are more than twice as likely to be in disadvantaged schools as non-immigrant students.*'

A Centre on Dynamics of Ethnicity report (2013) found that 43% of white men and 45.6% of white women moved up to a higher socio-economic class than their father. But only 34.3% of first generation men of Pakistani and Bangladeshi ethnicity and 27.6% of women of Pakistani and Bangladeshi ethnicity moved up from the socio-economic class of their father.

So in Britain it is hard to disentangle the impact of social class from immigration.

The changing nature of jobs is part of the picture

One of the features of most of the twentieth century was the change in the skills mix of the working population. There was a decline in manual jobs and growth of 'middle-class' jobs: fewer miners, more bankers, and so on. So some working-class children ascended to these middle-class jobs.

In recent years fewer higher-paid jobs have been created. What is more, there are more lower-paid jobs in Britain than 20 years ago – so there is more room at the bottom. Bukodi *et al* looked at more than 20,000 British people born in periods from 1946, 1958, 1970 and 1980–84. Their results confirm that there has been no decline in mobility. In the case of women, there is in fact evidence of mobility increasing. However, among the members of successive cohorts, the experience of upward mobility is becoming less common and that of downward mobility more common.

Income inequality

For much of the past 100 years the distribution of wealth has been getting more equal. In 1923 the top 1% of the population owned 61% of marketable assets. By 1976, this had dropped dramatically so they owned only 21% (Snowden, 2015).

The Office for National Statistics measures income inequality in the UK using the Gini coefficient where 0 means total equality and 100 means total inequality (one person has all the income). The patterns shows *over the past five years income inequality has fallen faster than at any point since the 1970s.* Since 2007–8 the only income group to have seen a fall in real disposable income is the richest 20%.

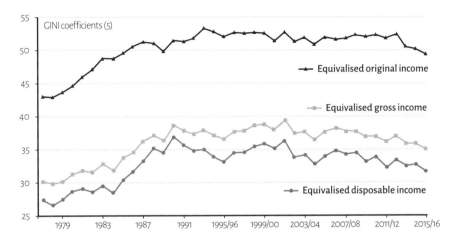

Source: Office for National Statistics Statistical Bulletin, 2017

Incomes are much higher across all groups today than they were in the 1970s. It is not true that the poor are getting poorer. The bottom 20% of earners have a disposable income that is 86% higher, adjusted for inflation, than in 1977 (ONS 2016). The average income in 2015 was twice what it was in 1977.

There is a danger of governments prioritising inequality as an issue at the expense of economic growth or the relief of poverty. It is possible for inequality to fall as living standards for everyone drop – as happened in the UK in recent years. In China inequality has risen in the past two decades but everyone is much better off than they were.

The regional dimension

A study by the Institute for Public Policy Research (IPPR, 2016) showed that northern secondary schools lag behind the England average. Even before they start compulsory school age the gap between pupils in London and those in the north of England is wide. In London 59% of pupils achieve a 'good level of development' by the end of the Reception year at age five compared to 49% in the north. The IPPR report found the proportions of pupils achieving the benchmark five GCSEs at grades A*–C were:

- 55.5% in the North
- 57.3% in England as a whole
- 60.9% in London

For free school meals pupils, the proportions achieving the GCSE benchmark were:

- 34% in the North
- 36.8% in England as a whole
- 48.2% in London

It also found that that the problem is not restricted to small towns and coastal areas, often singled out as areas where pupils perform poorly; rather, *'Even large cities such as Liverpool, Leeds and Sheffield need to raise their game'.* It points out discrepancies in school funding between regions, and backs measures to improve funding to northern schools through the new national funding formula. In the north in 2016 the annual funding per secondary pupil was about £5700 compared with about £7000 in London.

DfE data released in 2017 shows the proportion of schools falling below the Government's floor standard of -0.5 Progress 8 score:

Percentage of schools below the GCSE results floor standard in England in 2016

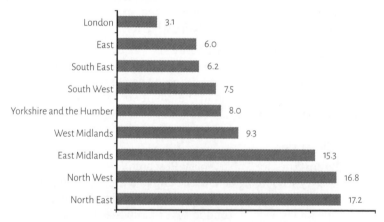

Source: Department for Education, Key stage 4 attainment data

The Social Mobility Commission (2016) found that over one-fifth of the children in failing schools in England live in ten local authority areas (Blackpool, Knowsley, Northumberland, Doncaster, Reading, Stoke-on-Trent, Oldham, Bradford, Telford and Wrekin, and Central Bedfordshire).

In 2016 only 28.2% of 18-year-olds in the south-west of England went to university, only 28.9% from the north-east, but 39.9% from London (UCAS).

There is a brain drain to London. Swinney and Williams (2016) found that London accounts for around 19% of UK jobs, but six months after graduation, of the graduates who moved city, London employed 22% of all working new graduates, and 38% of those working new graduates with a first or upper second class degree from a Russell Group university. This figure rises to 52% for Oxbridge graduates with a first or 2:1. London also has by far the highest graduate retention and return rates, with 77% of London students staying to work in the capital and 74% of those who left to become undergraduates elsewhere returning.

The problem of time lags

By definition you have to wait one generation to tell whether a group is experiencing social mobility. So even if improvement in state schools is creating good conditions for social mobility right now, we will not be able to prove it for some years.

Equally you cannot judge the prospects for social mobility of today's young people from the circumstances of those currently aged 40 or more, yet many of those who commentate on current conditions refer back to people born before 1960 (the number of privately educated judges *etc*).

The problem of the top 0.0001%

So the Social Mobility and Child Poverty Commission keep reminding us that 71% of senior judges and 62% of senior Armed Forces officers went to private school.

But it could also be a mistake to measure social mobility by looking at the background of senior judges, senior Armed Forces officers, Oscar-winning actors or members of the Cabinet. Because what really matters is not only what happens to the top 0.0001% but what happens to the rest.

In 2016 the Cabinet in 10 Downing Street swung from being quite private school to being more state school. What did that tell us about social mobility in the country *as a whole?*

Nothing much.

What causes social immobility?

1. Where you go to school

The quality of schools in England is variable. Schools that are apparently similar in terms of relative deprivation of area or disadvantage of intake can perform very differently. The large urban centres that were once the weakest performing are now among the strongest. Poorer children are more likely to attend worse schools, especially at secondary level, which doubles their disadvantage. In 2016 over half the pupils in Blackpool were being taught at schools regarded as failing by Ofsted. Weak schools find it harder to attract good teachers and this makes improvement much more difficult.

At the international level, PISA results suggest that segregation of schools by poverty tends to depress the scores of the already disadvantaged. In contrast, comprehensive, centralised and equitably funded school systems tend to produce both better outcomes overall and smaller attainment gaps between rich and poor children. Countries with lower segregation between schools, more egalitarian systems and low achievement gaps tend to have higher average attainment and also the highest percentage of very skilled students.

The OECD Education at a Glance 2012 report looked at where the children of 'low-educated' mothers are going to school – mothers who did not achieve five good GCSEs – and found that in the UK they were much more likely to be taught in schools with high numbers of disadvantaged children.

Among the children of immigrant families in the UK, 80% were taught in schools with high concentrations of other immigrant or disadvantaged pupils – the highest proportion in the developed world.

The existence of an independent or private sector in schooling increases segregation. But the Sutton Trust investigation of this issue concluded that *'most of the segregation of pupils by social class occurs within the state sector'*. A Sutton Trust 2013 report stated: *'We find that the overall rate of FSM uptake at the top 500 comprehensives measured on the traditional five good GCSE scale is just below half the national average, 7.6% compared to 16.5%, in almost 3000 state secondary schools.'*

In 2016 research by Schooldash showed that Ofsted-graded 'outstanding' schools, primary free schools and converter academies take in a lower proportion of pupils from disadvantaged backgrounds than is represented in their communities. Schooldash founder Timo Hannay said: *'The data presented here suggest that the postcode lottery is far from the only effect keeping poorer children out of good schools; even those poorer children who do live close to a high-performing school are less likely to end up going there'.*

We know that most of the schools with the best exam results are in middle-class areas and tend to push up house prices, making access to such schools impossible for all but the most prosperous. In 2016 Lloyds Bank research looked at 30 state schools with good GCSE results and found that local houses had a price premium of up to £630,000 above the rest of the county. Similarly, research by Stirling Ackroyd found that house prices close to the excellent Queen Elizabeth's School in Barnet were 34% above the average for the area.

2. The school curriculum

Cristina Iannelli of Edinburgh University studied a cohort of people born in one week in 1958 over the course of their lives (Iannelli, 2013). She found that pupils who studied certain subjects at school were more likely to be successful in their careers than other pupils – even pupils of the same ability and going to the same school type. These most valuable subjects were English, maths, sciences and languages. Pupils were more likely to study these subjects at grammar schools but those who studied them at non-grammar schools also did well. Subject choice mattered more than school type.

3. Intelligence

Peter Saunders suggests that the main thing which determines a person's socio-economic group is a combination of intelligence and hard work. People in low income jobs tend to be less intelligent than people in higher income jobs. He is scornful of the reluctance of his fellow sociologists to even consider the role of intelligence in determining social mobility, which he describes as politically motivated myopia (he claims that only 3% of sociology professors vote Conservative). Their research grants depend on their ability to prove that there is a problem.

Saunders states that the main way in which Britain falls short of the meritocratic ideal is that less able but wealthier children are prevented from failing. But able and hardworking children born into the lowest socio-economic group usually rise out of it.

Several authors have looked at the impact on brain development of weak parenting. A failure to stimulate babies means that they fail to develop synapses and this establishes an inferior brain by the age of three.

Professor Robert Plomin runs the Twins Early Development Study (Teds) of all twins born in England and Wales from 1994 to 1996. He compares the results of identical twins with non-identical twins in order to pull out the impact of genetics on the variability of results.

What his research shows is that nature is often more important than we like to think, particularly in the contentious area of intelligence. There is a complicated interplay of genes and environment, but even so it's striking how heritable intelligence is. Clever parents are more likely to have clever children.

In a twin sample of 11,116 16-year-olds, heritability was a high proportion of the explanation for GCSE performance for subjects such as English (52%), mathematics (55%) and science (58%) (Shakeshaft *et al*, 2013). In contrast, the overall effects of environment, which includes all family and school influences, accounts for about 36% of the variance of mean GCSE scores. So *individual differences in educational achievement at the end of compulsory education are not primarily an index of the quality of teachers or schools.*

In 2015 Plomin extended his results to A-levels and found a similar pattern: the results are 60% explained by genes and 20% by school.

4. Income

Children from better off families tend to go to better schools because house prices are higher near better schools. Children from richer backgrounds are also more likely to have private tuition, even if they go to state schools. In the early years, children from poorer backgrounds are less likely to attend good quality childcare or early education, partly because there is less good quality childcare available in poorer areas.

Children and parents who live in poor quality or overcrowded housing have worse physical and mental health. They are more likely to move house frequently, which has a very negative impact on children's attainment. Educational resources such as a computer and a room of one's own are expensive. Poverty also affects families through stress and a higher risk of depression, making it much more difficult for parents to support their children's education.

In addition to financial and economic disadvantages, children from poorer backgrounds are also disadvantaged by a lack of cultural and social capital – they are less likely to visit museums, go abroad or read books.

Families where both parents are educated spend an average of 110 minutes a day on educational activities with young children compared to 71 minutes where parents have a low level of education.

By the time that students receive their GCSE results, around 32% of the variation in performance can be predicted on the basis of indicators observed at or before age five (Washbrook, 2010).

Low income families are also less likely to have the benefit of two parents. In 2001 those at the top of the socio-economic tree (so-called Class 1) were 25% more likely to be married than those at the bottom (Class 7). That has now grown to 50%. Children in richer neighbourhoods are far more likely to have a father at home.

Serafino and Tonkin (2014) established that growing up in a workless household has an impact on your future poverty in the UK. Holding all else equal, those who lived in a workless household at age 14 are around 1.5 times as likely to be in poverty compared with those where one adult was working.

The father's level of education had the largest impact on the likelihood of low educational attainment in the UK out of the factors they examined. Holding all else equal, people are 7.5 times more likely to have a low educational outcome themselves if their father had a low level of education, compared with having a highly educated father (Serafino and Tonkin).

However, there is nothing deterministic about the relationship between poverty and exam results. The PISA 2015 tests (page 15) found that around one-in-three pupils in England overcomes a disadvantaged socio-economic background to achieve a top quartile score on the PISA science test, compared to an OECD average of around 29% (Jerrim and Shure, 2016).

5. The housing market

How you define someone's social position depends in good measure on their housing status. Because house prices have risen faster than salaries, it was easier to be a home-owner in the past – since 1990 we have seem a rise of tenants, a decline in home-ownership. Too few homes are being built and nearly a million more households with children rent privately than ten years ago.

Families are spending a higher proportion of their disposable income on accommodation: those born in the 1980s spend more than 20% of their income on housing compared to the 10% that was being spent at the same point in their lives by those born in the 1940s (Social Mobility Commission, 2016).

The rise in the value of housing since 1990, especially in the south of England, means that those middle-aged and older people who managed to get onto the housing ladder in the 1970s and 1980s are now living in homes worth vastly more than they paid for them. In great swathes of London the average house price is now over £750,000. As younger people cannot afford to buy houses the inter-generational wealth gap has grown. And the growing gap in property values between different parts of the country reduces the ability of people to move from one area to another.

6. Aspirations

There is some evidence that there is a general 'culture of low aspirations' among low income families. The Millennium Cohort Study shows that the mothers of seven-year-olds have almost universally high aspirations for them – 97% of both poorer and richer mothers say they want their child to go to university. However, children and parents from poorer backgrounds develop lower expectations as children grow older. They may still aspire to higher education and professional jobs, but their faith in their ability to achieve those ambitions is eroded.

This can arise from a combination of factors: lower achievement at school so far, a lack of social networks to provide knowledge and encouragement about how to achieve such goals, and a labour market with high numbers of low skilled jobs and limited opportunities to use qualifications to progress from those to better work. In addition, where parents themselves have not had good experiences in education, and have few qualifications, they may have limited knowledge, confidence and skills in helping their children in education such as reading to them and helping with homework.

The Sutton Trust report *Believing in Better*, June 2016, showed that one reason so many more girls go to university than boys is that they are much more likely to believe in the importance of a university degree. Even in Year 9 65% of girls said it was important to go to university compared to 58% of boys. 15- and 16-year-olds with similar GCSE results were twice as likely to go on to do three A-levels if they saw university as a likely goal for them. Disadvantaged students were less likely to think they would go on to university than their more advantaged peers, with only 27% having high aspirations compared with 39% of their better-off peers.

Forty per cent of all British children now go to university, but only 13% of white working-class do. This is not primarily due to poverty – other ethnic groups with the same low incomes are much more likely to go to university. It is poverty of aspiration.

7. Soft skills once in the workplace

The Social Mobility Commission has shown that bright children from poor homes do well but never reach the highest income levels of their peers from wealthier homes. This may be due to a relative lack of useful soft skills. This has been analysed by Ashley *et al* (2015) and the soft skills they identified included confidence, risk taking, the ability to speak well, accent, team working, being organised and punctual.

8. Networks and fitting in

Mike Savage's analysis of the Great British Class Survey (Savage, 2015) found that those whose parents work in professional occupations were much more likely to know other people in such occupations and this gave them access to networks of influence, networks which made it more likely they would be able to access such jobs.

In 2016 the SMC published research evidence that explained why young people from disadvantaged homes may struggle to become investment bankers. They find it harder to acquire work experience because they lack the necessary informal networks. They found that managers often selected candidates who fitted the traditional image of an investment banker and displayed polish in areas such as speech, accent and dress. They noted that this can disadvantage candidates whose upbringing and background means they are not aware of such things as City dress codes.

What can be done about low social mobility?

What should be done depends on what you think the cause is. If you think, like Peter Saunders, that the cause is the lower cognitive ability and motivation of pupils born in low income homes, then you need to focus on developing parenting skills.

Eliminate poverty

Children from poor homes start life at a disadvantage and find it very hard to catch up. The Social Mobility Commission, in their 2015 State of the Nation report, focus on the elimination of poverty: *'In a One Nation country child poverty would be a transient experience and would not inflict lasting damage into adulthood. But today as many as one in six children spend large parts of their lives living in households which are persistently poor. The one million children in this situation are often those from families characterised by ill health and low skills rather than simply by parental addiction or broken relationships.'*

Improve education

Mossbourne Academy, Durand Academy, King Solomon Academy – all schools achieving very good results in quite disadvantaged areas. In 2015, 18% of schools achieved a level of attainment for their free school meal pupils which was above the national average for *all* pupils.

Although it is early days, there is evidence that free schools and Academies can raise the standard of education in relatively low income areas. Porter and Simons (2015) looked at the impact of free schools on their local community and neighbouring schools and concluded there was a positive effect. When a free school opened in an area, other primary and secondary schools nearby improved faster than the national average.

In 2016 the Department for Education announced that £60 million would be spent on school improvement, teacher support and other schemes in social mobility 'coldspots', called Opportunity Areas. The first group would be Blackpool, Derby, Norwich, Oldham, Scarborough, and West Somerset, followed by Bradford, Doncaster, Fenland & East Cambridgeshire, Hastings, Ipswich and Stoke-on-Trent.

France: assigning teachers to unpopular areas and unpopular schools

Some parts of England find it harder to attract teachers than others. In France all teachers are regarded as civil servants and may only teach in schools in which the Government allows them to teach.

Primary teachers are recruited at the level of an *académie*, one of 30 educational regions; they can be appointed to any primary school in the *académie*. Secondary teachers are recruited at the national level and can be appointed to any secondary school in France. The school does not select the teacher, the State does. The teachers' unions support this because they think it is the role of the State to ensure equity between regions, schools and teachers, and that letting the schools choose their teachers would not be equitable.

Newly qualified teachers are sent to specific schools in less popular areas. Once a teacher has taught in an unpopular school for a few years they accumulate 'points' which permit them access to more popular parts of France.

The biggest problem, however, is the way the English education system fails the 30% of the population who do quite badly at school and who may not be suited to an academic style education. Our system of vocational education is very weak. In the UK 18% of the working population has a post-school non-degree qualification compared to 59% in Germany (Social Mobility Commission, 2016).

The Sutton Trust *Mobility Manifesto* (2015) made a number of proposals:

1. Ensure all disadvantaged children can access the best early years education and care. In particular, all disadvantaged two-year-olds should have access to nursery places with well qualified staff.

2. Make improving the quality of classroom teaching the top priority in schools, with effective appraisals and a guaranteed entitlement to good quality training for all teachers.

3. Create fairer school admissions to both state grammar schools and comprehensives at age 11, including through the increased use of ballots and banding in admissions.

4. Improve the impact of the pupil premium through greater use of evidence provided by the Education Endowment Foundation and incentives for schools that narrow the attainment gap.

5. Develop an effective national programme for highly able state school pupils, with ring-fenced funding to support evidence-based activities and tracking of pupils' progress.

6. Strengthen academies' support for low and middle income pupils by regular inspection of chains, publication of more data across chains and speedier interventions where academies are not working.

7. Break down barriers between state and private schools by promoting more partnership working and opening 100 leading independent day schools to all on the basis of ability rather than ability to pay.

8. Provide every young person with an entitlement to good quality personalised education and careers guidance, strengthening the national careers service to support schools and colleges effectively.

9. Introduce a new body, separate from individual universities, for the effective coordination of evidence-based outreach programmes, backed by more use of contextual admissions to improve access.

10. Greatly expand the number of good apprenticeships so that young people have real options at 18 and employers can develop the skilled workforce they need.

Are there arguments against trying to improve social mobility?

Yes – the counter-argument is that even the poorest people in Britain today are far better off than middle income people 50 years ago and that the best way to help those at the bottom is to generate more jobs and more higher-paid jobs. Focusing on inequality is dangerous because you are focusing on the wrong thing and risk compromising the main task – improving the economy. In education a concern about performance gaps between advantaged and disadvantaged children may be diverting energy from a more important consideration – raising the education level of all children in England in the face of growing international competition.

Social mobility policies can have other damaging side-effects. For example dilution of academic standards to allow more candidates to pass exams, as happened with the GCSE, led to less stretch for the top 50% of the ability range. There is growing evidence that the increase in numbers of students from low income homes going to low tariff universities has not improved their employment prospects while leaving them with debt.

All parents want is a good school locally. Not choice. Not social mobility. Just a good school with effective discipline and great teachers. Yet Michael Gove's Special Adviser could write, albeit a bit unfairly:

'Most of those with power in the English education system are much more interested in appearing to be 'on the side of the poor and less able' than they are in raising standards.'

(Dominic Cummings, blog, My essay on an Odyssean Education, 2014).

In 2016 Theresa May talked about the need to create a meritocracy. She said that the only thing which should 'count' in terms of success in life was innate ability and capacity for hard work.

This chapter started with a reminder that Michael Young, when he wrote *The Rise of the Meritocracy*, was fearful of the concept. The reason to be fearful is the fact that intelligence is to a large degree genetically determined, and that means that the middle classes are always likely to dominate the meritocracy at the expense of the working classes. If society is organised as a meritocracy then there is a danger that those at the top will feel they deserve their status and by the same token those at the bottom deserve theirs. Sympathy for the poor evaporates: they are poor because their lowly intelligence made them that way.

So there are those who think that a more meritocratic society will not result in social mobility, far from it, because meritocracy entrenches the privileges of the cognitive elite.

Chapter 20

So what should we do?

Conclusions for schools: things you need to do to ensure all pupils do well

School effectiveness has been extensively researched and the answer to the question of 'what works' is known. Most headteachers know the answer from their own experience, but some find it harder than others to implement in practice.

The fact that the answer is known does not mean that all successful heads are the same – far from it. Good heads range from those who are pretty authoritarian to those who believe in significant delegation of decision-making and responsibility to others.

A lot depends on the nature of the school. Schools which require huge and rapid change need different types of leader to those who are in good shape and need only to improve on what they are already doing. A brand-new school needs a head who is brilliant at marketing. If a school is well-established and successful, marketing is less important. Anyway, the research and my school visits suggest that schools whose pupils do well tend to have the following characteristics:

1. Good discipline

Without good discipline little else can be achieved. Fortunately, most children and parents want good discipline.

Good discipline generally comes from the head who very often has to:

- lay down clear rules which relate to behaviour in the classroom, behaviour in the corridors and public areas, behaviour on the way to and from school.
- have clear sanctions.
- assume that pupils will misbehave so all staff need to know the rules and sanctions and apply them fairly and 100% of the time.
- have a 'no excuses' policy.
- have detention after school on the same day the offence is committed.
- temporarily exclude pupils whose behaviour is disrupting others.
- speak in person to parents of troublesome children and enlist their support.
- have staff specifically responsible for the most troublesome pupils.
- provide support for staff who find discipline is a problem.

2. High expectations of every pupil

Every pupil must be expected to behave well and work hard. Every child must be expected to do well in every GCSE, BTEC and A-level. So there has to be regular questioning in class, marked homework and frequent testing to ensure the teacher knows whether pupils are keeping up with these high expectations. The school believes that effort is more important than genetically based intelligence.

The King Solomon Academy in London has some of the best GCSE results for disadvantaged pupils in England. Why? Because they work on the assumption that all their pupils will go to university – high expectations, from which everything else follows.

Expectations should not be limited by target grades or by a special needs label. Schools must be ambitious. Target grades are just as likely to demotivate a child as encourage them to work harder. The best teacher at a comprehensive school I visited said *'I ignore the school's target grades because my target is a top grade for every child. I will not achieve that, but MY targets influence everything I do.'*

If a pupil is NOT keeping up with expectations there must always be a response. The response will depend on the circumstances but will include:

- retests in the case of bad test marks.
- homework repeated after school when homework is late or of poor quality.
- seeing parents.
- extra tuition.
- pastoral assistance to pupils who are being held back by emotional or family problems – which will never be accepted as an excuse for poor behaviour or poor work.

There will also be plenty of rewards and praise for effort.

The curriculum should be stretching, especially but not only for the more able. That means studying hard texts in English literature, learning to read music in music lessons, doing life drawing to a good standard in art, making demanding pieces in product design.

Having high expectations of all pupils, and systems to force the less able to keep up, is far more important than issues about selection, setting and streaming.

3. Good teaching staff

Good schools invest a lot of time thinking of ingenious ways of attracting and retaining good staff. Good teachers tend to have good subject knowledge, they are enthusiastic about their jobs and their subjects, they plan lessons well, they check learning in lessons, they test pupils and mark work regularly. They set high expectations, command genuine respect and have the authority to create a scholarly atmosphere that allows pupils to be scholars.

We know that there is variation in results within schools as between schools. So a good head will nearly always have to focus on getting his weakest teachers and subject departments up to the level of the best.

4. Regular testing

Pupils have to learn how to commit work to the long-term memory. If material is committed to memory it makes it much more likely that pupils will have a better understanding and think analytically. They must all have good notes and revision guides. They must be tested on their work at least every three weeks or so, ideally across a whole year group for any one subject. Work should be *retested periodically to cement it in the memory.* The results should be send to parents and put up in a public place. Pupils who do badly should be set the target of improving their ranked position and be given help so that they do.

5. Routines and systems

It was clear that all the best schools I visited had trained staff and pupils to follow routines and systems designed to save time and ensure good discipline. For example, good schools have agreed routines for movement between classes, queueing for lunch, going into the classroom, what to get out of your bag before the lesson starts, how to end a lesson, how to hand in work, how a teacher will mark work, what to do if an adult comes into the room, how to address staff, how to wear uniform *etc.* If a child knows exactly what to do in the first minute of a lesson, this saves a huge amount of time – time which can be used for teaching.

6. Emotional commitment

Pupils must believe that their school is a good school and they are proud to be in it. They must like their teachers while knowing that they are strong on discipline. They must want to work well to please the teacher. They must be taught that good exam results are perfectly possible and lead to a better job and better life. They must see the point of it all.

Good teachers regard teaching as having a moral purpose and they have a sense of urgency about the task.

7. Cultural capital

Children from disadvantaged homes may not see much of the world. So they must be forced to visit museums, art galleries, classical music concerts, plays, lectures ... and write about these experiences. They must also be compelled to read good literature.

8. Parental involvement

There needs to be very good involvement with parents – regular reports on their children, visits to parents who appear to be invisible, newsletters, invitations to events, routine parents' meetings. Parents should be explicitly told which rules they should insist on in the home and how to help their children do homework.

9. Good English

Many pupils do not speak English at home and/or they have parents with a limited vocabulary. But good English is the *sine qua non* of success in most school subjects and many jobs. So all pupils coming to secondary school without good English at the age of 11 must have extra English lessons. And all pupils must be taught to speak well.

10. Extracurricular activity

Sport, debating, music, drama, Duke of Edinburgh Award Scheme – things which help develop lifelong interests and friendships and which provide something good about school for those who find academic work burdensome. The key is to find ways of compelling all pupils to be involved in something every term.

11. Collaboration

Many good secondary schools now benefit from being part of MATs or loose federations of local schools where they *draw on each other's strengths*. There is a sense of responsibility for the whole community and no school stands alone. Resources are focused on the weaker schools. The most successful MATs receive performance data regularly and they expect steady improvement.

And of course there is a number 12 – **good heads**. They are the people who make sure that numbers 1–11 happen. They need to be clear-sighted and determined.

Many of the successful heads I spoke to said two things:

'Keep it simple'; and

'Focus on what matters most'.

Policy conclusions

1. The main problem with the English education system is the long tail of underachievement. In 2016 57% of pupils in state schools gained five GCSEs grade A*–C including English and maths. This is a low figure – after all, a C grade in a GCSE is not a great achievement for most pupils. For pupils on free school meals the figure was 33.1% (DfE, 2016).

    In 2016 69% of all GCSEs were passed at grade C or above but 36% of those who passed only achieved a grade C – a bare pass.

    At the top end our pupils do well. A-levels are a secure and challenging qualification and many of those taking A-levels go on to good universities.

    Given that a high proportion of those not achieving the five GCSEs benchmark are from disadvantaged backgrounds, **it makes sense for the Government to focus on this group – the tail of underachievers.** According to the OECD this tail is what distinguishes England from other developed countries.

    PISA 2015 found that the difference between the top and bottom 10% of 15-year-old pupils in England is the equivalent of over eight years of schooling in both science and maths – a larger gap than in most OECD countries (Jerrim and Shure, 2016). If we are going to move from being a low-pay, low-productivity country to a high-pay, high-productivity country we need to do much more. What is more, we know that ill-educated parents beget ill-educated children. So we must break this cycle of deprivation.

    With Brexit we are on our own. To survive we have to become one of the most competitive countries in the world; in this context our current standards of education are not good enough.

    The London Challenge (pages 26-28) showed *what* could be done. In ten years London went from being the worst performing part of England in terms of school results to the highest performing.

    A small number of non-selective schools have eliminated the underachieving tail and much more needs to be known about how they have done it.

2. For disadvantaged children the gap in achievement is already apparent at nursery age. This is where government investment is needed – in nursery schools and parenting courses of the sort found at Tollgate Primary School. **We should be prioritising policies to increase the quality of age 2–4 childcare and education.** More Early Years teachers

should be trained because if children can be got to a good level by the age of five their life chances are hugely improved.

The focus for pupils from poorer homes should be on developing vocabulary, social skills and behaviour, not on teaching reading and maths at a young age. Children who are taught well at primary school will learn to read and do maths as long as the school readiness skills are in place.

3. Decisions about whether children should pursue an academic route or a more vocational route should be taken after GCSEs, not before. All children are capable of accessing a conventional academic curriculum up to the age of 16 and they have a right to do so.

The 2016 Sainsbury Review, with its recommended fifteen post-16 vocational courses, should be implemented. But this will be ineffective if the teachers of these courses cannot be found.

In 2015 only 266,000 students completed A-levels out of a total cohort of 633,000 (DfE, 2016). The main providers of full-time education for 16–18-year-olds were FE colleges (484,000 students), school sixth forms (433,000 students) and sixth form colleges (157,000). There is a strong social mobility argument for **focusing reform and spending on the FE colleges that deliver technical and vocational courses to huge numbers of students**: this is the group who need and will benefit most from extra investment.

As Vince Cable said during his tenure as Secretary of State for the Department of Business, Innovation and Skills:

Our post-secondary education has become distorted. The OECD concluded that our post-secondary vocational sub-degree sector is small by international standards – probably well under 10% of the youth cohort, compared to a third of young people elsewhere. In the US, more than 20% of the workforce have a post-secondary certificate or an associate degree as their highest qualification. In Austria and Germany, sub-degree provision accounts for around 50% of the cohort (Cable, 2015).

The conversion of polytechnics to universities removed the thrust of technical education in the UK. In the constant push to increase the proportion of students going to university such institutions have been trying to do everything but, often, doing nothing really well. The proposed Institutes of Technology are a good idea – if good teachers can be found and trained. But there have been endless reports and plans to create something similar to the Institutes of Technology since the Second World War, so this is an issue with a terrible history of policy failures.

The Government should refocus its apprenticeship programme from low level courses, which have little financial benefit to those taking them, to higher level, technical apprenticeships of the kind that are commonplace in Germany.

Once we have good vocational and technical pathways available after GCSEs, it will be necessary to persuade parents and teachers that these are much more valuable for some children than academic alternatives. At present schools have an enormous financial incentive to keep students on to take A-level courses for which they are ill-suited.

4. In general terms there should not be too much emphasis on school organisation. Variation in the quality of results *within* individual schools is much more important than variation between different types of schools (maintained schools, Academies *etc*).

    Some Academy chains are succeeding, others are not. There needs to be a much more open competitive bidding process. At present the process by which Academy chains are formed is opaque.

5. The most important influence on a child's performance is their individual teachers. Policy needs to be focused on the recruitment and retention of excellent teachers and in this respect we have some way to go. There is limited evidence that Teaching Schools or School Direct will in themselves solve the problem of teacher shortage. More money needs to be spent on teacher recruitment: a more educated workforce would more than repay the investment. The economist Eric Hanushek estimated that replacing the least effective 5–8% of teachers in the US with just average teachers would increase the annual Gross Domestic Product by 75 to 110 trillion dollars (Hanushek, 2011).

    There should be incentives to get good teachers into the most challenging schools, in the way they do in Japan and Singapore. These teachers should have access to a generous house-purchase scheme.

    The Brexit negotiations must make it easy for teachers from the EU and outside to come the UK to teach subjects where there is a supply shortage.

6. Teacher training and professional development of teachers is still quite weak compared to the standards being achieved in other countries, not least those in East Asia. There needs to be a careful appraisal of the systems

used in places like Finland, Singapore and Shanghai, together with an evaluation of the effectiveness of in-school teacher training in England.

7. One of the things which influences the effectiveness of a teacher is their teaching method (pedagogy). Excellent progress has been made in the past six years promoting phonics and maths mastery methods. This should continue.

There is evidence that textbooks are more effective than handouts or digital alternatives. Teachers must be encouraged to use textbooks.

The DfE should take set up a unit to co-ordinate the best online resources for schools and continue to encourage publishers to produce textbooks which are stretching.

8. Grammar schools should follow the example of the King Edward's Birmingham Foundation which lowers the 11+ pass score to grammar schools for pupils on free school meals in order to get the FSM proportion up to 20%. Only in this way can grammar schools benefit the group who needs them most.

9. The academic elements of the examination system (GCSEs and A-levels) have only recently been reformed. Many of these reforms are excellent. They should be allowed to settle down before any more changes are made. Constant change to the exam system diverts the energy of teachers away from things which matter.

GCSE reforms have made these qualifications more demanding. This was essential because the standards expected in England have fallen behind other countries (page 14). As Kuczera *et al* (2016) found '*the evidence points to upper secondary programmes in England which require lower levels of basic skills than many other countries.*'

If existing exam boards fail to show a high level of competence we should consider moving to one exam board per subject.

10. It is very important that Ofqual continues to clamp down on unwarranted grade inflation which gives the nation the impression that education is improving when it is not.

11. The supply of school places needs to increase in many areas as the school-age population grows. Free schools should be set up driven by staff from the most successful existing free schools, academies, Academy chains and local authorities.

There is some confusion about the role of free schools – are they being built to deal with the shortage of places or are they supposed to provide parents with choice in areas with sufficient places but few high quality schools? There is a case for developing two separate programmes: a basic need new schools programme, where the Schools Commissioner's office would work closely with local authorities to identify the local need and find a suitable provider to meet it; and a quality schools programme, through which the DfE would allow new schools to open in areas of generally low quality.

Meanwhile too many free schools are failing to find sites; planning rules need to change urgently.

12. Independent schools should be used to help solve the supply of good school places. Parents from low income homes (pupil premium qualified) should be allowed to use the money that would have been spent on a state school place to buy a place at an independent school if they wish, the school making up the difference in price.

Independent schools should also be encouraged to help state schools that want that help. Independent schools are not a good source of advice if the task is to educate disadvantaged pupils. But they *are* a good source of advice when it comes to subject-specialist teaching at primary level, boarding, university entry, modern languages and science teaching, cocurricular activities like sport, music, drama and cadet forces.

13. Schools alone cannot reduce gaps in achievement because a high proportion of the attainment difference between advantaged and disadvantaged pupils is caused by non-school factors such as poverty or weak parenting. It is a policy mistake to assume that schools alone are capable of creating a more equal society. Something has to be done about weak regional economies, house prices, income distribution and quality of parenting.

14. A myth has grown up that English society is becoming less equal. We must improve social mobility further but should also attend to the average level of achievement of all our children. It would be great to eliminate all gaps but even greater to lift our average standard of education in England to that of the best in the world. In the UK 40% of young people go to university and a minority study STEM subjects. In South Korea 75% go to university and the majority study STEM – so the gap is quite wide.

Gaps between the results of pupils of different ethnicities, genders and socio-economic groups persist in most schools. But the best schools get much better results for disadvantaged pupils than other schools.

Focusing on gaps between sub-groups is less valuable than raising the bar for *all* children in a school.

15. If society cannot or will not fund schools and colleges well, the progress of the past few years will stall.

The important thing to remember is that, while the data suggests that schools in England do quite well compared to other countries based on average pupil performance, average performance conceals an important truth – our top 20% do incredibly well, our bottom 40% do rather badly. So that tells us where government priorities should lie.

Schools in England have improved greatly in the past twenty years. The system shows much promise. But poor pupil performance correlates too well with low household income, which is why those schools achieving good results with disadvantaged pupils should be of great interest. The teaching methods and levels of discipline which lead to success in these schools are what really matters.

Bibliography

Acton Smith, M. (2015) *Calm*, Penguin.

ALCAB (2014) *The A-level Content Advisory Board Reports*, ALCAB.

All-Party Parliamentary Group on Education, Governance and Leadership (2015) *Twenty-one questions for multi-academy trusts*, APPG and NGA.

Allen, R., Parameshwaran, M. & Thomson, D., (2016) *Social and ethnic inequalities in choice available and choices made at age 16*, Social Mobility Commission.

Andrews, J., Hutchinson, J. & Johnes, R. (2016) *Grammar Schools and Social Mobility*, Education Policy Institute.

Armstrong, P. (2015) *Effective school partnerships and collaboration for school improvement: a review of the evidence*, DfE.

Ashley, L., Duberley, J., Sommerlad, H. & Scholarios, D. (2015) *A qualitative evaluation of non-educational barriers to the elite professions*, Social Mobility and Child Poverty Commission Report.

Atteberry, A., Loeb, S. & Wyckoff, J. (2013) *Do First Impressions Matter? Improvement in Early Career Teacher Effectiveness*, National Bureau of Economic Research.

Baars, S. *et al* (2014), *Lessons from London schools*, CfBT.

Belfield, C., Cribb, J., Hood, A. & Joyce, R. (2015) *Living standards, poverty and inequality in the UK 2015*, Institute for Fiscal Studies.

Berliner, D. C. (2014) 'Exogenous Variables and Value-Added Assessments: A Fatal Flaw', *Teachers College Record*, Volume 116.

Birbalsingh, K. (2011) *To miss with love*, Penguin.

Birbalsingh, K. (ed) (2016) *Battle Hymn of the Tiger Teachers; The Michaela Way*, John Catt.

Black, B. & Newton, P. (2016), '*Tolerating differences of opinion*', Ofqual paper.

Blanden, J., Goodman, A., Gregg, P. & Machin, S. (2001) '*Changes in Intergenerational Mobility in Britain*', Centre for Economic Performance.

Blanden, J., Gregg, P. & Machin, S. (2005) '*Intergenerational mobility in Europe and North America, Centre for Economic Performance*', LSE.

Blanden, J., Gregg, P. & Machin, S. (2005) '*Social Mobility in Britain*', CentrePiece.

Blanden, J., Gregg, P., & Macmillan, L. (2007) *Accounting for Intergenerational Income Persistence: Noncognitive Skills, Ability and Education*, LSE.

Blanden, J. (2009) *How much can we learn from international comparisons of intergenerational mobility?*, CEE DP 111, Centre for the Economics of Education.

Blanden, J. (2013) 'Social mobility matters, and the government can affect the mechanisms which promote it', LSE blogs, 4 November

Blanden, J., & Machin, S. (2007) *Recent Changes in Intergenerational Mobility in Britain*.

Blatchford, P., Chan,K., Galton,M., Lai, K. & Lee, J. (2017) *Class Size: Eastern and Western Perspectives*, Routledge.

Blatchford, P. (2003) *The Class Size Debate: Is Small Better?*, Open University Press.

Bloom, B. (1956) *Taxonomy of educational objectives: the classification of educational goals*, McKay.

Bolton, P. (2014) *Oxbridge elitism*, House of Commons Library

Bowes, L. *et al* (2015) *Understanding progression into higher education for disadvantaged and under-represented groups*, Department for Business, Innovation and Skills.

British Educational Suppliers Association (2015) *Research report: ICT in UK State Schools 2015 – Vol I: Opinions and Trends*

Britton, J., Dearden, L., Shephard, N. & Vignoles, A. (2016) *What and where you study matter for graduate earnings – but so does parents' income*, Institute for Fiscal Studies.

Brophy, J. E. (1979) *Teacher behavior and its effects* (Occasional Paper No. 35). East Lansing, MI: Institute for Research on Teaching, Michigan State University.

Broughton, N. *et al* (2014) *Open Access*, Social Market Foundation.

Bruner, J. (1960) *The process of education*, Harvard University Press.

Buffardi, L. & Campbell, W. (2008) *Narcissism and social networking web sites*, Personality and Social Psychology Bulletin.

Bukodi, E., Goldthorpe, J.H., Waller, L. & Kuha, J. (2015) *The Mobility Problem in Britain: New Findings from the Analysis of Cohort Data.*

Bukodi, E., Erikson, R. & Goldthorpe, J. H. (2013) *The Effects of Social Origins and Cognitive Ability on Educational Attainment: Evidence from Britain and Sweden.*

Bukodi, E., Goldthorpe, J. & Waller, Kuha, J. (2014) 'The mobility problem in Britain: new findings from the analysis of birth cohort data', *British Journal of Sociology.*

Burgess, S. (2014) *Understanding the success of London's schools*, CPMO, University of Bristol.

Blanden, J. Greaves, E., Gregg, P., Macmillan, L. & Sibieta, L. (2015) *Understanding the improved performance of disadvantaged pupils in London*, Centre for the Analysis of Social Exclusion.

Burgess, N. (2016) *A tale of two counties*, King's College London.

Campbell, D. T. (1975) 'Assessing the impact of planned social change', in Lyons, G. *Social Research and Public Policies*: The Dartmouth/OECD Conference.

Carter, A. (2015) *Carter Review of Initial Teacher Training.*

Carter, S., Greenberg, K. & Walker, M. (2016) *The Impact of Computer Usage on Academic Performance : Evidence from a Randomized Trial at the United States Military Academy*, SEII

Casey, L. (2016) *The Casey Review: a review into opportunity and integration*, HMSO.

Centre on dynamics of ethnicity (2013) *Addressing ethnic Inequalities in Social Mobility: Research findings from the CoDE and Cumberland Lodge Policy Workshop*, CODE.

Chingos, M. & Whitehurst, G. (2012) *Choosing blindly: instructional materials, teacher effectiveness and the common core*, Brookings.

Chua, A. (2011) *The Battle Hymn of the Tiger Mother*, Penguin.

Christian, D., Brown, C., & Benjamin, C. (2013) *Big History: between nothing and everything*, McGraw Hill.

Christodoulou, D. (2014) *Seven myths about education*, Routledge

Christodoulou, D. (2017) *Making Good Progress?* The future of Assessment for Learning, Oxford University Press.

Churchill, W. (1930) *My Early Life*, Thornton Butterworth Ltd.

Civitas (2015) *The Ins and Outs of Selective Secondary Schools: a debate.*

Clifton, J. & Cook, W. (2012) *A long division: Closing the attainment gap in England's secondary schools*, IPPR.

Clifton, J., Round, A. & Raikes, L. (2016) *Northern schools: putting education at the heart of the northern powerhouse*, Institute of Public Policy Research.

Coe, R. (2013) 'Improving Education: A triumph of hope over experience', Inaugural Lecture of Professor Robert Coe, Durham University.

Coe, R., Aloisi, C., Higgins, S. & Elliot Major, L. (2014) *What makes great teaching? Review of the underpinning research*, Sutton Trust.

Coleman, J. S. *et al* (1966) *Equality of educational opportunity*, National Center for Educational Statistics.

Cook, C. (2013) 'Grammar School Myths', *Financial Times*, 28 January, 2013.

Cook, C. (2016) 'Why not bring back grammar schools?' BBC news report, 14 July 2016.

Cordingley, P., Higgins, S., Greany, T., Buckler, N., Coles-Jordan, D., Crisp, B., Saunders, L. & Coe, R. (2015) *Developing Great Teaching: Lessons from the international reviews into effective professional development*, Teacher Development Trust.

Crawford, C. (2014) *Secondary schools characteristics, HE participation and outcomes*, 2014, Institute for Fiscal Studies.

Crawford, C. (2014) *Socio-economic differences in university outcomes in the UK: drop-out, degree completion and degree class*, IFS.

Crehan, L. (2016) *Cleverlands: the secrets behind the success of the world's education superpowers*, Unbound.

Cribb, J. (2013) *Income inequality in the UK*, The Institute for Fiscal Studies.

Cullinane, C. & Kirby, P. (2016) *Class differences: Ethnicity and disadvantage*, Sutton Trust.

Cultural Learning Alliance (2017) *ImagineNation: the value of cultural learning.*

Cummings, D. (2013) 'Some thoughts on education and political priorities', *The Guardian*, 11 October 13.

Department for Education (2010) *The Case for Change*, London, DfE

Department for Education (2011) *The framework for the National Curriculum*. A report by the expert panel for the National Curriculum Review.

Department for Education (2014) *Governors' Handbook*.

Department for Education (2016) *Revised A level and other level 3 results in England.*

Department for Education (2016) *Revised GCSE and equivalent results in England.*

Department for Education (2016) *Schools, pupils and their characteristics, National Statistics.*

Department for Education (2016) *Specialist and non-specialist teaching in England: extent and impact on student incomes.*

Department for Education (2016) *National statistics: Participation in education, training and employment: 2015.*

Department for Education (2016) *Multi-academy trust performance measures: 2014 to 2015.*

Department for Education (2017) *Revised GCSE and equivalent results in England, 2015 to 2016.*

Dewey, J. (1897) 'My pedagogic creed', *School Journal*, vol. 54.

Dewey, J. (1907) *The school and society*, University of Chicago.

Dewey, J. (1916) *Democracy and Education*, Macmillan.

Duncker, K. (1935) *The psychology of productive thought*, Oxford.

Durlak J., Weissberg R., Dymnicki A., Taylor R. & Schellinger K. (2011) 'The impact of enhancing students' social and emotional learning: a meta-analysis of school-based universal interventions', *Child Dev* 82.

Dweck, C. (2007) *Mindset*, Random House.

Education Endowment Foundation (2016) *Testing the impact of project based learning in secondary schools.*

Elliott, G., Rushton, N., Darlington, D. & Child, S. (2015) *Are claims that the GCSE is a white elephant red herrings?* Cambridge Assessment.

Elston, J. (2013) *Technology in the Classroom: survey results*, CIE

Engleberg, E., and Sjoberg, L. (2004) *Internet use, social skills and adjustment*, Cyberpsychology and Behaviour.

Erikson, R., Goldthorpe, J. H. & Portocarero, L. (2010) *Intergenerational Class Mobility and the Convergence Thesis: England, France and Sweden.*

Erikson, R., & Goldthorpe, J. H. (2006) *Trends in Class Mobility: The Post-war European Experience.*

Evans, G. (2006) *Educational failure and white working class children in Britain*, Palgrave Macmillan.

Eyles, A., Machin, S. & Silva, O. (2015) Academies 2: the new batch, CEP Discussion Papers, LSE.

Robert W. Fairlie, R. & Kalil, A. (2016) *The Effects of Computers on Children's Social Development and School Participation: Evidence from a Randomized Control Experiment*, NBER.

Fellows, E. (2017) *The Two Cultures: Do schools have to choose between the EBacc and the arts?* New Schools Network.

Feltovich, P., Prietula, M. & Anders Ericsson, K. (2006) 'Studies of expertise from psychological perspectives', in Anders Ericsson, K. *et al* (eds) *The Cambridge Handbook of Expertise and Expert Performance*, eds, CUP.

Finn, J. D. & Achilles, C. M. (1990) 'Answers and questions about class size: A statewide experiment', *American Educational Research Journal*, 27.

Foreman, A. (2015) 'In pill-popping America even shyness is a medical condition', *The Sunday Times*, 22 March 2015.

Gates Foundation (2010) *Learning about Teaching: Initial findings from the Measures of Effective Teaching Project.*

Bill and Melinda Gates Foundation (2012) *Ensuring Fair and Reliable Measures of Effective Teaching, Measures of Effective Teaching (MET)*, Project research paper, 2012.

Gill, T. (2016) *Assessing the equivalencies of the UCAS tariff for different qualifications*, Cambridge Assessment.

Goldthorpe, J. (1987) *Social mobility and class structure in modern Britain*, Clarendon Press.

Goldthorpe, J. & Jackson, M. (2007) 'Intergenerational class mobility in contemporary Britain: political concerns and empirical findings', *British Journal of Sociology*, 58.

Goldthorpe, J. & Mills, C. (2008) 'Trends in Intergenerational Class Mobility in Modern Britain: Evidence from National Surveys, 1972—2005', *National Institute Economic Review*, 205(1): 83–100.

Goldthorpe, J. (2012) *Understanding – and misunderstanding – social mobility in Britain: the entry of the economists, the confusion of politicians and the limits of educational policy*, Barnet Papers in Social Research, Department of Social Policy and Intervention, Oxford.

Good, F. J. & Cresswell, M. J. (1988) *Grading the GCSE*, London: Secondary Examinations Council.

Goodwin, K. (2016) Every Chance to Learn website.

Gorard, S. (2016) 'The complex determinants of school intake characteristics and segregation, England 1989 to 2014', *Cambridge Journal of Education*.

Gorard, S., Hordosy, R. & See, B. H. (2013) 'Narrowing down the determinants of between-school segregation an analysis of the intake to all schools in England, 1989–2011', *Journal of School Choice: International Research and Reform*

Greany, T., Barnes, I., Mostafa, T., Pensiero, N. & Swensson, C. (2016) *Trends in Maths and Science Study (TIMSS): National Report for England Research report*, DfE.

Greaves, E., Macmillan, L. & Sibieta, L. (2014) *Lessons from London schools for attainment gaps and social mobility*, Social Mobility and Child Poverty Commission.

Greenfield, S. (2014) *Mind Change*, Penguin.

Gregg, P., Macmillan, L. & Vittori, C. (2014) *Moving Towards Estimating Lifetime Intergenerational Economic Mobility in the UK*.

Hall, J., Lindorff, A. & Sammons, P. (2016) *Evaluation of the Impact and Implementation of Inspire Maths in Year 1 Classrooms in England*, University of Oxford.

Hanushek, E. (2011) 'Valuing teachers: how much is a good teacher worth?' *Education Next*, Summer 2011, Vol 11.

Hart, B. & Risley, T. R. (1995) *Meaningful Differences in the Everyday Experiences of Young American Children*, Baltimore, MD: Brookes Publishing.

Hattie, J. (2009) *Visible learning: a synthesis of over 800 meta-analyses relating to achievement*, Routledge.

Hattie, J. (2012) *Visible Learning for Teachers*, Routledge.

Haydn, T. (2001) 'From a Very Peculiar Department to a Very Successful School: transference issues arising out of a study of an improving school', School Leadership & Management

HEFCE (2015) *Differences in degree outcomes: The effect of subject and student characteristics*.

HEFCE (2015) *Young participation in higher education A-levels and similar qualifications.*

Higgins, S., Katsipataki, M., Kokotsaki, D., Coleman, R., Major, L. E., & Coe, R. (2013) *The Sutton Trust-Education Endowment Foundation Teaching and Learning Toolkit*, London: Education Endowment Foundation.

Higgings, S., Xiao, Z. and Katsipataki, M. (2012) *The impact of digital technology on learning*, Education Endowment Foundation.

Hill, A., Mellon, L., Laker, B., & Goddard, J. (2016) 'How to Turn Around a Failing School', *Harvard Business Review.*

Hill, A., Mellon, L., Laker, B. & Goddard, J. (2016) 'The One Type of Leader Who Can Turn Around a Failing School, *Harvard Business Review*, October 2016.

Hillman, N. & Robinson, N. (2016) *Boys to Men: The underachievement of young men in higher education – and how to start tackling it*, HEPI.

Hirsch, E. D. (1987) *Cultural literacy: what every American needs to know*, Houghton Mifflin.

Hirsch, E. D. (1996) *The schools we need and why we don't have them*, Anchor.

Hirsch, E. D. (2009) *The making of Americans*, Yale University Press.

Hirsch, E. D. (2016) *Why knowledge matters: rescuing our children from failed educational theories*, Harvard Education Press.

Hood, M. (2016) *Beyond the Plateau*, IPPR

House of Commons Education Committee (2014) *Underachievement in Education by White Working Class Children.*

Hutchinson, J. & Dunford, J. (2016) *Divergent Pathways: the disadvantage gap, accountability and the pupil premium*, Education Policy Institute.

Hutchinson, J. (2016) *School Inspection in England: is There Room to Improve?*, EPI.

Iannelli, C. (2014) 'Widening access to higher education: social inequalities in school subject choices matter', *British Journal of Sociology of Education.*

Iannelli, C. (2013) 'The role of the school curriculum in social mobility', *British Journal of Sociology of Education.*

Independent Schools Council (2017) Annual Census.

James, O. (2007) *Affluenza*, Vermillion.

Jacques S., Berkowitz, M., Kuehn, P. & Smith, K. (2003) 'The relationship of character education implementation and academic achievement in elementary schools', *Journal of Research in Character Education.*

Jerrim, J., Vignoles, A., Lingam, R. & Friend, A. (2014) 'The Socio-economic Gradient in Children's Reading Skills and the Role of Genetics', *British Educational Research Journal*, 41.

Jerrim, J. & Shure, N. (2016) *Achievement of 15-Year-Olds in England: PISA 2015 National Report*, DfE.

Jerrim, J. (2017) *Global gaps: comparing socio-economic gaps in the performance of highly able UK pupils internationally*, Sutton Trust.

Jepsen, C. & Rivkin, S. (2002) *Class Size Reduction, Teacher Quality, and Academic Achievement in California Public Elementary Schools*, Public Policy Institute of California.

Kidscape (2011) *Young people's cyber life survey.*

Krasnova, H., Wenninger, H., Widjaja, T. & Buxmann, P. (2013) *Envy on Facebook: a hidden threat to users' life satisfaction?* International Conference on Wirtschaftsinformatik (WI). Leipzig, Germany.

Kuczera, M., Field,S. & Windisch, H. (2016) *Building skills for all: a review of England*, OECD Skills Series.

Kynaston, D. & Kynaston, G. (2014) 'The 7% problem', *New Statesman*, 6 February 2014.

Lambert, P., Prandy, K. & Bottero, W. (2008) 'By slow degrees: two centuries of social reproduction and mobility in Britain', *Sociological Research Online*, 13(1).

Laurison, D. & Friedman, S. (2015) *Introducing the Class Ceiling: Social Mobility and Britain's Elite Occupations.*

LeBlanc, J. (2012) *Cyberbullying and suicide: a retrospective analysis of 22 cases*, American Academy of Pediatrics.

Lemov, D. (2010) *Teach like a champion*, Jossey-Bass.

Lemov, D. (2012) *Teach like a champion field guide*, Jossey-Bass.

Lemov, D., Woolway, E. & Yezzi, K. (2012) *Practice Perfect: 42 rules for getting better at getting better*, Wiley.

Lessof, C., Ross, A., Brind, R., Bell, E. & Newton, S. (2016) *Longitudinal Study of Young People in England cohort 2: health and wellbeing at wave 2*, DfE.

Li, Y. & F. Devine (2011) 'Is social mobility really declining? Intergenerational class mobility in Britain in the 1990s and the 2000s', *Sociological Research Online*, 16(3)

Lindley, J. & Machin, S. (2012) *The Quest for More and More Education: Implications for Social Mobility.*

Lukianoff, G. & Haidt, J. (2015) 'The coddling of the American mind', *The Atlantic*.

McAfee (2010) *The secret online lives of teens*, McAfee.

McGregor, D. (1960) *The Human Side of Enterprise*, McGraw-Hill.

Macmillan, L. (2009) *Social Mobility and the Professions.*

McKinsey and Company (2007) *How the world's best-performing school systems come out on top.*

McKinsey and Company (2010) *How the world's most improved school systems keep getting better.*

McKnight, A. (2015) *The glass floor*, Social Mobility and Child Poverty Commission.

McNally, S. (2015) *Schools: the evidence on academies, resources and pupil performance*, LSE.

McNally, S., Ruiz-Valenzuela, J., and Rolfe, H. (2016) *ABRA : Online Reading Support Evaluation report and executive summary*, EEF

Mangen, A. & Balsvik, L. (2016) 'Pen or keyboard in beginning writing instruction? Some perspectives from embodied cognition', *Trends in Neuroscience and Education*.

Mangen, A. & van der Weel, A. (2016), The evolution of reading in the age of digitization: an integrative framework for reading research, Literacy, John Wiley.

Mangen, A. (2016) The Digitization of Literary Reading, *Orbus Litterarum*.

Martin, I. (2016) 'Why Clinton and the smug liberals lost the culture war', *Reaction*, 12 November 2016.

Matthews, P. (2009) *Twelve outstanding secondary schools*, Ofsted.

Matthews, P. (2009) *Twenty outstanding primary schools: Excelling against the odds*, Ofsted

Matthews, P., Rea, S., Hill, R. & Gu, Q. (2014) *Freedom to lead: a study of outstanding primary school leadership in England*, NCTL.

Mauri, M., Cipresso, P., Balgera, A., Villamira, M. & Riva, G. (2011) 'Why is Facebook so successful?' *Cyberpsychology, Behavior, and Social Networking*, Vol.14.

Medrich, E. A. (1992) *International mathematics and science assessment: what have we learned?*, US Department of Education Office of Educational Research and Improvement.

Moss, G., & Washbrook, E. (2016) *The Lost Boys*, Save the Children.

Moss, G. & Washbrook, E. (2016) *The Gender Gap in Language and Literacy Development*. Bristol: University of Bristol.

Mueller, P. A. & Oppenheimer, D. M. (2014) 'The Pen is Mightier Than the Keyboard: Advantages of Longhand Over Laptop Note Taking', *Psychological Science*, 1–10.

Ndaji, F., Little, J., & Coe, R. (2016) *A comparison of Academic Achievement in Independent and State Schools, Centre for Evaluation and Monitoring*, Durham University

Niven, J., Faggian, A. & Ruwanpura, K. (2013) 'Exploring "Underachievement" among highly educated young British-Bangladeshi women', *Feminist Economics*, 19.

O'Shaughnessy, J. (2016) *A tide that lifts all boats: a response to the Green Paper*, Legatum Institute.

Oates, T. (2014) *Why textbooks count*, Cambridge Assessment.

Oates, T. (2015) *Finnish fairy stories*, Cambridge Assessment.

OECD (2013) *OECD Skills Outlook 2013: First Results from the Survey of Adult Skills*, OECD Publishing; Paris.

OECD (2014) 'Are grouping and selecting students for different schools related to students' motivation to learn?' *PISA in Focus* 39, OECD.

OECD (2015) *Education at a Glance*, OECD indicators.

OECD (2015) *The ABC of Gender Equality in Education: Aptitude, Behaviour, Confidence*, PISA.

OECD (2016) *Education at a Glance*, 2016.

OECD (2016) *Society at a Glance*, 2016.

OECD (2016) *Programme for international student assessment results from PISA 2015*.

Office for National Statistics (2016) *Families and Households in the UK, 2016 Statistical Bulletin*.

Office for National Statistics (2017) *Household disposable income and inequality in the UK: financial year ending 2016*.

Ofqual(2015) *Comparability of different GCSE and A level subjects in England: an introduction*.

Ofqual (2016) *Using differential step functioning analysis and Rasch modelling to investigate interboard comparability of examination standards in GCSE*, Ofqual.

Ofqual (2016) *Marking consistency metrics*, Ofqual.

Ofsted (2008) *White boys from low income backgrounds: good practice in schools*

Ofsted (2009) *Twenty outstanding primary schools: excelling against the odds.*

Ofsted (2009) *Twelve outstanding secondary schools: excelling against the odds.*

Ofsted (2016) *Annual Report 2015/16.*

Oliver, B. & Plomin, R. (2007) Twins Early Development Study (TEDS): A multivariate, longitudinal genetic investigation of language, cognition and behaviour problems from childhood through adolescence, *Twin Research and Human Genetics*, 10.

Ouston, J. (1999) 'School effectiveness and school improvement: Critique of a movement', in Bush, T., Bolam, R., Glatter, R. and Ribbins, P. (eds) *Educational Management: Redefining theory, policy and practice*, London: Paul Chapman.

Paterson, L. & Iannelli, C. (2007) 'Patterns of absolute and relative social mobility: a comparative study of England, Wales and Scotland', *Sociological Research Online*, 12(6).

Peal, R. (2016) *Early Modern Britain 1509–1760*, HarperCollins.

Pearson (2016) *Global survey of educator effectiveness.*

Perera, N. & Treadaway, M. (2016) *Education in England: Annual Report 2016*, CentreForum.

Pink, D. (2011) *Drive: the surprising truth about what motivates us*, Canongate Books.

Policy Exchange Integration hub (2016) http://www.integrationhub.net/module/education/

Porter, N. & Simons, J. (2014) *Five reasons why a return to grammar schools is a bad idea*, Policy Exchange.

Porter, N. & Simons, J. (2015) *A rising tide: the competitive benefits of free schools*, Policy Exchange.

Power, S., Whitty, G. & Sims, S. (2013) *Lasting benefits: the long-term legacy of the Assisted Places Scheme*, Sutton Trust.

Rasbash, J., Leckie, G., Pillinger, R. & Jenkins, J. (2010) 'Children's educational progress: partitioning family, school and area effects', *Journal of the Royal Statistical Society*, 173.

Recht, D. & Leslie, L. (1988) 'Effect of prior knowledge on good and poor readers' memory of text', *Journal of Educational Psychology*, 80.

Reeves, R. (2016) *How much social mobility do people really want*, Brookings Brief.

Robinson, M. (2013) *Trivium 21c: preparing young people for the future with lessons from the past*, Independent Thinking Press.

Robinson, M. (2016) *Trivium in practice*, Independent Thinking Press.

Roediger, H. L. & Karpicke, J. D. (2006) 'Test-enhanced learning: Taking memory tests improves long-term retention', *Psychological Science*, 17(3).

Ruiz-Valenzuela, J. & McNally, S. (2016) *An Evaluation of Teaching Assistant-Based Small Group Support for Literacy*, EEF.

Sahlgren, G. (2015) *Real Finnish lessons*, Centre for Policy Studies.

Saunders, P. (2010) *Social Mobility Myths*, Civitas.

Sammons, P., Mortimore, P. & Hillman, J. (1995) *Key characteristics of effective schools*, Ofsted and the Institute of Education.

Sammons, P., Kington, A., Lindorff-Vijayendran, A. & Ortega, L. (2014) *Inspiring teachers: perspectives and practices*, CfBT.

Sammons, P., Toth, K. & Sylva, K. (2015) *Subject to Background: what promotes better achievement for bright but disadvantaged students?* University of Oxford Department of Education.

Savage, M. (2015) *Social class in the 21st Century*, Pelican.

Sax, L. (2005) *Why gender matters*, Potter/Ten Speed/Harmony.

Sax, L. (2007) *Boys Adrift*, Basic Books.

Scherger, S. & Savage, M. (2010) *Cultural Transmission, Educational Attainment and Social Mobility*.

Schmidt, J., Shierholz., H. & Mishel, L. (2013) *Don't Blame The Robots: Assessing the Job Polarisation Explanation of Growing Wage Inequality*.

Schurtz, M. *et al* (2015) 'Clarifying the role of mind areas during visual perspective taking: issues of spontaneity and domain specificity', *NeuroImage*, 117.

Siegler, R. & DeLoache, J. (2003) *How children develop*, New York: Worth.

Seldon, A. & Hupkau, C. (2014) *Schools United*, Social Market Foundation.

Serafino, P. & Tonkin, R. (2014) *Intergenerational transmission of disadvantage in the UK & EU*, ONS.

Simons, J. (2016) 'Forget mavericks, we need 'factory schooling', *Times Educational Supplement*, 3 June 2016.

Shakeshaft, N., Trzaskowski, M., McMillan, A., Rimfeld, K., Krapohl, E., Haworth, C., Dale, P., & Plomin, R. (2013) *Strong Genetic Influence on a UK Nationwide Test of Educational Achievement at the End of Compulsory Education at Age 16*, PLOS One.

Shaw, B., Menzies, L., Bernardes, E., Baars,S., Philip Nye, N. & Allen R. (2016) *Ethnicity, Gender and Social Mobility, Social Mobility Commission*.

Slater, H., Davies, N, & Burgess, S. (2009), *Do teachers matter? Measuring the variation in teacher effectiveness in England*, Centre for Market and Public Organisation Working Series.

Slater, J. (1992) *The Zulu Principle: Making Extraordinary Profits from Ordinary Shares*, Orion.

Smith, J. (2000) *The Learning Game*, Little Brown.

Snowden, C. (2015) *Income inequality: the facts*, IEA.

Social Mobility and Child Poverty Commission (2015) *State of the Nation*.

Social Mobility and Child Poverty Commission (2015) *Social and Emotional Learning: Skills for Life and Work*.

Social Mobility and Child Poverty Commission (2015) *Downward Mobility, Opportunity Hoarding and the Glass Floor*.

Social Mobility and Child Poverty Commission (2015) *Non-educational Barriers to the Elite Professions Evaluation*.

Social Mobility Commission (2016) *Socio-economic diversity in life sciences and investment banking.*

Social Mobility Commission (2016) *State of the Nation 2016: social mobility in Great Britain.*

Sparrow, B., Liu, J. & Wegner, D. (2011) 'Google Effects on Memory: cognitive consequences of having information at our fingertips', *Science,* 333.

Stevenson, H. & Stigler, J. (1992) *The Learning Gap: why our schools are failing and what we can learn from Japanese and Chinese education,* Summit Books.

Strand, S. (2010) 'Do some schools narrow the gap? Differential school effectiveness by ethnicity, gender, poverty and prior attainment', *School Effectiveness and School Improvement,* 21.

Strand, S. (2011) 'The Limits of Social Class in Explaining Ethnic Gaps in Educational Attainment', *British Educational Research Journal,* 37.

Strand, S. (2015) *Ethnicity, deprivation and educational achievement at age 16 in England: trends over time,* DfE.

Strand, S. (2013) *What accounts for ethnic achievement gaps in secondary schools in England?*

BERA Insights, Issue 4, British Educational Research Association.

Strand, S. (2014c) Written evidence submitted to the House of Commons Education Select Committee inquiry into Underachievement in Education by White Working Class Children.

Strand, S. (2014) 'Ethnicity, gender, social class and achievement gaps at age 16: Intersectionality and 'Getting it' for the white working class', *Research Papers in Education,* 29.

Strand, S. (2014b) 'School effects and ethnic, gender and socio-economic gaps in educational achievement at age 11', *Oxford Review of Education,* 40, (2), 223–245.

Strand, S. (2014c) *Mind the gap: An analysis of the FSM gap in Buckinghamshire County Council.* Buckinghamshire: Buckinghamshire County Council.

Strand, S., & Demie, F. (2005) 'English language acquisition and educational attainment at the end of primary school', *Educational Studies,* 31, (3), 275–291.

Strand, S. & Demie, F. (2006) 'Pupil mobility, attainment and progress in primary school', *British Educational Research Journal,* 32, (4), 551–568.

Strand, S., & Fletcher, J. (2014) *A Quantitative Analysis of Exclusions from English Secondary Schools.* University of Oxford: Department for Education.

Strand, S., & Lindsay, G. (2009) 'Evidence of ethnic disproportionality in special education in an English population', *Journal of Special Education,* 43(3), 174–190.

Strand, S., De Coulon, A., Meschi, E., Vorhaus, J., Ivins, C., Small, L., Sood, A., Gervais, M. C. & Rehman, H. (2010). *Drivers and challenges in raising the achievement of pupils from Bangladeshi, Somali and Turkish backgrounds (Research Report DCSF-RR226).* London: Department for Children School and Families.

Strand, S., Malmberg, L. & Hall, J. (2015) *English as an Additional Language (EAL) and educational achievement: An analysis of the National Pupil Database.* London: Educational Endowment Fund.

Sturgis, P. & Buscha, F. (2015) *Increasing Inter-generational Social Mobility: Is Educational Expansion the Answer?*

Sullivan, A, Parsons, S., Wiggins, R., Heath, A. & Green, F. (2014) 'Social origins, school type and higher education destinations', *Oxford Review of Education*, Vol. 40.

Sutton Trust (2010) *Education mobility in England.*

Sutton Trust (2011) *Improving the impact of teachers on pupil achievement in the UK.*

Sutton Trust (2012) *State funded places in independent schools before 1976.*

Sutton Trust (2013) *Lasting Benefits: the long-term legacy of the Assisted Places Scheme*, Sutton Trust.

Sutton Trust (2013) *Selective Comprehensives.*

Sutton Trust (2015) *Private pay progression.*

Sutton Trust (2016) *Believing in Better.*

Swinney, P. & Williams M. (2016) *The great British brain drain: where graduates move and why*, Centre for Cities.

Tiggemann, M, & Miller, J. (2010) 'The internet and adolescent girls' weight satisfaction and drive for thinness', *Sex Roles*, Vol. 63.

Tinsley, T. & Board, K. (2016) *Language Trends 2015/16: the state of language learning in primary and secondary schools in England*, Education Development Trust.

Tomsett, J. (2015) *This Much I Know About Love Over Fear … Creating a Culture for Truly Great Teaching*, Crown House

Tomsett, J. (2017) *This Much I Know About Mind Over Matter … Improving Mental Health in Our Schools*, Crown House.

Tough, P. (2013) *How children succeed: grit, curiosity and the hidden power of character*, Random House.

Tough, P. (2016) *Helping children succeed: what works and why*, Random House.

Turkle, S. (2012) *Alone Together: why we expect more from technology and less from each other*, Basic Books.

Twenge, J., Konrath, S., Foster, J., Campbell, W. & Bushman, B. (2008) 'Egos inflating over time: a cross-temporal meta-analysis of the narcissistic personality inventory', *Journal of Personality.*

UCAS (2016) *End of cycle report, 2016.*

Wakefield, M. (2013) 'Revealed: how exam results owe more to genes than teaching', *The Spectator*, 27 July 2013.

Warwick Commission (2015) *Enriching Britain: culture, creativity and growth.*

Waldfogel, J. & Reardon, S. (2016) *International Inequalities*, Sutton Trust.

Waldman, M., Nicholson, S. & Adilov, N. (2006) *Does television cause autism?* National Bureau of Economic Research.

Walker, S. (2016) *The Tribe Effect: measuring the non-cognitive impacts of state day, independent day and boarding education*, Mind.World

Washbrook, E. (2010) *Early Environments and Child Outcomes: An Analysis*, Commission for the Independent Review on Poverty and Life Chances.

Waterhouse, L. (2006) 'Inadequate evidence for multiple intelligences', *Educational Psychologist*.

Waters, M. (2013) *Thinking aloud on schooling*, Independent Thinking Press

Willingham, D. (2005) 'Ask the cognitive scientist: Question: What does cognitive science tell us about the existence of visual, auditory and kinesthetic learning?' *American Educator*.

Willingham, D. (2007) 'Critical thinking: why is it so hard to teach?' *American Educator*.

Wolf, A. (2011) *Review of Vocational Education – The Wolf Review*, Department for Education and Department for Business, Innovation & Skills.

Woodworth, J. *et al* (2015) Online charter school study, Center for Research on Education Outcomes.

Young, M. (1958) *The Rise of the Meritocracy*, Thames and Hudson.

Index